'A powerful, honest story of courage, purpose after experiencing so much h◠ the Australian SAS in Afghanistan.'

BEAR GRYLLS OBE
British adventurer, author and SAS veteran

'In Special Forces it is often said the thinking is at least as important as the fighting. Through these pages Mark Wales is shown as a thinking soldier. And further, a person of magnificent generosity, taking us to rarely trespassed ground, the battlefield within.'

CHRIS MASTERS PSM
Gold Walkley award-winning journalist and author

'Mark Wales is one of those men to whom we have outsourced the responsibility to kill – and be killed – so we may live as we do. If you read one book about the SAS, Afghanistan, those Australians who fought the war on our behalf and the price they have paid for it, this is it. The power is in the story. In this one, discover your own and be inspired to be a better person and a better Australian.'

HON DR BRENDAN NELSON AO
Former Director of the Australian War Memorial and
former Minister for Defence

'Searing, humbling and uplifting by turns, this story vibrates with the energy of a former SAS officer and his empowering search for peace and a new life. This man is a remarkable package: elite warrior, hungry entrepreneur, and a survivor determined to overcome his emotional wounds. Mark Wales is a true inspiration.'

MAJOR GENERAL JOHN CANTWELL AO, DSC
Bestselling author of *Exit Wounds* and
retired Australian Army general

'Mark's book is a great lesson that even the strong can feel weak, and that allows the weak to feel strong in the face of adversity. *Survivor* is action-packed and reminds us all that a veteran's sacrifice is not for a period of time in a foreign land. It is here and it is eternal.'

MERRICK WATTS
Comedian and joint winner of *SAS Australia* (2020)

'When I met Mark on *Australian Survivor* I knew instantly he was a big tough guy with an even bigger heart the size of Texas. What I didn't know was the daunting rollercoaster ride of courage and pain, risk and terror that he had been through to arrive there. A true survivor! His book is a must read – the tribe has spoken.'

JONATHAN LAPAGLIA
Actor and host of *Australian Survivor*

'Modern war can be confounding, confusing and unyielding, but this modern warrior's story invites the reader to understand the fear and resilience, strength and incredible innovation of the Australian combatants involved. A very personal story with an international scope, this is an engrossing book that's about triumphing in life during and after a war that was often less than triumphant.'

BEN MCKELVEY
Author and journalist

'This is a story of a man tested by both war and peace – a gripping read for young Australians.'

HON ANDREW HASTIE MP
Federal Member for Canning and SASR veteran

Mark Wales grew up in the red dirt of Western Australian mining towns in the Pilbara. While still in high school, he decided he wanted to join Australia's elite military unit, the Special Air Service Regiment (commonly referred to as the SAS), and embarked on a career that would eventually lead him to the battlefields of Afghanistan. There, as a troop commander in charge of 30 elite soldiers, Mark led combat missions deep behind enemy lines.

Like many who survived this unique and harsh environment, Mark's experiences made a searing impression, allowing him the chance to forge greater resilience and undergo personal growth. Today he is an accomplished corporate speaker, reality TV star, and CEO and founder of a tough luxury fashion label. He lives in the Dandenong Ranges, Victoria, with his wife and son.

Find out more at www.markwales.com.au.

SURVIVOR

LIFE IN THE SAS

MARK WALES

MACMILLAN
Pan Macmillan Australia

Pan Macmillan acknowledges the Traditional Custodians of country throughout
Australia and their connections to lands, waters and communities. We pay our
respect to Elders past and present and extend that respect to all Aboriginal and
Torres Strait Islander peoples today. We honour more than sixty thousand years
of storytelling, art and culture.

First published 2021 in Macmillan by Pan Macmillan Australia Pty Ltd
1 Market Street, Sydney, New South Wales, Australia, 2000

A catalogue record for this
book is available from the
National Library of Australia

Typeset in 11.7/16 pt Sabon by Post Pre-press Group
Printed by IVE

The paper in this book is FSC® certified.
FSC® promotes environmentally responsible,
socially beneficial and economically viable
management of the world's forests.

To Harry and Samantha. Turns out the light at the end of the tunnel was both of you.

To Keegan and Leigh, as promised.

CONTENTS

It makes no difference what men think of war, said the judge. War endures. As well ask men what they think of stone. War was always here. Before man was, war waited for him. The ultimate trade awaiting its ultimate practitioner. That is the way it was and will be. That way and not some other way.

Cormac McCarthy, *Blood Meridian*

AUTHOR'S NOTE

THERE IS A SIDE OF WAR THAT IS RARELY TOLD BY THOSE WHO experience its rough embrace. Most military books focus on the hard-won battle but not so much on the blaze that war starts in your mind and which follows you home, where it continues to burn, often scorching those around you. Combatants, civilians, families – the survivors . . . war costs us all dearly.

I joined the military as a young man, wanting to rescue people in need. I had studied battles and wars as a history under-graduate; I had listened in awe to the stories of men – including my own relatives – who had fought in the jungles of New Guinea and Vietnam. I decided my mission in life would be to join the SAS, the famous unit that terrorised the Afrika Corps in World War II and, 70 years later, would earn the nickname 'the red beards' in the mountains of Afghanistan.

I passed selection to join the revered unit (with an unusu-ally high population of redheads). Standing on the shoulders of giants, we helped grow the unit into a 21st-century combat outfit. Over six years, I fought alongside my mates in Australia's longest war – the twelve-year Afghanistan campaign. I was professionally trained in warfighting by then, so I believed I knew enough to survive . . . How wrong I was.

I did survive the conflict but what I didn't anticipate – had no idea of – was the cost of the war. Cost in every sense: personal, professional and human.

In the decade that followed, a blaze smouldered away in me every single night. The residue of combat was insoluble. I tried to wash it away, hide from it, mask it, outrun it, outdrink it, outwork it and even bury it. Sitting alone in a one-bedroom apartment in Canberra, then Perth, Philadelphia and New York City, my mind never quite left the mountains and muddy aqueducts of Afghanistan. I tried to move on into new professions. I wandered the corporate landscape in a grey suit and leather shoes, bewildered, hoping to find a new tribe, trying to fit in – only to realise I would never fit in again. Eventually, I stopped trying. I knew I would have to find my own path.

This book is my record of those years, from the battlefields of south-central Asia to the silent battle fought within, and how I overcame their legacy. It is my intention to reveal the human side of special operations soldiers – a side that is rarely seen, given the secrecy in which we operate – and to show that, despite the way we might be characterised, we are not robots, devoid of the normal range of human emotions. Like everyone else, we feel fear, anger, empathy, embarrassment, sadness, wonder, grace, humour, anxiety and hope. I have come to believe that, far from representing weakness, emotions such as these are our greatest assets.

I hope that my story will help you to harness your own blaze, and inspire you to hope, to love and to stay in the fight, no matter what the battlefield.

SURVIVOR

PROLOGUE

I EMERGED FROM THE FREEZING RIVER WITH TWO DOZEN crouching soldiers. Green ghosts in the dawn light, we held our weapons ready. We were in enemy territory, uninvited. Our mission: to wrest back the valley from the 100 Taliban that occupied it. We had no doubt that blood would be shed in the attempt.

Cold water drained from our boots as we continued our silent patrol towards the ambush site. There was no movement in the fields, which had been freshly tilled by the lumbering ox-drawn ploughs, the October harvest reduced to rows of earth and wheat stubble. This was rare, unsettling. I strained to hear a noise from the nearby farms or the deep water channel we followed.

Nothing.

No birds. No cows. No goats. No breeze in the river willows.

I felt a shiver of unease in my chest. This was my first tour in Afghanistan, so I was not yet fluent in the language of the unconscious body: a tingling scalp; a prickling between the shoulder blades; a silent voice from deep within warning: *something isn't right.*

Be careful in the green belt during the day – someone'll get shot. Advice from an old hand stuck in my head. Yet here we were, in the green fields of the Chora Valley, with the sun rising behind us. This particular valley had shot to infamy in a clearance operation in 2006, just a year before, when Dutch and Australian troops fought the Taliban in a battle that saw more Australian soldiers wounded than in any other engagement since the Vietnam War.

We carried guns. Lots of guns. Long, camouflaged rifles with glass optics on top and grenade launching tubes underneath. Black boxes with aiming lasers clipped to our barrels. Black, compact pistols holstered to our hips. Serrated knives were sheathed horizontally across our chests. Ceramic armour plates that stop high-powered rounds caged our thumping hearts. I favoured bombs, so I carried many. Gold-topped grenade bullets lined my chest plate. Two hand grenades were clipped to my belt: one for my enemy and, in a nightmare scenario, one for me. To be captured by the enemy was to be skinned alive, stoned, beheaded. The worst Taliban fighters alive called this valley home. In the summer prior, the Taliban commander in the valley had cut off the hands of the police chief's wife while he watched, then beheaded him. *Top bloke*, I had thought during the intel briefing.

Scanning the fields, I was worried. The quiet was palpable. No kids shepherding goats or rolling spare bike tyres along the trails. No 'pattern of life'. We patrolled beside the river in a broad formation, my gaze caught by a cornfield off my right shoulder. The shrivelled stalks were a blight against the lush greenery blooming from the low aqueducts. If I had been seasoned already, I would have stopped mid-stride, realising that the corn offered superb concealment: those within could see out, but no-one could see in. But at the time, it didn't occur to me.

We crept along the cornfield, pausing to listen. Our weapons were up, parallel to the ground, following the direction of our gaze. A cold bead of sweat ran down my painted green brow, but I didn't dare take my hands off my weapon to wipe it away. Looking from under a bush hat, I scanned the field until my eyeballs hurt. The body armour plates cladding me made hot knots out of my back muscles. I wanted to shift the weight, but I couldn't afford to make any jarring movements that might catch the eye of the enemy.

As we crept forward, we dodged the narrow dirt trail, dry sticks and leaves, and patches of sunlight. We sought shadows and bushes for concealment and noted depressions in which we might take cover from fire. We communicated through looks and tiny nods of the head to avoid movement of our hands, which remained on our weapons at all times, trigger finger propped right next to the trigger guard. At the end of each scan of the terrain, I would look ahead at my lead patrol commander, Sergeant Matthew Locke.

I felt confident with a warrior like Lockie at the front. He was as agile and muscular as a Bengal cat. The summer before, in this same valley, he had scaled a cliff and countered a Taliban attack against his patrol's position. He was considered one of the best fighters in the unit. Now, he was leading the first patrol in our formation as we slunk further into the valley. As I was the officer present, Lockie and the other men were under my command, but the bench was deep; these were highly experienced combat soldiers. They guided me and helped me lead – it was in their best interests that I grew into my job quickly.

A team of snipers parked on a small ridge amid a boulder outcrop over our left shoulders provided us with what is known as overwatch. They were a 'foot on the ground', scanning with rangefinder binoculars as we ventured across the river towards the cornfield. Three sniper pairs were set up to fire a weapon as long as a canoe oar which launched exploding bullets the size of a car wheel nut. They focused on the trees lining the river, looking for the shimmer of a dark shadow or the sparkle of a watch face, a creeping man or an uncovered hand.

A voice sounded in my earpiece. *'You're clear to the south-west. We can't see forward line of troops – cover's too thick.'*

Two squat, black, wasp-like Apache gunship helicopters circled high overhead, scanning the ground ahead of us for enemy. Hellfire missiles were stacked in four packs on the stubby winglets. Each missile packed 20 kilos of explosive power and thousands of flechette darts. Protruding from each helo's nose was a 30 mm cannon, a weapon famous for decimating cars, buildings and hordes of people. The steady thrum above us was reassuring. We would soon need all the firepower we could summon . . .

'Bravo, on foot, south side of cornfield,' chattered through my earpiece.

I paused. *Why is a woman fleeing?* I wondered. I would have my answer soon enough.

The Taliban were waiting in that cornfield for us, in chest-deep trenches, fingers on the triggers of their belt-fed, heavy machine guns. They had waited until we were *real* close. So close that artillery could not support us. So close that the B-1s would not be able to drop their bombs to our front. So close that the Apaches would have to hold their fire.

I was staring at the woman fleeing, holding the hand of her tiny child, when the shooting started. That deafening bloody sound.

Those shots would echo for thirteen more years, lodged deep in the corners of my mind. It was the start of a long downward spiral, as the dream I'd had since I was a kid turned into a nightmare.

ACT I

THE ROAD TO WAR

You do not know what things you set in motion, he said. No man can know. No prophet foresee. The consequences of an act are often quite different from what one would guess. You must be sure that the intention in your heart is large enough to contain all wrong turnings, all disappointments. Do you see? Not everything has such value.

Cormac McCarthy, *The Crossing*

1

MEN IN BLACK

A KID SAT NEXT TO ME IN JAPANESE CLASS. HE WAS AN ARMY cadet in his spare time. He acted like a junior soldier, too. Buttoned up, smiling, on time to class. Aaron was his name.

It was a stinker of a Perth summer day, nearly 40 degrees. Fans spun on the ceiling; the state school had no budget for air conditioning. The kid had a small magazine. On the front cover was a black-and-white image of black-clad men with grim-looking gasmasks and compact submachine guns. Their dark menace stood out against the pristine white masonry of the balcony on which they stood.

'What's that?' I asked.

'It's the SAS at Prince's Gate,' said Aaron. 'In London.'

In 1980, terrorists had stormed the Iranian embassy in London, taking 26 hostages. When a hostage was killed on the sixth day of the siege, Prime Minister Margaret Thatcher lost patience with negotiations and signed off on Operation Nimrod, authorising the British SAS to force their way into the building and rescue the hostages. They were authorised to kill or capture the terrorist occupiers. The image on the magazine cover showed a four-strong SAS team balcony-hopping towards their entry point.

These events had taken place thirteen years earlier, but the images felt very urgent and real to me, a year nine kid living in an outer suburb of Perth. I sensed an electricity in the pictures: these men, intent on their task with their submachine guns covering all angles, looked like a single organism. Their mission was a success, but the unit was so secret that few people knew their identities and even fewer knew the work they did. They performed their heroic job then disappeared from the scene without fanfare. I was intrigued.

We were only looking at pictures of the operation. We did not feel it. The concussion of the window charges that blew the points of entry, the heat of the velvet curtains on fire, the smell of burning carpet. We did not see the looks in the eyes of the terrorists as the SAS team swarmed in, did not witness the terrorists gunned down and left in a tangle of ashes, blood and urine. We knew nothing of how the soldiers themselves felt in that moment. None of this occurred to me and, in truth, none of it mattered. I wanted to be one of the soldiers in black, storming that building. Saving people from hell. A good guy.

In one photo, I could see a man's gloved hand placed on the back of the soldier in front of him as he negotiated a window ledge. It looked reassuring, like your father's hand on your back as you navigated a dangerous forest. Years later, on the cusp of entering a room with enemy nearby, I would feel the same reassuring touch on my arm: *You're not alone.*

That single image was enough. I ran from Japanese class to the library. I asked the librarian for all the books she had on the SAS. She produced three, their covers emblazoned with winged daggers and explosions. I borrowed them all, ran home, and started reading about the mythical unit.

By bedtime, I had decided I would become an SAS soldier. I would dedicate myself to a brave and noble cause.

2

THE LAST SAMURAI

Before we moved to Perth and I had that fateful Japanese class, our family had lived in the Pilbara, in the north-west of Western Australia. My dad Rob and my mum Jane had met in Maffra, a small town to the east of Melbourne, in the 1960s. Dad was a bank teller across the road from the car yard where Mum – a tall strong farm girl originally from Western Australia – worked as a secretary. Dad offered Mum a lift to Sale, and that offer led to me as the middle of three boys. The first was Steve, born two years ahead of me. I arrived in November 1979, just in time to see the last of the decade's orange carpet and floral wallpaper, and bearded men with tight shirts, flared pants and hairy chests – mirroring the iconic Australian cricket team's fast bowlers. Dan, the youngest, was a feisty addition to our family in 1985.

I was born in the Western Australian iron ore mining town of Newman, where Dad worked shifts as a truck driver. He eventually landed a job in customs, which was a ticket back to Perth, where the sun set over the Indian Ocean. I didn't mind the ferric red dirt of the Pilbara, but in Perth I found the first love of my life: the coast.

We didn't stay long in the city, though. I'd just finished

year two when Dad moved the family 400 kilometres up the coast to Geraldton. It was all limestone and white beaches and wheat silos. My entrepreneurial brother Steve had figured out we could head to a beachside tavern on weekend mornings to collect aluminium cans and sell them. We would descend the limestone cliff down to the beer garden, sometimes finding a stray $20 note or a gold coin. Often there were used bongs made from plastic drink bottles. They smelled like baked cow shit. Drunken men slept in the gardens between hedges as we worked away. Well, my brother worked. I would watch as Steve scooted around picking up all the cans while I wandered about looking at plants and dreaming about Ninja Turtles and Transformers. I was a shit labourer.

Not only did I lack a work ethic, common sense also eluded me. One year I bought a commando survival knife from a tele-phone marketing company. I destroyed as many objects with it as I could. I would throw apples in the air and cut them in half with the razor-sharp blade. Mum would watch me with concern. 'You'll cut your bloody throat with that thing,' she'd warn. 'Be careful.'

Sure enough, I ended up shoving the knife tip into the webbing of my hand while stabbing a piece of paper. I spent the next day trying to conceal the wound from Mum. Not long after that, I tried to cut a cork in half using my thigh as a cutting board. I cut the cork all right – and plunged the blade two centimetres into my thigh in the process.

One of my best friends in school was a young Canadian girl, Megan. My parents had met hers at a parents night at the school and they struck up a friendship – the Canadian family was so far from their home, and Geraldton was not renowned as a cosmopolitan city.

Megan was my height with brown hair and a funny accent. She was 'born without her plumbing', my mum explained. Born without a bladder and bowel, she had to urinate and defecate into a colostomy bag. The other kids in the class would all hold their noses and wave their hands in front of their faces when she passed. She spent recess and lunch wandering the playground alone, singing to herself. It broke my heart; I hated to see people alone. So I took to sitting with her. The class joker would come up to me and say in a Canadian accent, 'Hello, Mark, I'm your girlfriend,' and try to hug me. It was far less bothersome than seeing a person ostracised when they did not deserve it. Megan's parents had lamented to my mum that every morning they sent their daughter off to school, and every evening they had to 'put her back together again'.

I was starting to learn that was life was anything but fair – not everyone was born equal, and the weak were picked on.

My brothers and I grew up watching war films. One that scared me was *The Beast of War*, a film about a Russian tank crew abandoned in Afghanistan. Left to fight the locals alone, they met a grisly end. Steve and I loved *Tour of Duty*, a kitschy American series about the Vietnam War. As soon as we heard the theme song – 'Paint it Black' by the Rolling Stones – we went running for the TV to watch it. It seemed an impossibly hard war. My mother was working at the cinema in Geraldton when the biopic *Born on the Fourth of July* was released. Tom Cruise played Ron Kovic, a paralysed Vietnam War veteran. In one distressing scene, he screams drunkenly at his mother, confessing they had killed babies. My own mother turned to us and said: 'This is what happens – don't you boys go to war.' We believed her, because of Grandad.

Mum's father, George McEwin, had fought in World War II. A gentle giant, when he wasn't working the farm he was reading books. I can still picture his tattered copy of *All Quiet on the Western Front*. One summer I read his copy of *First Blood*, about a disaffected Vietnam vet who goes on a killing rampage in a small American town.

When I told Grandad I would be joining the SAS, he stood up from his cream recliner chair and gestured for me to follow him. He strode down the hall to his bedroom, where he rummaged in the wardrobe for a few minutes before producing an old Japanese samurai sword. Holding it horizontal in both hands, he offered it to me. I felt its heft then drew the sword from its sheath. Noticing rough chips on the edge of the blade, I ran my thumb along them. 'What are these from?' I asked.

'It's from hitting our boys,' he said.

He took the sword from me, and held the blade and sheath for a moment without speaking. I felt the gravity of the moment without quite understanding its cause; *Grandad and his comrades must have damaged the sword*, I thought. (It was only later that I realised the blade had been damaged when it struck the bones of Australian soldiers.)

'Would you ever give it back to the Japanese?' I asked.

'I'll burn it before I give it back,' Grandad said as he rammed it home in the sheath. His eyes flashed with a fury I had never seen before. For the first time I had an inkling that whatever had occurred in the jungles of Morotai still smouldered in him to that day.

As Grandad replaced the sword in the wardrobe, I asked about the weapon he had carried in the jungle. 'A .303 when I could. Sometimes an Owen gun. They weren't much good at range, though; only good as far as a footy kick.'

He didn't tell me many stories, but my mother told me his platoon commander had been killed when he rolled over what he believed to be a dead Jap soldier. The cadaver was holding a pistol and shot the lieutenant in the face.

War was a part of Australia, evident in the stone obelisks covered with names of the fallen from both wars. The memorials in Yarloop, where my grandparents lived south of Perth, paid homage to the 220 farm men who had been lost in that region. I wanted to share in the experience that soldiers spoke of among themselves in quiet whispers: the trials of combat, death, loss and sacrifice.

My first encounter with weapons was down on Grandad's farm back before we moved to Geraldton. He took out his .22 Ruger rifle at the farm and let us kids shoot at cardboard boxes on the fence. I loved holding a lethal weapon; the polished wood-grain and black metal in my hands made me feel dangerous and older. One day, when I was able to handle the rifle well, Dad let me hunt rabbits. Prone beside hay bales in the paddock, I was a sniper for an afternoon. As terrified rabbits scattered from my harassing fire, I learned that a close miss is still a miss.

3

A SINGLE STEP

ABOUT THE SAME TIME I DISCOVERED I WANTED TO BE AN SAS soldier, as a year nine kid in Perth, I got a job at Red Rooster as a kitchenhand. We slaved over the vats of hot oil, frying chips in 20-kilo batches. The air conditioning would break down in the summer and we would wipe sweat from our faces all day. I burned my hands on hot racks of chicken and slipped on the greasy floors. But at $5 an hour, we were rich.

I had been working alongside a classmate, Jim, who shared my love of computer games and science fiction novels. At one point he came up with the idea: 'Hey, with all this cash we're making, I think we can pull a root.' I knew what he was talking about – we had joked about a brothel we had seen in a northern suburb. We were not fanatics, but we were at an age where the opposite sex had become a whole lot more interesting.

Go to a brothel? 'No way,' I said. It was an outrageous idea; we were only fourteen years old. But then I considered it. We looked mature for our age: I had a solid build and Jim pretty much had the facial hair of a grown man. It was a long shot, but we decided to pick up the phone directory and call them. The woman who answered told us it cost $50 for half an hour with a lady. Whatever that entailed.

We came up with a plan to head to the city under the guise of watching a movie and then walk to Northbridge. I was nervous – if we were caught, we risked humiliation at best and a run-in with the police at worst. Not to mention the consequences if our parents found out. They would most likely disown us.

I was expecting red lights and girls in the windows, but the brothel had an innocuous appearance: a white colonial-style two-storey home with a wrought-iron gate and tiny letterbox. We loitered in a cafe over the road, watching the place.

'I don't think this is a good idea, man,' said Jim.

I agreed – but I was also determined. We had made a plan, and I was keen to see it through. 'Let's just go look,' I suggested. 'We can decide once we're in there.'

Hesitantly, we walked up the path and entered the house. Inside we found lush carpet and a staircase with a polished wooden bannister. A woman seated at a reception desk asked us if we were after a '30 minute session'. We said yes and, after we had each given her a $50 note, she pointed to a waiting room. Jim and I sat side by side on a couch, bolt upright. Around us were four bored-looking women, a mix of ethnicities and ages. One had some papers on her lap and was writing away. I asked her what she was working on.

'It's just some TAFE homework,' she replied. She sounded British.

'Oh, cool,' I said.

I glanced sideways at my mate. He was wide-eyed, gaze fixed towards the stairs. I looked over and saw a woman in faded white lingerie walking a fat man with spectacles down the grand staircase. 'Now you make sure you come back soon,' she was saying in a mock-scolding tone. The fat bloke scared me, even though I was sure he was an accountant. *Okay, time to leave.* We were in over our heads.

I stood and slunk over to the woman at the desk. She was frowning over a ledger. I asked if we could get our money back.

Without looking up she said, 'Sorry, love, we don't do refunds.' She made another entry in the ledger.

I crept back to the couch where my mate was sitting; he was looking even more uncomfortable than I felt. He looked at me, expectant, and I sensed his mild panic when I shook my head.

I sat down next to him and motioned with my chin towards a woman using an emery board on her nails. Jim's eyes darted between me and the emery board lady. I had never communicated so much without words.

Finally, one of the girls asked if we wanted to 'see' anyone. Dressed in a negligee, she had a Spanish accent and was attractive and polite.

'Can I go with you?' I asked.

'Sure!' she said, and she led me upstairs. I was nervous, but happy to be moving. I had left Jim in the den, hoping he would follow suit. Leave no man behind was a fine motto, unless you were trapped in the waiting room of a brothel – in which case it was every man for himself.

We walked along velvet carpet to a neat room containing a double bed and a shower.

'Take off all your clothes,' said the Spanish woman as she slipped out of her negligee. She was a real woman, my height, and with contours to her hips and bust and shoulders that I did not see on the girls in high school.

I did what I was told. I was pretty scared by now, but I had to hold it together, because if she found out my age, I was in serious shit.

'How old are you?' she asked.

'Eighteen,' I lied.

'Do you play football?'

'Yes. I play for . . . a team south of the river.' I'd almost said Bull Creek under-fifteens.

'I thought so. You look strong.' She put a hand on my shoulder. It was warm. She stepped closer.

17

I wasn't afraid anymore; she knew I was nervous and she was careful with me.

I fumbled through the encounter, but it wasn't a bad experience at all. I had been a virgin until then, so in a sense I felt like I had cheated the whole process of persuading a girl to have sex with me. I didn't care. It was getting away with it, that's what mattered now. I knew I was never going to tell a soul about this. I would take it to my grave, and I hoped Jim would too.

Afterwards, as we lay together in the bed, she asked how old I really was.

'I'm fourteen,' I confessed.

'Oh shit.' She sat up in bed, hand to her mouth. 'My God, I was meant to check your licence when you came up here.' Then she laughed. 'Well, at least you know how to screw now!'

I met Jim across the road at the cafe. He looked a bit shaken.

'I picked that British girl,' my friend told me. 'She was a ball breaker. She wasn't nice.'

Neither of us was hungry. We got the hell out of there, and rode the bus home in silence.

We had been in way over our heads. I probably should have just given up the $50 and done a runner. But I learned a lesson that day: once you step in the arena, you're committed. Don't ask for a refund. We were in the shit the moment we crossed the threshold of that property, and a retreat might have given us the worst of both worlds: ignominy, and no good story to tell. Years later, I found the same overseas. The minute you cross into another person's territory uninvited, you breach their world and you belong to them, unless you can find a way through.

I was learning lessons, too, from the SAS books I was reading. *The Quiet Soldier* by Adam Ballinger was a reservist's account of the British SAS selection course from contender in a group of 100 to one of the last men standing. It was a rare glimpse into the workings of the secretive unit. I devoured it. Lying on my single bed, with a tiny reading lamp clipped to the bedhead, I read for hours. The author's stories of scaling the Brecon Beacons in Wales in driving sleet and snow with an enormous Bergen backpack on his back had me enthralled. Even the profanity was exotic: 'It's as black as a witch's tit up there,' one of the instructors said. The suffering seemed almost unendurable.

The book led me to a few conclusions. First, I needed to be very strong and fit even to consider joining. Second, I needed to be able to absorb severe punishment: not inflicted by the instructors but from within myself – my own desire to keep going would hurt the most. In the black of night there would be no instructors shouting; I would be the one driving myself forward. And finally, holding my nerve would be paramount. It seemed that consistent overwhelm was the normal setting of the unit – people would quit in search of relief or in exasperation at their own flaws. My mind would play tricks on me as a result of the severe lack of sleep, stress and disorientation. I needed to start training right now.

I decided to do fifty sit-ups in my bedroom, right then and there in my pyjama shorts.

I was grunting and puffing as I jerked and threw my arms about for momentum, sweat running down my face. Just as I was gasping through my final ten, Mum barged in. Her unannounced room invasions were a habit of hers that really shat me. On this occasion, however, I couldn't even shout at her – I was too buggered.

'What the *hell* are you doing?' Mum asked, incredulous.

'Sit-ups,' I panted. 'I'm training.'

'Get to bloody bed, it's eleven o'clock. Christ Almighty.' She left, slamming the door behind her.

I puffed through the last ten sit-ups and then, exhausted, hauled myself up to sit on the edge of bed. I could not believe how far I was from where I needed to be. Still, as I lay awake thinking of the barren, frozen Brecon Beacons, I felt good taking a first step. It felt strange to take a physical action to prepare for something that was at least ten years distant.

Tomorrow, I'll run before school, I vowed.

But when I climbed out of bed the next morning, my midsection burned with pain. I couldn't even bend forward to put my shoes on. There would be no running before school – I was unable to twist any part of my body.

It was 38 degrees that afternoon. We were so far inland that the Fremantle Doctor, the famed afternoon sea breeze, rarely reached us. I jammed a peanut butter and honey sandwich down my throat for fuel then pulled on my school gym clothes – red parachute silk shorts and a thick black polo shirt – and worn basketball shoes.

I ran through the windless streets as the sun beat down on the black bitumen. After a few blocks my lungs began to burn. It felt like I had sandbags wrapped around my ankles. My stomach jiggled with each step.

By the time I got to the school oval, I was doubled over with a stitch. I had run 600 metres. I dropped to the grass and lay there until I had recovered enough to walk home.

I had a long, long way to go before I would be physically fit enough for selection into the SAS, but I began looking for a path into the military. I knew that would be the first of many steps. A close mate of mine, a rangy Brit from Yorkshire, told me he was going to join ADFA, the Australian Defence Force Academy. It was an officer training school in Canberra, he explained. If you got in, you did a degree there and then went to Royal Military College, Duntroon and became an army officer. He showed me the brochure. There were cadets with short haircuts and crisp white uniforms wearing swords and hats and saluting; lifting weights and smiling; walking around with mates laughing. I was impressed. This was a path to university and the military at the same time. If you graduated, you got to lead a platoon of 30 people. After reading Michael Crichton's *Jurassic Park* the year before, I had decided to study genetic engineering so I could build dinosaurs, but this was even better.

I told my parents about the career path I'd decided on. Mum looked nervous. She had seen what war had done to her father. Dad cautioned me: 'You know soldiers are kind of . . . they do shit jobs, right? What about the air force? Or the navy?'

'Nah, I want to be a foot soldier,' I said. (Actually, I had flat feet and wore orthotics to correct them.)

I told another family friend my plan and he laughed at me. 'Bend over and clean those toilet bowls, boy!' he mocked in a drill sergeant's voice.

Fuck you, I thought. But it only made me more determined to join up.

In the winter of the same year, I asked my year coordinator if I could do work experience with the SAS at the army base in Swanbourne.

An older woman who taught home economics, she was perplexed. 'I'll have to ask about that,' she said. 'It's never been done for a year ten student before.'

But I persisted, returning each day to ask if she'd had a response from the base.

Eventually they agreed to allow me to do two weeks work experience at Campbell Barracks.

In the first week, I was assigned to a workshop as an apprentice armourer. I saw all the weapons racked up in the armoury – long, black, with desert beige paint on them. I asked the armourer who was supervising me about the history of the unit as I watched him marking use-by dates on small silver gas cylinders. He told me the SAS hadn't been used for operations in ages. It's like training your whole life for a game of footy that you never get to play, he said. They almost went overseas to get the Aussie hostages in Cambodia in 1993, but they didn't, and the hostages were killed in the end.

In the second week, I was sent to the gymnasium. I shook hands with the physical training instructor. He was built like a granite statue; his quadriceps looked like they were carved out of hardwood. He appraised me. 'You'll be training with us this week.' He walked me into the gym, where black-and-white images of the infamous selection course adorned the wall.

I stayed on the fringe of the group before class, too shy to talk to anyone, as the men joked around with each other. But they were true gentlemen, shaking my hand and asking my name.

The circuit started. I strained in the push-ups and dips and general movement, where everyone else seemed to be cruising. It was a brutal introduction. I went home on the bus a physical wreck, unable even to look out the window.

But I had survived my first brush with the SAS.

4

PHANTOMS

EVENTUALLY I BEGAN TO RUN FASTER. I WAS RUNNING STEADILY, now, on the front of my feet, where before I had lumbered along. I would head out on the baking hot nights of summer to complete my 6-kilometre route. My record time was 24 minutes 30 seconds. I was always trying to break it.

At Red Rooster, I swapped the nuggets for bread rolls and the Coke for water. My apron, tight around my waist a year before, was now loose. I sometimes declared my ambition to join the SAS when I was at Red Rooster. I worked with an older manager, genial with grey hair and beard, who listened to me talk then said, 'I knew an SAS guy who was in Vietnam. His friend was being airlifted out of the jungle on a rope dangling from a helicopter when he fell. My guy went back to look for him but they never found him. He's gone to psychics and clair-voyants to ask if his mate survived or not.' I remember feeling so moved to hear that, decades later, this warrior still pined for his mate who had been left behind. I thought there might be a force that bound those men which was stronger than family. It was a great feeling when, in 2008, I learned that Private John Elkington Fisher had been found and his body was repatriated, to be greeted by his old comrades from 2 Squadron.

I had studied hard to keep up in all my year twelve classes. I had learned in year eleven that when you keep up week to week, you don't need to panic-study at the end. I had taken chemistry, for my love of bombs; history, for my love of war stories; and biology, for my love of dinosaurs. But the army, the SAS – that was the dream. That's what made me pull my shoes on every night and train when not a soul was watching.

One weekend the national newspaper ran a spotlight story on the unit. The reporter had travelled into the outback to get pictures. The final shot was of four men walking along a desert road towards the camera, carrying their rifles and packs, wearing Oakley Frogskins sunglasses. They looked like rock stars.

As well as studying, working and exercising, I continued to read. I bought a book called *Phantoms of the Jungle*. The title was a reference to the nickname the Vietcong gave to the SAS soldiers who crept through the jungles of Vietnam completely undetected, covering their footsteps over with dirt, not speaking a single word, for weeks at a time. It was a long account of the Aussie SAS in Borneo, Malaya and Vietnam. It wasn't all recon and hiding; there were some savage battles. During ambushes, SAS patrols would deploy long lines of mines that would explode and kill NVA soldiers. When clearing one apparently dead enemy, a soldier recalled a junior NVA scout 'full of holes' reaching up and grabbing his wrist as a dying act of defiance. He gripped it so hard his fingernails left puncture marks in the soldier's wrist. Another patrolling SAS soldier recalled being so well camouflaged for an ambush that he had to lean back from the edge of the jungle trail he was following as an entire NVA unit walked past him. They would have walked into the barrel of his gun had he not moved.

The stories seemed unreal, but I believed them absolutely, and I wanted to be part of that world, wanted to witness a historic event, like a battle, not just as an observer but as a participant, fighting there alongside my men.

*

I was getting ready to head to school one June morning in 1996 when a news item on the TV caught my eye. In a field near Townsville was the charred wreckage of two Black Hawk helicopters that had collided during a counterterrorism training exercise. Eighteen soldiers had died. Black 1 exploded on impact with the ground, with only two out of the fourteen soldiers aboard surviving. Team leader Gary Proctor stated: 'We went back to collect them, some we had to leave, some blokes were on fire. There were explosions.' I saw footage of a man on a stretcher being loaded into an ambulance. His green coveralls had a torn sleeve and his muscular forearms were smeared with black dirt and smoke. He was gesturing to the emergency staff, issuing directions even as he lay wounded. The pilot of one of the downed aircraft described how SAS men soaked in jet fuel and with broken bones had run back into the flaming wreckage to pull their mates out.

I later watched the *Four Corners* report into the incident. I wanted to hear what had happened but I was also keen to see these men, these heroes of mine whose comrades had died before their eyes. The regiment soldiers spoke in neutral tones that contained a touch of dry humour. They were articulate, honest and even-keeled in their delivery. I noticed that they referred to themselves as 'you' rather than the first-person 'I'. None of them cried, but I sensed numbness in their words.

Reflecting, patrol commander Gary Proctor said, 'I was the only one in my . . . don't s'pose there's too many days go by you don't think about it, sometimes you might have a bit of trouble sleeping, but . . .'

It was a national tragedy that made world headlines. For me, it brought home the high stakes of SAS training. At Campbell Barracks there was a stone memorial for dead soldiers etched with more than 50 names. Most of these lives had been lost in training exercises. Parachute crashes, propeller strikes to the head, motorbike crashes, scuba diving accidents, plane crashes, accidental shootings. It was a dangerous job. But far from putting me off, I wanted it more than ever.

I kept training. One day when I was walking to school in shorts, a friend pointed at my thighs. 'You've been running a bit,' he observed. I had never had anyone point out a change in my physical appearance. My parents bought me running shoes and a singlet for my birthday. I was running faster over longer distances. I would run at night, when no-one could see me and I could work as hard as I wanted. It felt good to have my own secret mission to train for.

My marks improved, too. I was spending long nights at my desk at home. I had an army sticker on the side of it that said: *The Army. The Edge.* I was dead keen on the army, to the point where my yearbook listed my stated ambition as being to become a 'six-star general'. The rank did not exist, but I wanted it anyway.

I finally received a letter requesting my attendance before an ADFA selection board. I arrived at a riverfront barracks near Fremantle and saw a group of enthusiastic young men, bright-eyed and polite. We began by doing some physical exercise with a barrel-chested captain who made us sprint and do push-ups together. Thanks to all my training, I was able to keep up. Next we attempted an obstacle course which required us to work as a team to complete various challenges. At one obstacle we needed to use some planks of wood to get ourselves across a poisoned area. But there were not enough boards, and we argued over the best way to proceed. The instructors watched us and took notes.

Another exercise had us standing in front of the group and delivering a short presentation on crime management in Western Australia. One of the speakers let everyone know that he carried a knife when he went into the Perth CBD; he was looking us each in the eye and nodding as he talked, like he was looking for more carriers. From then on the group referred to him as 'Knife-man'.

At lunch, I saw an army captain in dress uniform leaving the mess. He was stocky with red hair and a bushy moustache – dashing in a 1980s kind of way, he looked like he'd come straight from the Falklands battlefield. His blue beret marked him out as aviation, and I remembered where I had seen him before.

'Is he from the Black Hawk accident?' I asked the barrel-chested captain who had been training us.

'Yup, the inquiry is underway here just now.'

I knew the man; I had seen him in the news. He was the pilot of one of the helicopters that had crashed.

A letter arrived at home with a Defence crest in the corner. It was slightly damp from the lawn sprinkler, so I opened it carefully with Mum standing next to me. We both read it. She squealed and hugged me. I had been accepted into the Australian Defence Force Academy. I would not be studying dinosaurs; I was joining the army.

5

SHIT FIGHT

DAD RUMMAGED THROUGH HIS WARDROBE.

'Try this,' he said, offering me an old off-the-rack suit. I pulled on the jacket and realised I looked like a used-car salesman. The shoulders were too wide, and the sleeves gaped. 'No worries,' said Dad. 'As long as you have a shirt and tie you'll be good.'

I was getting nervous. The letter from ADFA had specified 'formal' attire for my induction ceremony at the recruiting station in Northbridge. I had worn a tux and a bow tie to my year eleven formal, but surely that's not what they meant.

Dad put the tie around his own neck and tied a half-Windsor knot, then slipped it over my head and adjusted it. He was concentrating; this was not a daily ritual.

I left home with my suitcase and an ironing board, wearing Dad's suit pants with no jacket. Mum had packed my suitcase with me, and she had given me a small address book with Australia-themed cartoons of kangaroos, koalas, kookaburras and the Sydney Opera House. She had handwritten phone numbers and addresses for my four aunties and my grandparents, and at the front she had written in cursive:

To Mark,
You will make it!
Love,
Mum & Dad '97

Steve had given me a silver hip flask, on the back of which was engraved: *To Mark, the 'six-star general'*.

I walked up the road in Northbridge adjusting my tie, looking at the other new recruits milling on the path ahead of me. All wore blazers, navy or maroon, their ties in full Windsor knots. Their trousers were neatly pressed and their shoes were real leather. It was the first time I realised that private schools actually had real uniforms that looked like formal wear. They looked like actors in a play about British schoolboys – the type where they talk about rugger and flick towels at each other in the washroom. They were all pleasant handshakes, strong eye contact, and plummy western suburbs accents. I recognised a few of them from my selection boards, and I went and chatted to them. Knife-man was nowhere to be seen.

An ancient brigadier with a grey moustache marched down the stairs. He looked like an extra from a *Blackadder* episode. He invited us all inside to an auditorium and we took our seats. At his signal, the students stood, and we raised our palms to pledge allegiance to the Queen. By the end of the ceremony I was technically a soldier. In reality, I was still an adolescent in ill-fitting business casual. The entire cohort lined up for a photo and I realised that of 22 kids I was the only one who had no jacket and a tie pointing diagonally left.

We drank hot tea and I pretended to eat a stale muffin. I felt like I was being charmed before being yanked away from my family. My parents helped me load my suitcase and ironing board onto a sleek green bus with the yellow slogan: *The Army. The Edge*. We were all silent. My throat had tightened and I was afraid to speak for fear of saying the wrong thing. We walked out on the street at midday, no shadow in sight. My dad shook my hand and hugged me. I knew he was proud of me, and that he was sad I was leaving. Mum hugged me long and close, a real mother's hug. Dan held out his tiny hand for me to shake, and then it was Steve's turn – he was more excited than I was.

I waved through the window at my mum as the bus pulled away, headed to the airport. She was wiping away tears and waving a white tissue. I had no idea when I'd see them again.

A navy officer cadet leaned forward to inspect the corner of my single bed fold of an army blanket that smelled like a horse. It may have been surplus from the Gallipoli campaign.

I was standing at the side of the bed.

'That's not a hospital corner,' he said. 'Do a hospital corner.' The navy man looked to be barely twenty. He was wearing bright white shorts, white socks pulled up to the knee and white dress shoes. Under the offending blanket, I pulled at a diagonal swathe of starched bedsheet and tried to turn it into the hospital corner he had just showed me. I rushed it. It was a mangled corner of folds and kinks, worse than before.

'DO A HOSPITAL CORNER!' he screamed at full volume, his hot breath in my ear.

My anus clenched in abject terror. I had never had anyone shout at me at full volume. Even my dad kept his shouts to a civilised level. This was DEFCON 1.

I leaned forward again. This time my hands were shaky as I once again tried the hospital corner origami steps. It was a limp, slack corner that I presented the second time.

'This is abortionate, Mr Wales.' He pointed at the origami pile. 'An *absolute* shit fight. You will bog properly in this section. Get down into the breezeway in dress uniform. You have one minute.' He strode out of my room. I undressed and put on my unironed uniform. I knew I would be shouted at in the breezeway.

My eyes stung with tears. I didn't know what a shit fight or abortionate was, but I gathered they were not complimentary terms. Bog, that sounded like a shit, but I had no idea.

I was a bloody long way from the beaches of Perth and my family.

We marched down to a store and were issued with two large black bin bags worth of clothing. I had a parachute silk tracksuit, Defence Force home brand running shoes, leather boots, an entrenching spade and army camouflage uniforms. It felt like Christmas.

'*No* – you do not have to bloody pay for this! It's a gift from the army,' a female private with broad shoulders and an oversized jaw bellowed from behind a counter. She looked at me like I had shat in front of her. 'No. You sign for it.' She was pointing at a clipboard. I signed on the dotted line for my first batch of army gear.

The soulless white buildings that housed cadet divisions were nicknamed Legoland. One of these buildings was the armoury and we marched there to be given weapons. It was our first sighting of the new issued weapons. I recognised them because a bad guy had used one in *Die Hard*; they were futuristic and sleek.

'That's an F88 Austeyr,' I heard the storeman say as I stepped up to the counter. A hefty bald corporal, he was reading out the rifles' serial numbers while a junior soldier handwrote them in a ledger.

'Regimental number,' the corporal barked, not looking up.

'Five-eight-oh-three-one-five-oh,' I recited.

The corporal looked up, wild eyed. 'It's *zero*, not *oh*. *Oh* is the sound that *faggots* make when they fuck each other!'

He checked the barrel, then handed me the weapon and a silver metal receiver. I grabbed it with one hand on the butt stock and the other under the barrel. It felt like a serious, weighty tool.

'Thank you, sir,' I said, then added, 'Nice gun.'

'It's a WEAPON! It's not a fuckin' *gun!*' He bawled the last part down the whole line of the cadets. 'If one more cadet calls it a *fuckin'* gun, look out,' he yelled.

A wiry man in dress uniform appeared out of nowhere and motioned to the storeman. The man looked relaxed but serious. He seemed to be talking about the shouting.

'That's the XO,' said someone behind me. 'He's an SAS guy – see the beret?'

Everyone was impressed that he had saved us from the nasty storeman. The corporal was much more civil when he resumed his job.

I decked my single bedroom out with my portable CD player and Pearl Jam's album *Ten*, plus some Led Zeppelin and Smashing Pumpkins albums. I had a poster of an American football player running through flames. I put my SAS books up on the shelf: they were my signal to the world of what I had in mind. I did not have the courage to speak my ambition aloud.

That night, an enormous teenager knocked on my door. He barely fit in the doorframe.

'I'm Toby,' he said, extending a large hand.

'I'm Mark,' I said.

Toby walked in and plopped down on the spare chair. He surveyed my posters and books.

'How good are these guns? Rifles, I mean.' He pointed at the rifle locked against the wall in a metal collar and brace.

'Unreal,' I said. I detected a potential nerd-brother. He spoke fast and his eyes were bright with the thrill of our new life. 'What does bogging mean?' I asked.

He laughed out loud. I liked him for it.

'It means cleaning, man. Everyone knows that.'

We made small talk about football and rugby and the states we came from. He had played under-21s for the Wallabies. He stood and walked over to my bookshelf.

'Good books! Do you want to join the SAS?'

'Yeah,' I said, downplaying it, but he was just as keen as I was – and just as well read on the subject. He knew a lot about the SAS and its history, and the fire rate of our new weapons. It seemed I had made a friend.

That night, the third years called us into the breezeway in formation.

'Come down in patrol order!' they screamed. That meant uniform, rifle and webbing. We each unlocked our weapons from the braces and ran downstairs with them. There was shouting and commotion; cadets skittered about like rabbits while fully uniformed third years terrorised us. Some were clearly relishing the 'bad cop' role, screaming in people's faces.

We all lined up. The lead cadet was an army man, no older than twenty, muscled with thick veins running down his forearms. He paced along the front rank, not looking at anyone. His hands were behind his back, and he was frowning under his dress cap as though deeply troubled.

'It appears that not every cadet here is the same.'

I felt a bolt of fear. Was it me? Had I forgotten something?

'One of the staff cadets' – he stopped mid stride and turned to a tiny female soldier with an oversized bush hat – 'does not have *her weapon*!'

I glanced to my left and saw that her hands were by her sides, empty. Everyone else had their weapon. Shit. I felt bad for her.

The lead cadet continued. 'Your personal security is not up to standard, and now there is a rifle missing. How are you going to fight without a RIFLE!' His words rose to a shout as he towered over her, glaring.

'ARRRGH!' A green-clad figure with a green-painted face, wearing a green helmet with hessian strips hanging off it, ran out of the darkness towards the front rank. It looked like a soldier, but all I could see was the black metal bayonet on the front of his rifle, pointing at us as he charged.

He skidded to a stop in front of the female soldier, brandishing the bayonet. His eyes were wild. I could see the girl was trembling. The green blob stalked along the front rank, his bayonet inches from our faces. It was our first lesson in security.

Winter came, bone cold and wet. I ran about in the dark at football training, and all I could think about were the warm beaches of Perth. I had started academics. I studied chemistry and politics and geography. We seemed to live in the dark, and the days were grey and freezing. I marched to class in my uniform. Like a fool, I had committed to the 'no jumper' challenge for 1997, and was hurting as I strode across the campus in only a dress uniform shirt in single-digit temperatures.

Later, sitting in my room, I picked up the address book Mum had given me and read her encouraging message: *You will make it!* As I looked out across Legoland I felt pretty homesick. This was not the army, I thought. This was a boarding school run by children. But it was part of the path, I reminded myself. Three years at ADFA then, after I graduated, Duntroon. One year in Duntroon, hoping that I was good enough to graduate to an infantry unit. Then work hard in the unit for two years until I could take selection, where I figured I had a 10 per cent chance of passing, at best. It was six years of eating shit for a 10 per cent chance at being selected for the SAS.

The odds weren't great, but I had to stick at it. If I went home, that was it. I would be starting from scratch, and the SAS would never be a part of my future.

*

After six months in Canberra, I flew home to Perth for the first time. I was so excited I travelled in my army uniform, clutching a copy of Tom Clancy's *The Hunt for Red October*. When I arrived, Mum hugged me like I'd been lost all that time, and everyone admired my new uniform.

Later, I went for a drive with Dad. I was sitting in the passenger seat and complaining about how hard ADFA was and how cold, and how I wanted to come home. I was shovelling little strawberry cream lollies into my mouth as I wept.

Dad listened for a while in silence. Then he said, 'You know it's gonna get better.'

I stared at his hand resting on the gearstick of the family Tarago. He wore a silver wedding band and his hands were tanned from his weekends in the garden.

I cried more as I reached into the lolly bag to grab more strawberry creams. 'I want to leave, Dad. It's shit. It's not what I thought it would be.' I listed a dozen other reasons why I should quit.

Dad's face was impassive. I was not convincing him.

'Maybe you should just harden up and finish it,' he said, without taking his eyes off the road. He spoke with casual ease, knowing it would land on me like a bomb. It was a challenge. Dad knew how I ticked.

I sat up straight in my seat, on the defensive. I swallowed the last of the lollies and collected myself – I was ashamed of my conduct.

Dad had told me before that adversity was not a bad thing. 'Did you ever see a cornered animal that's depressed?' he asked me as a kid. 'A bit of struggle keeps you alive.' His family had grown up poor in freezing Victorian winters, with dirt floors and no electricity. They had been stressed about making a living, but they were a strong family. He knew a bit of struggle would be good for me. Dad only had a few rules for us: no drugs, no motorbikes, and do your best, always.

At the end of the week, I packed, had a beer with my brothers, then flew back to Canberra.

Dad's words had had the desired effect. I knew I wouldn't be going home until I was done.

6

THUNDERSTRUCK

AFTER THREE YEARS AT ADFA, I STILL HAD ONE YEAR TO GO before taking the next step towards selection – a year at the Royal Military College, Duntroon. There was just one problem: I was a disaster as a cadet. I felt like my dream of heading to the infantry unit, 2 RAR, was doomed. The regiment was next in line to tour East Timor as peacekeepers, and as it would be our first warlike mission since Vietnam, I wanted the experience and credibility of leading a platoon on operations.

I had fucked many a mission by now. The last one was the stuff of legend – ranked in the pantheon of the best cadet field disasters of all time.

I had been leading a platoon attack against a small enemy squad. This was considered a fundamental skill for any officer in the military, regardless of whether they were going to lead a bunch of mechanics or a tank troop. There was a standard tactic: you fired on the enemy group then, leaving a team in position to keep the enemy pinned down, you took another two teams around the left or right flank of the enemy and attacked from out of the protection of low ground – or 'dead ground', as we called it. You could then clear the enemy position with your fire support pinning down the enemy at right angles to your attack. The concept was called 'fire and manoeuvre' and had been developed to avoid the carnage of World War I. It was basic, in theory.

I had initiated the attack, put a fire support position in place, and led two teams on a long semicircular walk to flank the enemy. I reckoned we had walked about 300 metres in a long arc, and were now sitting 50 metres from the enemy position, hidden from view in the low ground. We waited, spread out with 5-metre spacing, as I took a bearing to the enemy with my compass. I could hear their machine-gun fire and yelling just over the top of the ridge. I walked down the line to each section commander and pointed out the angle of attack, checking off all the tasks. Team spread out, check. Attack angle allocated, check. Smoke grenade ready, check. Time to advance – one minute. I stood, my mind spinning, excited that I was about to execute my first decimation of an enemy squad. I would be victorious, the envy of the team. I crouched over my carbine, with its blank rounds loaded. I stared into the grey banksia scrub to my front and paused in the crisp morning air, waiting to go 'over the top' and hit the enemy flanks. I held up my hand and looked down the line. Everyone was up on their feet, crouched forward, ready for the attack. I dropped my arm in the direction of the enemy, and we crept forward towards the distracted enemy. As we crested the ridge, I saw Kris Reilly pause and shoot a clatter of blank rounds at the opposing force. It was a decisive action: we were now 20 metres away, right on top of them before the battle had even started. This was certain victory. It would mean a pass in Platoon Command assessment, maybe even a barracks promotion. I shouted out to the forward sections to advance and wipe out the enemy.

After a couple of rounds, Kris looked back and shouted: 'CEASE FIRE! It's our fire support position!' He was making a cutting motion across his throat, eyes wild.

Slack-jawed, I stared at Kris. I had attacked my own section. During the 300-metre loop, I had lost my bearings and not advanced far enough towards the enemy. When we set up in low ground, with the clatter of fire and the stress of getting my people in position on a time crunch, I had not advanced far enough and was too close to my own team. It was as bad a result as you can get: both inept and dangerous.

The instructor stormed between the two teams, his arms pumping, branches cracking under him. He pointed at two soldiers and bawled: 'You're DEAD!' He shifted his aim to two more piles of green huddled in each other's arms. 'You two fucks – you're dead. Shot by your own *mates*.' He spat and strode around the position as we collected the 'bodies' of our own troops. My mates were huffing and sweating as they worked, glaring at me as they pulled their 'dead' friends' bodies into the circle. The centre of the position resembled a mass grave. As the farce became too unbearable to watch, the instructor stopped us. The dead came back to life and walked in for the debrief. There was just the crunch of leaves as everyone settled in the centre.

'So, how did you go, Platoon Commander?' the captain asked.

The question was rhetorical. We all knew it had been a massive fuck-up.

'Ah, not good,' I said. 'We attacked our own position. I think I came up short in the recon.'

'*Came up short*. Yes. Yes, you could say that.' Pause. Long stare. 'In *fact*, you came up so short you need to consider a bloody *career change*, Staff Cadet Wales!'

It was a humiliating fail, and widely discussed in my class. Not exactly where I wanted to be only six months from graduating ADFA.

*

41

The first fingers of dawn stretched out across the scrub and the first waves of screaming galahs headed west, looking for a drink. I was sitting on the cold clay with a wet arse, my rifle next to me, scrawling my ambush orders in a tiny green notebook. I could feel the tightening in my chest of an approaching deadline. Ambush orders are detailed, complex and hard to execute. I had made it to Duntroon and was determined to perform well and complete a good ambush – this could set me up as a cadet leader and increase my chances of getting into a light infantry unit. Get into light infantry, and you increased your chances of taking part in the new East Timor peacekeeping mission – which gave you a better chance on the SAS selection course.

'Ambush is legalised murder,' a glowering instructor would proclaim to his students. The line was relished and parroted by cadets. 'I like ambushes – it's legalised murder,' the senior cadets would say to each other, nodding. The official notes were more professional. *It is an attack by an organised force lying in wait in terrain of your choosing.* Ideally, you would have set this up in advance with machine guns, mines and other explosives. You could land a hammer blow on your enemy in the opening seconds of the battle with withering machine-gun fire and exploding mines and rockets. This was the 'kill zone' – the area where the enemy would be shot at and blown up – though the term was later changed to 'engagement area', which was much less offensive from a public affairs perspective.

Australian forces had executed some very effective ambushes in the jungles of Vietnam, a perfect example being the 'tractor job'. An SAS patrol had noticed a tractor that was used to shuttle a trailer load of weapons along a track in an enemy area. So they planned an ambush that would allow them to destroy the tractor and fighters in one hit. They set up roadside bombs and a series of small mines, and lay in wait alongside the track. When the tractor drove through the ambush site, it detonated the mines and the entire team of enemy soldiers was wiped out.

At Duntroon, we were practising the art of platoon-level ambushing against a fictional Soviet-esque military called the Musorians. This involved leading three teams of nine people into an ambush site, and initiating against the enemy. It required detailed planning because once you were in position, you could not move or talk lest you be detected. You would need to plan who went where, what order you walked in, what tasks had to be completed, what equipment you needed and set a time. You would also need to determine some control measures: Who initiates it? What if civilians walk through or detect us? What if the enemy are travelling with a lot of civilians? The orders were completed in a standard format. This was known as SMEAC, an acronym for Situation, Mission, Execution, Admin and logistics, Command and signals. The format was easy to remember and easy to follow. You could use it if you had four days or four minutes of planning time. I had written my orders in this format. Well, most of my orders. Unfortunately, I hadn't quite finished when I heard someone say: 'Staff Cadet Wales, let's go.'

A captain had strolled over and the entire platoon was lining up for orders, a mass of 30 green uniforms seated in front of a small map of the site that had been prepared by a mate. We called it a 'mud map', and it showed the order of battle – the practice went back to the days when armies used rocks on the ground to illustrate their tactics. We used paper discs to mark the team locations, red string for the road, and blue string to indicate our path into the ambush site.

I started off with the orders. 'We have all section commanders?'

Three people put their hands up. One of the section commanders was Kris Reilly: a strong blond soldier with an amazing karaoke voice, he would sing Pearl Jam ballads at full volume in Canberra as a small band of fans swooned in front of him. We had been in the same squadron at ADFA, and now we were both platoon sergeants in Kokoda company at Duntroon. Our rooms were in the same position, one floor apart. The floors all had identical layouts, and one night a shirtless Kris had staggered into my room drunk, thinking it was his room. I woke up to see a giant dark silhouette hovering over my bed, while I cowered under the sheets trying to talk the intruder out of landing on me.

The rest of the platoon sat in a semicircle around the map, and a hush descended over the team; everyone cooperated when a cadet mate was on the hook for a job.

'The following are ambush orders for 3 Platoon. No questions until the end. Situation: Enemy. We are expecting an enemy team of six Musorians to approach from east to west. Enemy is dressed in woodland camouflage and is carrying a combination of weapons. They are known to conduct aggressive counter-ambush drills. Their morale is high. Their intention is to reinforce an enemy unit up the road.'

I could see the captain instructor standing beside the group, jotting down notes.

'Mission: 3 Platoon is to destroy enemy force no later than 2200 in order to deny enemy village reinforcement.' I repeated this; the mission is considered so important, you always say it twice. I was going well: I had completed the first two steps of orders with good control and authority. I was on my way, my voice steadying and slowing, my confidence rising.

'Execution: This will be a two up, one back ambush formation. It will be a four-phase mission. Phase one will be the insertion into the ambush site; phase two: setting up the ambush; phase three: the ambush; phase four: extraction. Phase one in detail.' I explained how we would walk the site and set up the ambush, then moved on to phase two. I flipped the page of my notebook to find . . . nothing. Just a blank page. I flipped

44

to the next page, thinking I must have skipped one. Surely I'd got further than this!

Nope. Just more blank pages. *Shit!*

Remain calm, I urged myself. *Theatre is all a part of this*. I felt my heart rate creep up a little. I cleared my throat. I was off the map. In the wilderness, without my notes.

'Once in position in phase one, there is to be no eating at all to ensure we remain undetected.' I considered this for a moment; I love eating and I am always hungry – I knew I would need to eat. 'Actually, you can take a small snack in the ambush site, just some chocolate or something.' I was off script, talking about chocolate. I saw the two section commanders look at each other, one frowning.

Moving on to phase two, I described what would happen when the ambush was initiated. 'I will initiate the ambush once I detect the enemy. I will do it with a burst of machine-gun fire. Then we will take out the enemy in the engagement area.'

Someone in the back chuckled. I saw the instructor was still writing, but now he was shaking his head, like a disappointed parent.

Feeling rattled now, I gestured at the mud map.

'If the enemy counterattack, I want the rear section to piss-charge down the back from support position and help us fight the enemy.'

One patrol commander laughed aloud, then the whole platoon broke out into laughter – that term was not in the official NATO tactical dictionary. Block, advance, clear and feint were. Pisscharge – that was not even a colloquialism. The captain was shaking his head even harder.

I covered the clearance of the engagement area and the withdrawal with barely any of the detail needed to make it work. I was in a hurry to wrap it up before I said any more stupid shit.

'Okay: questions, section commanders?'

The section commanders all shook their heads. This was cadet code: 'Don't jack on your mates.' You never questioned your mate's orders, lest they appear unclear. You acted as though you understood it all. You would need your mates to support your own leadership tilt later.

The rest of the troop, having already completed their command assessments, had no such misgivings. One thrust his hand into the air and fluttered it.

'Walesy, you said we could eat in the site. What can we take in?' It was a trap: the bastard was asking me to elaborate on my stupid point about eating.

'Well, take in some chocolate, but no M&Ms – they're too bloody colourful and would give us away.'

The entire platoon erupted into laughter, even the instructor.

The tragedy of my delivery had tipped into full-blown comedy. The entire team relished seeing their mate squirm – it was obvious I had run out of orders and was winging it, and I had been found out. The mission was off to a bad start.

Needless to say, we fucked the entire job. The teams got lost in the dark. One patrol walked off to the flank of another and could not reconnect. Once we were in the ambush site, there were twenty people walking in every direction, bumping into each other, hissing and waving each other away. It was a total mess. And it was my mess, M&Ms and all. The enemy walked in from the left flank when we were setting up the ambush, and one of the cadets actually spoke to them, asking for help to site a machine gun. The enemy opened up with rifles and routed the entire team. I tried to bring in depth reinforcements, but they were half asleep and too slow to get to us. We had been ambushed in our own ambush.

I walked out chastened, and spent a restless night waiting for the morning debrief. I had thought I was one of the best cadets in the team, strong, fit and fast, but I had fucked a difficult yet achievable test. I knew from the laughs and chatter that came out of the night that people were talking about the mission, and that I was the butt of the joke.

'So, how do you think you went?' asked the captain the next morning.

'Well, I think the orders were okay, but the set up of the ambush was a bit of a mess.'

'A bit of a mess?' The captain shook his head. 'I gotta tell you, I've been in the army twelve years and it's the first time I have heard soldiers laughing during a set of orders.' He was keeping a straight face, but I could tell that he was suppressing a smile: clearly he had been laughing too. He opened his notebook and began to read out his list. '*Contradiction in phase two orders. Team lost on infiltration. Wrong march in sequence. Late initiation. Surprised by enemy. Five dead soldiers* . . . I have about ten more points, but I'll stop there.' He closed the notebook. 'Not your best effort,' he concluded. 'A bloody shambles setting it up. Ambushes are hard, I get it. This one was bad.'

I felt a stab of shame. I knew I had blown it, but his words still stung.

He wasn't done, though. 'But . . . I noticed that people listen to you. To my absolute bloody amazement, they followed you. They wanted to work for you. That's a good thing. You can lead, you have that skill – you just need more technical work.'

It was a small boost for me, but I needed something.

My next fuck-up involved live ammunition on a grenade course. We had been throwing live grenades all day, and we had been safety staff for our mates. We waited in the stand-by bunker listening to the booms and hearing debris landing on the roof from the assault course. There were two grenades left at the end of the day – a staff sergeant walked into the bunker and asked who wanted to throw them. I was always keen to take on extra work to improve myself so I volunteered to throw, with a mate acting as safety supervisor.

We went to the firing bunker for the first throw. I pulled the grenade out and held it with the lever positioned in the web of my hand between thumb and forefinger, and wrenched the pin free. While I was holding the lever, it was still safe. Once thrown, the lever disengaged, and a thrower had 4.5 seconds before detonation. The 'kill radius' was 5 metres.

I pulled the pin and lobbed the grenade at a target. We both crouched under the timber railway sleeper ledge to our front as the grenade went off with a solid bang, shredding the target.

I pulled out the second grenade and held it in my hand to pull the pin. I was holding it with the lever now positioned against my thumb. I pulled the pin, shouted, 'Grenade!', cocked my arm, threw – and fumbled it. I watched in horror as the grenade fell on the timber beam right in front of our faces. My world shrunk to that grenade: spinning on its end like a top, turning in slow motion, every revolution of the bomb showing off its nudity – no pin, and no safety lever cladding its flank. I had never seen a naked grenade. The clock was ticking. Four seconds left: we both stared at the spinning grenade right in front of us. Three seconds left: we climbed to our feet and ran out of the bunker, holding each other, whimpering as we ran. Two seconds left: we dived to the ground, arms still around each other's shoulders. The bomb was 4 metres away as we lay face down in lush grass. One second left: I ran a quick damage prediction. Back of right thigh, backside, foot and lower back and neck were exposed to the 400 ball bearings that would soon be headed our way. I braced for the blast.

BOOM!

The blast and frag washed over the top of us, missing us by half a metre. We got to our feet and stood looking at the pit. The parapet beam had been shattered to kindling.

A short, bald range instructor ran over, chest heaving, red moustache trembling.

'Are you blokes all right? *Shit* that was close! Good drills!'

He was pumped. He ran over to the grenade bay and admired the damage, picking at the shattered timber beam. 'We'll have to write that up!' he shouted, thrilled at the prospect of arranging a safety investigation.

My mate's face was devoid of colour, and his right leg was trembling. I was stone silent.

More range officers gathered around the pit, frowning at the damage and pacing the distance to the flattened grass where we had lain.

My mate and I wandered back to the waiting bunker in a daze. My peers had already texted out to the wider army that I had dropped a grenade in a pit. Everyone was laughing and cheering and asking for the fine details.

In the years that followed, I heard that my example was still used for new trainees on the grenade range. The red-moustachioed man would declare: 'It doesn't matter if you're as strong as an ox – this one trainee . . .' And he would then go on to recount the tale of my shit throw.

My mates all thought it was hilarious, but not me. I knew there was no way the SAS would take a soldier who would either attack his own team or blow his mates up with grenades he could not throw.

Weeks before graduation, our class was marched into a room so we could find out what corps and unit we had been allocated. I would find out if I had made the fabled light infantry unit, heading to East Timor. Three of my mates had made it – and to my surprise, I had too. My determination to improve had paid off. I was about to take my first step towards operations and, I hoped, SAS selection.

7

JUNCTION POINT

I STOOD IN THE MAKESHIFT HUT IN EAST TIMOR, THE SWEAT gluing my jungle uniform to my back while my eyes were glued to the TV screen, watching the crises unfold in Afghanistan. The brown ridge lines of Tora Bora erupted in gouts of dirt and rock as the B-52s went to work against al-Qaeda positions. The mountains were being pounded into gravel. You could sense their proximity to Osama bin Laden from the urgency in the war correspondents' voices. Not one military or security planner had predicted a campaign in Afghanistan. The Soviets had met their end there, had withdrawn, humiliated, as the rest of the world cheered. Now the Allies had strayed into the Graveyard of Empires, hungry for revenge.

I had miraculously passed Duntroon in 2000 and was allocated the position of Commander of 5 Platoon, 2 RAR. After a year of training the platoon, I had just embarked on my first tour of duty in East Timor. I had 30 light infantry soldiers and we were protecting the locals from the marauding pro-Indonesian militias. Tropical humidity hung over the island, and our long uniforms were always soaked with sweat. The wet season – you could set your watch by the 3.30 pm downpour. Skin broke out in prickles, rashes and itching. Mosquitoes would swarm at dusk and bite our testicles through our uniforms. Each night, we would fog our camp with insecticide to ward off the insects.

This had been exactly what I was looking for: an operational deployment. There was danger in East Timor, but by early 2002 it was a stretch to call it a war zone. This would give me valuable experience on my way to the SAS. I was also lucky to have been allocated the best cohort in the battalion. My platoon sergeant, Darryl Egan, was tough and capable; he had mentored me for a full year. I had improved alongside him. He helped me run an ambush with my platoon in jungle training, and with the clown ambush from the year before still burning, I was determined to succeed. This time I planned it down to the tiniest detail, and in the dark jungles of North Queensland, we pulled off a ripper ambush. I was getting better at writing and issuing orders, and I was growing in confidence.

The company officers were top notch; the company commander was considerate, exacting and placed a lot of trust in me. My platoon commander mates were senior to me, but they had welcomed me into the fold. Over Guinness and $10 steak sandwiches at an Irish pub, they told stories of old battalion officers and exercises from years before. I loved a night out in Townsville; it was warm and had the feel of the Wild West, like Fremantle. One night I was even thrown out of the saloon doors of the Mad Cow bar onto the main street. After watching spaghetti westerns as a kid, I had always wanted to be kicked out of saloon doors.

In Timor I had been assigned to Junction Point Alpha, a tiny outpost that sat on the border of East Timor and West Timor, which was Indonesian territory. A mere 100 metres from us there was an Indonesian platoon at their checkpoint, with a heavy machine gun pointed at our hut. My commanding officer, then-Lieutenant Colonel Angus Campbell, had described Junction Point Alpha as his 'strategic vulnerability'. Campbell appeared somewhat aloof in temperament, and was tall and rangy, with a beak-like nose. The soldiers called him 'Creeping Jesus', due to his ability to infiltrate your office and be seated at your desk when you least expected it. He was intelligent – a Cambridge graduate who'd majored in astrophysics and philosophy – and had a mind like a steel trap. He was personally invested in his soldiers, and he took the time to explain his strategy in East Timor to every person in the battalion. Despite his eccentricities, I loved him. Later he would go on to join the Department of the Prime Minister and Cabinet as a civilian, and he would eventually lead the entire Australian Defence Force. He was also a former SAS squadron commander, and it was clear they bred capable leaders. We had asked him why he didn't stay there, and he had told us the SAS was a 'menagerie' at the time.

My platoon's job in late March 2002 was simple. Protect the 3000 returnees that would cross the border back to East Timor in time to spend Easter with their families. For a Catholic nation, it was akin to a pilgrimage. We stood in the cover at JP-A as thousands of returnees stood in long queues waiting to be searched on their way home. They had been living in refugee camps in West Timor for nearly two years and were carrying their meagre possessions home with them. Cane chairs, mattresses, rocks, baskets, pigs hog-tied and inverted on poles, grunting in distress. Chickens were dangled by their feet in bunches, a deranged bouquet of feathers and wings and squawks. The air was a warm, still blanket, and the junction smelled of sweat, spices and petrol.

A Brazilian military policeman in a tight-fitting dark uniform, sunglasses and a red beret manned the front of the line. He was the lead searcher of all the returning families.

A young woman, slender and pretty in a black sarong, approached him clutching a small wooden box to her chest. Her parents stood on either side of her, each with a hand on her shoulder.

The MP gestured to the box with his metal detector. '*Aberta*,' he commanded in Portuguese. 'Open.'

The young woman obeyed. Inside, nestled in a bed of straw, was a tiny brown baby – dead. Its dermis had shrivelled over its tiny limbs and its hands were like hooks as the tendons had shrunk and contracted. The dead infant's bulbous head was fixed and staring at the side of the box. A few small bugs crawled around in the straw.

The MP scanned his wand over the baby, like he was looking for signs of life, then he waved the small family through.

In that moment, we all felt the young woman's loss. She walked through the checkpoint to freedom clutching a death in her arms. I felt bloody empty. She had lost her baby, and that day I realised life was a long way from fair. I had grown up with white sand beaches and parks and safety. Other people had a shit sandwich from birth, if they were lucky enough to survive that. Afterwards, when I replayed it in my mind, I could not quite believe what I had seen. That would become a common experience through my twenties. But I realised, too, that, as soldiers, we could actually be a force for good for some people in their personal chapters of pure bloody dark.

My first break of the tour came when I went to the battalion boxing night to fight my arch nemesis: Stanley 'The Hacksaw' Goodman, a massive man with a broad head, a sandy moustache and a tattoo of a Viking wielding a double-sided battleaxe on his left shoulder. The year prior, at my boxing debut, he had beaten me on points in front of a drunken battalion on a warm night in Townsville. This was the eagerly anticipated rematch. Stories had leaked to me of Stanley breaking a boxing bag while training.

The crowd in the old Portuguese building hissed as I walked out to avenge my loss. One of my platoon commander mates barracked for me, and the whole crowd turned to stare daggers at him for supporting the officer.

I punched and dodged and got smacked around by Stan's giant fists. My defence was poor, and my legs could not handle the intensity of boxing. He made mincemeat of me.

At the end of the fight I stood with Stanley and the referee, my nose bloodied, as the ref held up Stan's hand and declared him the winner. It was now 2–0 to the Hacksaw. I would have to do something about that, one day.

I had a hard time adjusting when I returned to Townsville after our East Timor trip. I was reading a book called *Captain Corelli's Mandolin*, the World War II love story of an Axis soldier and a village girl in occupied Greece. I cried often and for no reason at all. I felt different, but I could not pinpoint why. Was it the Lariam we had been taking on deployment? The administering of the weekly anti-malarial pill was designated 'nightmare night' as the entire team would descend into a mild psychosis; you could hear the screams across the stretchers as people thrashed about inside their mozzie domes. Talking about nightmares was a common topic: 'I was eating someone's leg,' the team joker had said, but not joking. The pills were sending us mad. Years later, Lariam would be banned in America and designated a psychotic drug after the US Food and Drug Administration reviewed its side effects.

With time, I slowly returned to normal. I wasn't sure what else could have brought on the bout of mild depression.

I took a Contiki tour through Europe for three weeks in the northern hemisphere summer, drinking cheap wine and spending time with some new civilian mates in Italy and France. They wanted to hear about East Timor and what I had been doing. I occasionally logged on to email at internet cafes to send pictures home. When I logged on in Venice I found an email from Dad asking me to call home. I went straight to a payphone.

'Your mum has some cancer in her lymph nodes,' Dad told me. 'She's going to have a small operation to have it cut out.' He was acting like it was no big deal, but in my bones I knew something was not right.

I arranged to return to Australia. Between my tour in East Timor and the trip to Europe, I had been away for almost nine months. It felt good to be going home.

Then I saw Mum. I knew immediately this was no 'small operation'.

8

JANE

I walked up the driveway of the family home with my suitcase. Mum was standing by the door with Dad. Her face was pale and drawn, gaunt. She was afraid – I could see it in her eyes.

'Mark,' she called.

She hugged me tight and we cried together.

'We're going to get chemo tomorrow in Fremantle,' Dad said. I could tell he was also pretty tense. The sense of dread was palpable.

Mum held my hand tight as we walked back to the house. She always had hands like a farm girl: strong enough to wrestle a calf or throw a hay bale. Despite her frail appearance, her grip was as tight as ever.

I walked into the backyard and found my beautiful dog Josie waiting for me. She yelped and squirmed and crawled all over me as her tail wagged her body. She was smiling. I had walked her twice a day for five years when I was in high school; I loved that animal.

After months and months of dirty huts in East Timor, and a stint in Europe, I was finally home. The garden was blooming, as always. Dad was a weapons-grade gardener. He planted silver birches and azaleas and cleared land and mulched and kept the lawn immaculate. He was always out the back in an over-sized slouch hat, often shirtless. The yard front and back had been a sandy wasteland when we arrived in Perth, but Dad had transformed them each into an oasis, one weekend at a time. From the beginning he'd had a vision. 'This will be a limestone retaining wall. I might put some limestone slabs over there . . .' His passion for limestone was legendary. Limestone liners, limestone pavers. Concrete made from limestone that covered the backyard trellis. Limestone brick walls. Driving the Tarago slowly past neighbours' houses: 'Look at that limestone feature wall,' Dad would enthuse. He had a cherished photo-graph of a natural limestone bridge he had seen in Europe.

When I was a kid, Dad came home from work by 5 pm and would come out and kick a footy with us. As a kid, I took this for granted. Dad was only away once: his work in border control had taken him on a seaborne patrol up the coast through the wild Abrolhos Islands. He was gone for two weeks, and it was the longest absence we had ever known. He attended every one of my football matches and would give me advice at the half-time huddle. Only later did I come to appreciate that not all parents made the choice to be there for their kids, but mine always were, no matter what.

And, in a similar vein, Dad was by my mother's side during this hard time. As the chemo treatments progressed, I would sit with her at Fremantle Hospital as she took a full dose through a large gauge needle. 'It's like having a crowbar in my arm,' she complained. Since my mum *never* complained, I knew she was really suffering.

Over time, though, she seemed to improve. Her dark hair had fallen out and my parents went shopping to buy her a wig. Dad was kind enough to ask the wig specialist if he could give mum a 'little blonde number', explaining that was what he had always wanted. The specialist, who had never been exposed to

Dad's dry sense of humour, took the request seriously, and Mum emerged from the shop with a blonde bob she wore with pride.

We holidayed in Bridgetown, in the south-west, and walked in the forests. Mum would hold her wig down on her head as she ducked under branches. 'If I'm not careful, some branch will fling it into a tree and it'll become a bloody bird's nest,' she would exclaim.

When it was time to return to Townsville to rejoin my unit, I was certain Mum was on the road to recovery. By early 2003, the US Army was flooding into Kuwait and threatening Saddam Hussein's iron grip on Iraq, and the Aussie army was on a major naval exercise in the Pacific. I joined the exercise with my unit, and was miles out in the Pacific Ocean when a call came in for me on the ship's satellite phone. The captain went to the trouble of seeking me out himself, and he lent me his cabin so I could speak to Dad in private. I knew it was bad news.

'The cancer's spread. The doctor said Mum has two weeks left. You have to come home.' Dad was so stricken, he could barely talk.

The navy arranged for a Black Hawk to fly me all the way back to Rockhampton. I had no spare clothes, just a stale army uniform I had been wearing for a week. I spent a night in a motel in Rockhampton then flew to Brisbane and from there caught a flight home to the west coast. When I arrived at Mum's bedside, she was in better shape than I'd feared. We were at the local hospital, and it was much more pleasant than Fremantle. I leaned down to hug her. She was skinny now, but her arms were still strong as she squeezed me tight and rubbed my back. I was crying. Me, my brothers, my dad – we were all upset. She held our family together like concrete with her big heart, a lack of any verbal filter, and her propensity to laugh long and hard without shame. She had loved us boys, even when we were turds, which was often. I knew that, to my mother, we were the most important thing on earth.

I asked Mum what she was thinking.

'These things are sent to test us,' she said. 'I wish I had seen your apartment in Townsville.' She did not have many regrets, but I knew she had wanted to travel more.

I still couldn't grasp that she was referring to a world without her in it.

'I don't feel bad for myself, but I don't want to leave you. I'm sorry.'

She had lost half her body weight, and her eyes had sunk into their sockets. They had dulled and lost some of their sparkle. This battle had sucked much of the life from her. She was a shell of the farm girl who used to throw us over her head in the backyard pool.

Eventually we took Mum home; there was nothing more they could do for her in hospital. We cared for her in the main bedroom, changing her diapers and washing her, bringing her ice cubes to suck on. We brought Josie the dog into her room, and she sniffed at Mum's hand and wagged her tail, sensing the weakness in her and wanting to help. It was heartbreaking.

It was late March by now. American forces had stormed the borders of Iraq and were headed to Baghdad. I told Mum that a war had started and she just sighed; she was too tired to care.

One night, Dad brought us to Mum's room as she struggled for breath. Mum's sisters filtered into the room to say their goodbyes, and Dad and I sat on the edge of her stretcher bed, holding her hand in the low light of the room's lamp. It was a still, warm evening, and we felt certain it would be Mum's last. Finally, Mum's closest sister, Christine, arrived and she hung a small glass angel over the top of Mum's bed and kissed her. Mum had been waiting for her, and she seemed less restless once Christine was there.

Mum breathed, and breathed, and she opened her eyes, lucid and alive, to look at her sons and husband and family. She couldn't talk, but everything she was saying to us was written in those green eyes. She loved us, she knew we loved her. And Jane, the farm girl who had crashed our BMX bikes at Christmas as we howled with embarrassment, who stood at the dances with her long legs and a cigarette as Dad courted her, who nursed the elderly in their final moments, finally had her own last moment.

9

WONDERLAND

'But I don't want to go among mad people,' Alice remarked.
'Oh, you can't help that,' said the Cat. 'We're all mad here.
   I'm mad. You're mad.'
'How do you know I'm mad?' said Alice.
'You must be,' said the Cat, 'or you wouldn't have come here.'

Lewis Carroll, *Alice's Adventures in Wonderland*

September 2004
Day 0

'TAKE YOUR CLOTHES OFF – EVERY LAST STITCH,' THE SAS instructor told us.

I felt cold to my bones, the concrete floor of the hangar sucking the heat from my legs. It was day one, week one of the SAS selection course held in the SAS facility in Bindoon, 85 kilometres north of Perth – a moment eleven years in the making. I stood in the front rank of 89 hopefuls. All our eyes were trained on the SAS instructors. They were real men. Thick shoulders and necks, stubbled chins and beards, eyes that betrayed not one hint of uncertainty.

We trembling hopefuls had accepted their invitation for the three-week selection course after passing a battery of tests.

This was their domain: fear, uncertainty, discomfort and chaos were intensely familiar to these men. And they *were* all men – except for one. She paced steadily along the front ranks, arms by her sides, a look of professional curiosity as she inspected our bodies and genitals as if she were looking at real-estate listings. My hands were clasped to my front in an attempt at modesty. I glanced up the ranks to see what others were doing with their hands. Nearly all were standing tall, chest out, chin up, hands behind backs. Oh. We weren't doing modesty. I switched my hands to the back.

I'd heard rumours of what parts of the course would entail – food and sleep deprivation, extended solo navigation, a separate module for officers, and endless physical punishment – but no details. We weren't given an itinerary at the start. We would find out as we went along, the hard way. Officers were expected to do all the same training as a soldier, plus the added burden of planning, leading and executing missions. The pressure on officer candidates on selection was extreme.

The men facing us wore sandy-coloured berets and green camouflage.

'What you're about to undertake is one of the hardest courses on earth. More people have climbed Mount Everest than have entered this regiment. If you want to bow out now, you may do so and we will send you back to your unit.'

No-one moved.

'It is not enough to survive this course. You must be deemed suitable to join our regiment. You will be given a form.' He held a piece of paper aloft. 'This is a Withdraw at Own Request form. It is to be kept in your left breast pocket at all times. If you wish to be removed from the course, sign the form and hand it to an instructor.' He paused and stared across the ranks. 'If you are physically or mentally incapable of signing your withdrawal form, simply state to the instructor that you wish to withdraw, and you will be removed.'

I was alarmed. What did he mean by 'mentally incapable of signing your withdrawal form'? How was that even possible? I felt a niggle of trepidation at the back of my mind. I thought of Ron Kovic in *Born on the Fourth of July* screaming at his mother from his wheelchair in a drunken rage. That must be what mentally incapable looked like.

'We have a course schedule of events. We will print a few out and give them to the duty student.' He looked across at the other instructors as he said this, and one nodded to him. I saw the same instructor quickly suppress a smile. *What does that mean?* I wondered.

'All right, reach into your bags and pull on your new uniforms. Place your old uniform in your echelon bag immediately.'

Rustling broke out across the room as 89 candidates leaped into to action. I folded and placed my old uniform next to my bag and searched the bag for my new clothes. I heard heavy boot strikes headed my way – my arsehole clenched as I saw one of the instructors coming directly for me. *Oh shit.*

'Candidate, weren't you told to put your old uniform into your bag immediately?' he asked in a surprisingly thick Scottish accent. He was pointing at my canvas green bag on the ground.

'Yes, sir,' I whispered. I was wide-eyed with fear. I could manage only a shallow breath.

He leaned forward a half-inch, his face calm like a bomb, his dark eyes locked into mine. '*Immediately* means exactly that.' The air hummed as his eyes bored into me. His restraint terrified me. I had been made an example of. Lesson number one: we would be told things once only.

These men were my heroes, but they scared the fuck out of me. I had survived that encounter without evacuating my bowels, but barely. Some negative self-talk started in my head. *Has he been told to target me? He came for me in the first five minutes. Have I just been labelled a half-wit?*

'Not fast enough,' said the lead instructor, barely raising his voice above normal speaking volume. 'A hundred push-ups, count 'em off.'

Eighty-nine men dropped to the concrete floor of the hangar.

'One, two, three . . .' we recited as we pumped out repetitions.

'Louder, or you'll be here all night.'

We believed him.

'FOUR, FIVE, SIX, SEVEN . . .'

The hangar reverberated with our shouts. Nervous energy made us fast. The polished concrete was cold under my hands. I had waited eleven years to be on this concrete floor, and now I was wondering what the hell I had been thinking.

Day 1

'Welcome to day one, week one of the selection course.'

I turned my head a touch and looked at my mate with a small frown. *Isn't it day two? He must have lost count.* Six candidates were gone, 83 of us stood on the red pea gravel in the pre-dawn light. I had a black number written on a red shoulder brassard: 87, my candidate number. We had been roused at 2 am with a hand-operated air-raid siren, a noise like a stray cat being strangled.

It was a jarring start, but I'd felt ready when I came on the course. I'd completed two deployments – to East Timor and the Solomon Islands – as a platoon commander, and after losing my mum I'd felt a new sense of urgency. I knew my time on earth was limited. I was determined to either finish the course, or ruin myself trying.

'This morning you will be participating in a 20-kilometre forced march. You must complete it within 1 hour and 55 minutes in order to pass. Your packs will be 30 kilograms, and weapons and webbing are also required.'

That would bring my total weight to 137 kilos; I was sturdy in build, having shot up to 6 foot 3 inches in my late teens. I knew I had strength, but that was not enough in an endurance march.

The instructor was deadpan. 'As you're walking along through the forest, I encourage you to take in all the natural flora and fauna of the Bindoon forest. It's really lovely.' 'Lovely' was said with a hint of irony. He looked at another instructor, who was nodding. It was an early introduction to SAS humour. You could never tell if they meant what they said because their expressions were always the same: completely neutral, giving nothing away.

The other 82 men and I jockeyed for position on the four-wheel-drive track before the start was ordered. 'GO!' came the shout.

I walked as fast as I could along the gravel road lined with scraggly eucalypts and banksias. It was still early and fresh – the sky shifting from a deep lavender dotted with last night's stars to the orange of dawn. All I could see ahead of me were camou-flaged legs. When I looked up, I saw oversized packs adorned with orange panel markers, arms and legs sticking out of the flanks and bottom.

I would have to run, I decided. There was no way to complete the course in time otherwise.

By the 15-kilometre mark, I wasn't running. I doubled over with cramps in both my hamstrings. *Ahhhhh, fuck!* It felt like they were contracting into hot balls. The canvas and Cordura pack heaved and creaked on my shoulders; it looked compact against my large frame, but it was dense and heavy. I felt a stinging at the tip of my penis; I couldn't figure out if it was chafing or the need to piss. I looked around to check I was clear, then unzipped myself and started pissing on the move. There was no way I was going to lose precious seconds in a stop. My urine looked more like Coca-Cola than a healthy fluid. I pissed down the front of my pants and on my boots as I went. I didn't really care – I already stank of ammonia and fresh sweat. I had stopped seeing the flora, and I was a bit too busy to watch the kangaroos scattering away as we hiked the hill. I reached into the pouch at my rear and pulled a packet of colourful M&Ms from my emergency ration pack. We'd been told not to touch our emergency rations, but I took a chance because I knew I would burn out if I didn't eat soon. I was already seizing up. I barely chewed as I tipped the whole packet down my throat. It was the only thing that would stave off cramps.

I was now 18 kilometres down, two to go. Both my quadriceps felt like jelly. Raw skin chafed on my lower back from hard points on the pack. My right hand felt like a ham hock, all sensation gone from holding my rifle, which weighed as much as a 2-litre can of paint. My feet were bruised from the 137-kilo smashing they were taking at a rate of 1000 steps a kilometre. Ahead of me were three candidates on the trail. Three bobbing packs, orange plastic panels tied to their tops, legs pumping up and down like pistons, rifles swinging in their hands. Their gazes were locked on the horizon, and they look peppy and focused. I felt like I had been dragged the last 4 kilometres by my testicles. *I'm not sure if I'll get it. I'm not sure if I'll make the time.* Doubt coursed through my mind – I'd never really believed I could handle endurance work.

At the finish line I saw three men doubled over, a couple of instructors with small black notebooks recording their candidate numbers. 'You.' One pointed to me. 'Go over there. Drop your pack.'

I staggered over to a truck and slung off my pack, taking care to place it down easily. I was the second officer in the gate. I had finished in the top ten, only a few minutes ahead of the cut-off. It was a small boost to have survived that, but there were so many more days to come.

Day 5

As we finished the vehicle ambush on the second-last day of the officer module, I reached into the top of my pack to retrieve the precious radio antenna. Nothing. Fuck – I'd left it on the ground next to the jeep we had attacked in the dead of night. After packing the bodies onto a stretcher, we had walked all night to a morning stop 12 kilometres away. There was no going back for it. But without it, I was screwed. The staff would realise I had lost critical gear when I could not use my radio.

'Billy, the gooseneck is missing. What do I say?'

'Oh shit.' Billy's voice was full of sympathy. One of my mates from Duntroon, Billy was a star performer and had been the cadet leader at RMC. We had been in Timor together and he was a top candidate for the SAS.

'Maybe see if you can lift one from stores?' he suggested.

This was bad. I considered my options. As far as I could see, I had two: try to find another antenna and conceal the fact I had lost the original, or admit to the loss and get a new one. Either way, it would be a huge black mark against my name. Then a better option occurred to me. I sat on my pack and sketched out the ambush site. I drew a diagram of the vehicle and put a cross next to the wheel where the antenna had fallen out of my pack. I wrote notes on its location, including a ten-digit grid that located its spot to within a metre. I added my name to the top, and walked over to an instructor.

'I lost a gooseneck last night, sir. This is the location.' I handed him the diagram.

He folded the paper and put it in his pocket without comment. His face did not change a wink.

Day 6

I felt a presence hovering at eight o'clock, high. Left shoulder. 'Candidate 87, come with me. Leave your work.' The bearded man spoke just above a whisper in the concrete-walled room. I pushed my chair back from the desk and got to my feet, leaving my essay on Australian defence policy in the South China Sea where it was. I had been working on it for the last couple of hours. The page was marked with long stray pen lines where I had fallen asleep while writing and my pen had careened off the paper. It was 3 am, frigid, and we had not slept in the last two days of the officer module.

I was in a small group of officer candidates running through the component of selection that determined our ability to plan, lead and execute. The officer module went for around 96 hours. Sleep was rare, and broken. In scenario planning we were told that a tsunami had hit Samoa. We had one hour to present a full concept of operations to evacuate every Australian in country. None of us had ever seen or planned for a problem of this magnitude. We had no idea what to do. We were each handed a stack of nautical and land maps, and a ream of A4 paper on which to write operations orders. It would take a day to absorb all the information.

I knew I would be briefing a real SAS squadron commander and his squadron sergeant major. They watched us fumble through the maps. The savvy candidates sorted and prioritised quickly, discarding the immaterial items. What was left they interpreted fast: the key was to determine the mission, the information on threats and the constraints you would face to achieve the mission. We had to develop a rough plan and present it to a contemptuous audience. Some would walk out mid-briefing in frustration, just to rattle you.

This had gone on for four days: insertion plans with small aircraft into fictional countries; submarines into the South Pacific; hostage recovery missions in South-East Asia.

I picked up my webbing and weapon and threaded my way through the fifteen other desks in the room, their sleep-deprived candidates now perking up at the sight of one of their rank being led to slaughter. I followed the bearded man from the room. We walked through the dark maze of red-brick walls and concrete floors. My nostrils stung from the old tear gas in the building. I knew this was the famed 'embassy' building, a three-storey mock-up where close-quarter battle training was completed.

We stopped in a dark section of the hallway, and the bearded man pointed at a door to my left. Raw timber, with yellow light seeping at its edges. In a low voice, he said, 'Walk through that door.'

I pushed the door open and took two steps into a bare concrete room, and saw a horseshoe-shaped arrangement of desks, with a lone stool in the middle of the horseshoe. Men were seated behind the desks, staring at me. I stared back. There was a variety of shapes, sizes and ages. Most looked to be middle-aged, sinewy, with sharply etched cheekbones and jaws. One man was bearded and in standard uniform with a sandy beret, another was clean-shaven and dressed in a black polo shirt and windstopper. I felt like I had walked into a claw of panthers.

They were reviewing my posture, dexterity, heart rate, respiration and pupil dilation. These tiny observations told them what type of candidate they were dealing with. They sat in silence for a moment.

I walked forward into the U of the horseshoe, stopped next to the stool and saluted. Taking some action felt like a start. I could feel the eyes to my left and right burning into me.

'Sit.' A man who looked a lot like Buzz Lightyear gestured to the pathetic stool. A single dull light bulb dangled above it, casting yellow light. The stool was rickety, with a severe tilt to the right. I placed my rifle down on the bare concrete, barrel pointing away from the pack. My hamstrings screamed as I leaned forward; the lower half of my body still felt like it had been trampled by a bull after the punishing physical trials we had been subjected to. I sat on the stool and my whole body lurched to the right as it took the strain. I kept my bush hat on my head.

Buzz Lightyear spoke. 'Candidate 87, tell us your story. From the start.'

I told them.

'I grew up in Newman, in Western Australia, and decided at the age of fourteen that I wanted to join the SAS. I joined the army and went to ADFA and Duntroon, and from there went to 2 RAR. I did a tour of East Timor and one in the Solomons last year. I've wanted to do selection for a while.' *Steady. Keep your voice steady. Breathe.* I was staring at them from under the brim of my bush hat, which felt dumb considering it was 3 am and we were indoors.

'Let's cut to the chase. Tell us about the charges.' The speaker was a man in a woollen pullover. His voice was crisp, and he threw his notes onto the table as he waited. My job had been made easier by knowing they would target my charges. I was expecting this question, and a lot was riding on my response.

The charges he was referring to dated back to the year before, my last year in the infantry battalion. I had been doing well in the battalion, but I was brought back to earth by some ordinary judgements. The first one saw me storing explosive initiators that I had planned to use for training. A disgruntled soldier had found them and dobbed in me and my sergeant. We had been wrong to store such devices, but at least we'd had positive intentions. Strike one.

Strike two was a little awkward. While in the Solomons, I had been caught by the local police with my pants down – literally. I was on the wharf with a local girl I'd met while on a night out with my soldiers. We had been drinking in a local bar and one of my men had kindly depth-charged my beers with a shot of vodka each. Long story short, I was found in a compromising position and the local police had reported it to headquarters. I was hoping I'd got away with it, but oh no: this became big news in the camp. And fair enough – I'd been a bloody idiot. There were enough fatherless bastards in the region from the Vietnam War era; I did not need to contribute to the mess myself. We were meant to be helping the locals, not ruining them. I was brought before the commanding officer, John Frewen, who reprimanded me and docked me a few days pay. To my relief and enduring gratitude, he never raised the incident again. He could see I was mortified and I had admitted my guilt. The real problem, I knew, was that I would have to explain my indiscretion to the SAS.

The man in the pullover was staring at me as I prepared my response.

'The first charge relates to a mistake I made with ammunition. My plan had been to train my team with some rare ammo that we never get to use. But it was a stupid idea. The second charge involved a serious lapse of judgement. I had a bad night when I was drinking. I pleaded guilty to both charges, accepted my punishment, and now I'm here to get on with it.'

No-one spoke, but I saw one man give an almost imperceptible nod. I thought I detected a trace of appreciation; it seemed my candid approach had been the right one. The admission of guilt appeared to have dismantled a whole line of questioning, as no more was said about the charges.

'What are your weaknesses?'

'I'm sometimes slow to pick things up,' I said, 'but I work hard on comprehension and once I have grasped the concepts I move quickly. Sometimes I'm not punctual, but I always work on getting better.' Admitting that I was sometimes a little slow was not fun.

'All right,' said Buzz Lightyear, 'we've heard a lot about your flaws. Let's hear what yer good at.' He was throwing me a lifeline. I had known Buzz when I was training as an officer; he had been the adjutant in our unit. He later shot to royalty in Special Ops as the man who had led the invasion of the Western Desert in Iraq, with a full SAS squadron of assault vehicles as the first cruise missiles of the war screamed overhead towards Baghdad.

'Well, I'm a determined person, and I work hard when I set a goal. I persevere even when things don't go well. I just keep going.'

Neutral expressions across the board. This was a tough crowd.

Day 7

In the morning, I finalised my last essay on Australian fiscal policy post-World War II. As I put my pen down, the bearded man walked in and said softly: 'Candidate 87.'

I stood and followed him to an adjoining room. When he turned to face me he was holding a gooseneck antenna – my misplaced gooseneck antenna – and there was a hint of a smile at the corner of his mouth.

'Name your punishment,' he said. It was the price of recovery.

'One hundred push-ups?' I suggested.

He considered the exposed red-brick wall near me, and gestured. 'Squat hold.'

I put my back to the wall and sank down to a seated position. I held my rifle level in front of my eyes and braced my thighs. I was getting off lightly; I'd been expecting carnage over that loss.

'How's the knee?' he asked, his tone even.

'Good, sir,' I lied. I had strained it running down an airstrip and had been limping for days.

He held me there for half a minute then told me to stand. He handed me the gooseneck and sent me back to the room.

Day 13

I lifted my hand to my face to take another compass bearing. Ahead of me the landscape looked like Mordor: burned coastal scrublands with no distinguishing features. You had to be guided by compass bearing alone. The sun was high overhead, beating down remorselessly. I had traversed the sandy terrain alone for three days and nights on the Happy Wanderer phase of selection. Starved of calories, I had reopened my carefully sealed bags of rubbish to rummage through the scraps. I sucked old condensed milk tubes dry and licked the sugar sachets clean. My combat pants now hung low off my hips, exposing my lower back as my shirt bunched upwards under the bottom of my pack.

I collapsed under a small bush atop a sand dune, hot, exhausted and overwhelmed. Tears ran down my face as I sucked a warm tube of condensed milk. It was pathetic, but I knew no-one could see me. My legs were swollen and shapeless, like massive sausages. I was feeling completely fucked. I looked at the fine dune grass and watched a cluster of brown cattle ticks crawl towards my legs. I pulled my trouser cuffs up to check my ankles. There were four ticks on my left leg; one, which resembled a bulbous raisin, had clearly been feeding for a while. I yanked it off, not caring that he would probably leave his stem in my leg. My wrecked knee was the real concern. I had broken a critical rule of selection: don't get injured.

Five days earlier, I had been running down a long airstrip with my pack on when I felt a twang through the middle of my kneecap. Right away, I knew I had just caused a serious problem. Each day since, the knee had grown more aggravated and swollen. I compensated with my opposite leg, and now that was buckling under the strain of a heavy pack. My body was on a downwards trajectory. At this rate, I would be leaving the course on a stretcher. I still had at least a week to go and I could barely walk. My large toenails had turned purple and I could feel the blood blister tension underneath them. The blister on my heel was now a weeping mess of mushy pink flesh; it looked like a broiled pork chop. I tried to pull back the loose skin but my fingers wouldn't grip. I pulled off my Nomex glove to inspect my hand. It was swollen – the fingers and palm had inflated to double their normal size and I could barely close my hand. It was scratched and sunburned and swollen from gripping my rifle for days as I pushed through saltbush. Swelling in the hand had occurred because of a lack of lymphatic drainage. We had been on our feet 80 per cent of the last two weeks.

The skin on my heel came off on the third pull. I was worried about the blister. It could finish my selection course. Every step felt like sandpapering of raw skin, and my left knee groaned in protest as it took extra weight. I was exhausted from the pain; every step was a special ordeal.

Time and distance would be an issue now. I had walked 25 kilometres on day one and 17 kilometres on day two. I had walked 10 kilometres today and had only a few hours of sunlight left. I was getting worse by the hour.

I redressed and climbed to my feet. I considered my options. There were plenty of poisonous snakes around, I reasoned. When I saw one, I would step on it until it bit me. Then I would call for an evacuation. I would leave with my dignity intact. I would be flown to Royal Perth Hospital or to Lancelin. *That's a good idea*, I thought. *I'll keep going on this bearing until I find a snake*. I moved off on my next bearing – I was looking for either a checkpoint, or a snake.

After another hour of limping, I crossed a dune, and on the other side I saw an old brick building with a chain fence around it. Every other checkpoint had a soldier with a tent, the soldier doing weights, playing a guitar or reading a historical novel. I staggered up to the fence and saw an army jeep and a bristling array of antennas on the roof. *This must be a communications hub*, I thought. I staggered around the side of the building to a small tent and waited.

An instructor appeared in woodland cams and thongs. He looked not a day under 70. There was no meanness in his face at all as he looked me up and down. 'Farrrrk,' he said. 'Candidate

87.' He was shaking his head. He picked up his small notebook and checked it. 'You're miles behind.'

He took my notebook and checked the logs, shaking his head as he calculated my total distance covered. 'You won't make it – you're about 30 kilometres behind. You'll have to double-time it to finish.' He looked up at me.

Was this an act? I couldn't decide. He seemed genuine. I concluded that it was not an act, and I was in deep shit.

'Fill your water up and take a seat there,' he said.

A woman emerged from the tent, short and attractive. I recognised her immediately as the nude-candidate inspector from the beginning of the course. This was the second time she would see me in all my glory. 'Sit down and pull your boots off,' she said. I could smell her from ten paces – citrus shampoo, exquisite after two weeks of my own stink.

I sat down with my back to the wall, white crusty rings of sweat lining my armpits and back. My uniform was black from sweat. I smelled like a pile of ammonia and urea; march flies flew laps around me, looking to collect precious salts. I peeled my sock off my left foot, and the medic flinched as the smell of my foot caught her. I knew it was turning septic.

'See all this red crap around the blister, and the red tracks running off it?' She traced around the blister with her finger and pointed at the red lines radiating from it. 'That's an infection.' She was shaking her head.

Ah, Jesus. She's going to tell me to stop.

She looked at my knee and bent it a few times. 'That's a medial strain. You've probably torn it a little.'

I wanted her to say, 'Well, you're done – there's nothing we can do about that. Go get a brew and sleep on that stretcher.' Instead, she opened her medical bag.

Within five minutes, my heel was wrapped with 10 yards of tape. The knee was similarly swathed. She dropped a handful of grape-sized pills in my hands. They were pink, diamond-shaped and looked much too large to swallow. 'Anti-inflams. Have those two now, two more tonight.' She stood up. 'I'd get going if I were you.'

I pulled my boots on. My heel felt good. There was a little pain, but I could walk.

I walked a dozen yards into the head-high dune scrub, and paused. I was hydrated and my pain levels had dropped from ludicrous to bad. *Go, go*, I urged myself. I took a compass bearing and took off. Soon enough I hit thick scrub. The only way through was by falling forward to clear a patch, standing again, falling again to clear another patch. I had two hours of daylight left, and 20 kilometres to cover before the night was out.

Day 15

I collapsed on the dirt guttering along the side of the four-wheel-drive trail. I rolled slightly to my side, so my pack could lie on the ground, and I pulled out the sugar sachet that was stored in my pocket, next to my white withdrawal form. I moved it to my lips and tore the corner off, pouring its contents into my mouth. I chewed softly, and waited. The sun was setting out to the west across the yellow dune grass that bent in the breeze. That sachet was the last of my food. I had been saving it all afternoon for an emergency. I felt calm as the evening sky turned a layered orange, pink and lavender. I waited for the sugar to kick in. I knew it was my last push; I had nothing left. Food, spirit and water – all had been consumed. I went to stand, which, when you're wearing a pack, is an ordeal even when you're fresh. On day fifteen of SAS selection, it was like a sad comedy. I rolled to my side, tucked one knee up high. Forming a fist with my hand, I pushed myself upright and got to one knee. I collected my rifle from the ground with my good hand. It had taken me all of a minute to get to a kneeling position. I bucked and groaned as my rump ascended first, pack slipping forward and hitting the back of my head, cold air on my exposed lower back. My bush hat was pushed forward into my eyes, the suede toe caps of my boots had been shredded by countless sticks. I looked more like a ragged camel than a soldier. I stood up and straightened my hat with my left hand, always keeping my right hand on my weapon. The left hand was for taking bearings, wiping your arse and hand signals. The right was near the trigger, and it had to stay that way. I staggered in a drunk gait towards the low wire fence. I kicked a twig and then tripped, collapsing face down at the side of the road, rifle pinned beneath me. I rolled to my side and started the process again.

We had been given five days to complete the mission. It was day five, and I was looking at a setting sun. With my strapped heels and anti-inflam tablets, I had cleared 36 kilometres and 32 kilometres in the last two days. I calculated I had travelled about 120 kilometres through withering dry scrub, soft sand and tundra. I was done. There was nothing left in me.

My heart jumped as I saw a green tarp struck against the fence. It was taut and low, the mark of a fresh soldier. From the scrub to my left, I saw a broad-shouldered soldier walking towards me in pale desert uniform with a broad tan belt around his waist. He had shoulder-length blond hair. I stared at him from the mound I was lying against, my pack oblique against my head and my rifle pointing across my body towards my face. This was not my finest hour.

He squatted by my side and looked me over. 'Stop walking,' he said, stone-faced. He gestured with his chin towards the fence line. 'Set your hutchie up there and rest.'

This couldn't be real. I had made it! I had reached the last checkpoint. That sachet of sugar had been the difference between passing and failing.

'Oh my God,' I said. I released a breath I had been holding since he walked over to me.

He handed me something that had been concealed in his hand. It was a block of army-issue chocolate. I had never been so happy to see the rock-hard chocolate bar.

'Take this – you're gonna need the calories.' The corners of his eyes crinkled in a wry smile.

I couldn't believe it. Not only were these soldiers humans, they were nice people when not in character. I realised later that when they looked at us, they saw themselves only a few years earlier: scared, exhausted and on a path that could only be travelled alone. They cheered for us in complete silence. I had passed Happy Wanderer, but barely. It was a close call.

I staggered over to the fence and dumped my pack then stood upright and looked out over the sand dunes in the fading dusk. The clouds streaked across a sky of deepest amber as I breathed in the tangy salt air. I fished my tarp out of my pack and struck it against the fence. I pegged down the side facing the breeze as low as I could. I unrolled my sleeping bag and a foam mat then crept under my shelter and pulled my shirt off. It was like a sheet of wet leather. I summoned the strength to pull my boots and socks off, and placed them in a pair under my tarp. I paused to look at the white wrinkled mess of nail and skin and tape and blood of my battered feet. They were utterly fucked. I climbed into my sleeping bag, pulled the hood right up around my head and zipped it up, feeling its embrace. Tonight, no checkpoints would haunt me. A light ocean rain blew in across the Indian Ocean and over the dunes. I thought of nothing as the first squall of rain pattered on my tarp and sleep swallowed me whole.

Day 19

The man with the mock French accent pointed through the scrub up a giant hill. '*Tu m'y emmèneras. Au camp.*'

My five teammates and I looked at each other like we were on a bad trip. I didn't have a fucking clue what he had just said.

'He said he wants to go to the camp,' said my mate Billy, who had passable French. I was standing slack-armed, my rifle held by fingertips pointing at the ground. I did not have the strength to lift it up to a useable position.

The instructor was playing the part of a French revolutionary soldier called Henri, and it was our job to lead him and all his equipment to the camp in a bullshit scenario.

This was the final leg of the course. Impossible tasks with unachievable timelines. Deprived of food, sleep and cognition, we stumbled through the tasks. This was a simulation of team dynamics in combat. How well can you lead, contribute, and problem-solve with a group when, individually, you have nothing left? Does this candidate give his last biscuit to his mate, or does he hide it for himself to eat later? Only under these conditions does true character emerge, as all facades are stripped away.

A dozen instructors were watching us, assessing us according to a range of traits: resolve, adaptability, initiative, common sense, control of anxiety, self-discipline, confidence, integrity, leadership, strength and endurance, assimilation of information, teamwork, ability to work alone, and communication.

Each of these traits describes behaviours that define a capable soldier. Take adaptability, for example. Non-adaptable soldiers need structure and certainty, and are unable to cope with ambiguity. They fail to consider alternative options, make poor use of available resources and have no control over their emotions. Adaptable soldiers, by contrast, seek novelty and thrive on uncertainty. They are able to modify plans effortlessly and implement alternative solutions. They have total control over their emotions and use the resources available to them to enhance any situation.

Although I was aware of the selectors' scrutiny, I tried not to look at them and to instead focus on the task at hand. I felt self-conscious since I had torn the crotch of my pants on day seventeen. I had done my best to repair them with an army-issue sewing kit, but I hadn't done a terrific job and kept inadvert- ently exposing my genitals as I was trying to complete the tasks. Once I had to traverse a horizontal rope that ran under my chest and crotch and only narrowly avoided castration.

So in the current scenario 'Henri' wanted to be taken to the camp. I hated pretending in scenarios; I was shit at it. This time, though, I had no choice – I was the team leader. Henri had put me in charge of taking all his equipment up to the camp: four of us to carry, two acting as guards. Problem was, he wanted us to move a box containing an outboard motor. All six of us stood looking at the black box. It was the size of a large domestic refrigerator. I was pretty sure it was full of gravel, not a motor, as it rattled inside as we moved it. I estimated it weighed 200 kilos.

We had already tried to lift the box, but it had no handles and we struggled; we would have to improvise. Together the team and I chopped down a couple of slender ironbarks and lashed them to the sides of the box.

'Okay, prepare to lift.'

The men started grunting as they took up their positions and heaved.

'Why you grunt like a bovine? Be quiet, there are enemy here.' Henri was impatient.

'Prepare to lift,' I ordered. 'Okay: LIFT!'

We almost buckled under the weight. The box shifted forward an inch, scraping across the earth.

'Stop!' someone called. The log was rubbing against the back of my neck and I felt the cool burn of skin being scrubbed off in layers.

We tried again, starting in a lunge position with one knee bent then straightening our legs. As we stood, I could feel my entire core bowing and straining under the weight. The broad band of sinew that ran along the outside edge of my thighs tightened like a rubber band about to snap.

'Go! Go!' I urged.

We staggered two steps to the side before we made any forward motion.

'To the next row of trees!' someone shouted.

I could see the trees about 10 metres ahead, on the right. I had one hand on my rifle, the other on the load at my shoulders; we were disarmed. Flies swarmed my face, seeking the fluid in the corners of my eyes. When I sucked air through my nostrils, flies would get sucked up and I would sputter and snort them out. Sweat ran down my forehead, through green camouflage paint, stinging my eyes. My hand burned as I hefted the beam; I had already scraped half the skin off my palm one night when I fell on a rock.

We took three more steps and I walked face first into a crop of spiky bushes. I closed my eyes as the spiny leaves raked my cheeks and neck.

A blue-tongue lizard hissed up at me at me from the mass of branches and roots below. We'd interrupted its sunbathing. 'Blue-tongue! Pick it up!' I shouted. We had not eaten for two and half days; the lizard would be a feast.

We stalled, the box crashed to the ground, and we all dropped to our knees. We had covered 6 metres. We had 7 kilometres left to go to reach the enemy camp.

Henri lost his mind. 'You men are weak!' he berated us in broken English. 'You Aussies not strong. You make mooing sounds! Much noise!' He spat.

'Henri, we are very tired, and we have no food,' I said. I regretted the comment as it was leaving my mouth.

'You are no good, I finish you!' He pointed over my shoulder at one of the sentries. 'I pick your friend. He is real leader, a real man!'

My mate's face fell as Henri pointed at him.

I understood the dread he would be feeling. Being accountable for a mission was hard. How you performed could be the difference between passing and failing. I knew I had not performed well on the endurance walk and this was proving even harder.

We eventually managed to move the box to its destination: a rebel camp with several chickens and a small fire.

A bespectacled white-haired man dressed in an old woodland uniform emerged from a tent. 'I am Commander Undies,' he declared. 'Welcome to my camp.' He then goosestepped around the camp, arms swinging to shoulder height. He marched up to each candidate in turn and, stern-faced, offered a crisp salute and a handshake. He then kissed the hand of our team's leader then led him by the hand around the camp to inspect the men and the farm animals. The team leader had never held hands with a grown man for so long, and it showed. When he tried to recover his hand, Commander Undies just gripped it more tightly.

The commander beckoned us all over to the fire and addressed us with pomp and ceremony. 'You are such brave soldiers to bring this equipment. I have told my village we will make a feast for you.' Two minions brought forward a large plastic box with handles. I could see steam coming out of the edges of it. 'Please accept our offering.' The minions dropped the chest in the middle of our team, and we gathered around eagerly. I noticed that the instructors, normally distant, had crowded in to view the spectacle.

The metal latches were unhooked from the sides of the chest, and as the lid was lifted, the flies buzzed around us in excitement. A rancid, rotting odour filled the air. We murmured in disgust as the steam cleared and the meaty nugget appeared.

It was a hairy black hog's head, boiled. Its dead black eyes had a grey film over them. Dinner tonight would be skin, fur, snout and tongue with some tripe and rice on the side. One candidate pulled out a knife and proceeded to carve strips of dermis off the pig's head as everyone huddled around.

Metal cups were held up for a serve. Several of the instructors turned their heads from the scene in disgust.

Officers are expected to eat last, so Billy and I waited until everyone had eaten. My cup was loaded up with sheets of furry skin and rice. One strip of skin hung over the side of my cup, dripping fluid down my hand. I picked it up and shoved it into my mouth, furry side up. It was like trying to chew wet leather with a little rubbery bounce to it. I tried a sawing motion, sliding my bottom jaw forward and back like a cutting press. I could not defeat it. At one point, I had to reorientate the pig skin in my mouth and I felt the bristled fur, quite soft, on the back of my tongue. I gagged. I steeled myself to swallow it whole. I gave a hard swallow, and the long strip of skin sandpapered the back of my throat as it disappeared downwards, making my eyes water.

'All right?' my mate said.

I wiped my mouth with the back of my glove. I knew if I did not force myself to eat these strips of pig face, I would not have the strength to last three more days without food.

We kept eating until the pig was reduced down to a skull with a few shards of skin hanging off it. Someone had even eaten the eyeballs. We were full, but we could feel our bodies making short work of the food. Sure enough, within 30 minutes, I was hungry again.

After dinner, we sat around the fire. Commander Undies held court, singing a rebel ballad for us in French. He crooned and swayed without shame for a full five minutes. Afterwards, he told us it was a song about a rebel woman who had been squashed by a boulder in his village. We knew he was deliberately hamming it up but, committed to the scenario, we struggled not to laugh.

He asked us to sing an Australian song for his people, so we obliged by standing in a line and singing both verses of 'Advance Australia Fair'.

After an hour of sleep, we awoke and headed to the next

mission, which involved extracting a bogged jeep from a poisoned swamp. We fashioned pulleys and a road made from boards, then abandoned them to yank the jeep out with brute force.

Trucks came for us that afternoon, and we picked up large sticks as we climbed aboard, certain we were about to be abducted. We ended our trip at the front of the hangar we had entered on day zero. There was an SAS soldier dressed in full uniform, including the sandy beret, waiting for us. He looked clean and alert. He asked us all to sit down. There were already twenty other men gathered.

'You have completed the SAS selection course,' the soldier told us. 'Not all of you will be accepted into this unit, but no matter what happens, for the rest of your life you should be proud of what you have achieved here. Many people talk about doing this, fewer arrive, and only a small handful finish. Well done.'

I had tears in my eyes as he spoke. I knew that I had done my best, and the result was now out of my hands. I was okay with that.

We were instructed to eat and then shower. We walked into the hangar, and there we saw tables with trays of pies and sausage rolls, and platters of fresh fruit. I devoured four sausage rolls and one pie. Then I headed to the shower rooms with my mates. It was not a pretty sight: gaunt men with pale bodies and black faces, most with bleeding chafe on their backsides and bunches of ticks hanging off their shins. One candidate had a large tick in his groin and let everyone inspect it. We were all ribs and hollow faces and big smiles.

We took the bus back to Perth, and watched *Hamburger Hill* on the way home – nice easy watching for our traumatised minds. When we arrived, the officer group was separated from the others and directed to walk over to the regimental head-quarters. There were six of us officers, and we were ushered into a carpeted waiting room.

'Wait here until your name is called. No talking.'

We sat in silence as men were summoned in alphabetical order at five-minute intervals. One by one the others were called, until there was just me in the waiting room.

Eleven years – and it all came down to the next five minutes. I'd know in five minutes if I'd made it into the SAS. I studied the bandages covering my battered hands. I had entered the course at a solid 107 kilograms; I now weighed 91. I had lost just under a kilogram of body weight each day for twenty days straight.

A man poked his head into the room. He looked at me with narrowed eyes. 'Were you talking to yourself?' It was the bearded man who had given me my antenna back. He was smiling. Surely he wouldn't smile if I was getting binned?

'Nope,' I said, hoping he didn't think I was going mad. If he'd seen me 72 hours earlier, though, he would have been right.

I tottered into the CO's office in bloody socks, trying to walk upright.

The commanding officer was grey-haired and bespectacled with eyes like a hawk. There was an A4 dossier in front of him, and I saw my photo at the top of it. This was it: the final word. I swallowed, my mouth dry.

From behind his desk, the CO looked at me over the top of his glasses and said, 'So how do you think you went?'

'I found it hard,' I admitted. 'I was in bad shape, but I had a good team with me at the end. I found the officer module really difficult.'

He nodded, frowning slightly as he considered his next words.

Ah, shit, no. I can do it again. It's okay. I blinked. *Don't you dare cry if they say you didn't make it*, I warned myself.

'What happened on Happy Wanderer?' the CO asked.

'Well, my time wasn't that great. I think a few injuries slowed me down.' It sounded like I was making excuses.

'Maybe you just don't work well on your own?' he offered. It was a rhetorical question.

Fuck – I'm done. I felt a rising sense of panic.

'You have a chequered past' – he paused, glanced at the dossier – 'but we'll take a chance on you. You're suitable for further training and cleared to attend the reinforcement cycle.' He wore the slightest smile as he stood from his desk and walked around it, extending his hand to me.

I was stunned. I looked over at the bearded man and saw that he was smiling. They, too, had once sat in my place, and they knew it was a life-changing moment.

I clambered to my feet and shook their hands. The CO gripped my hand for a moment longer than necessary, and I could tell he was pleased to be giving a battered candidate some good news. I wept a little bit from joy, and said I had lost my mother the year before and she would have been proud. They nodded; they didn't seem embarrassed by my tears. After three weeks of displaying only impassivity and simmering hostility as instructors, they were now able to drop the mask and reveal their warmth, humour and protectiveness.

After a few minutes, it was back to business.

'You were good in the execution phases,' the CO told me, 'but too quiet in planning. We need you to be leading the whole time. You'll have to work harder on tactics . . .'

'*Yes, sir.*' I was going to agree with anything he said.

I'd made it. I was in the regiment: *the* regiment. I'd made it through selection: that fearsome beast that soldiers whispered about in awe. But I knew that selection was just the beginning. The real skills training started with the reinforcement cycle. In the next eighteen months I would be subjected to an intense training that would turn me and the others who'd made it to this stage into skilled fighters. The culture of the unit would be instilled in us: the relentless pursuit of excellence, the primacy of the mission and the sense of camaraderie. If I survived that, then I would be issued the coveted sandy beret.

When I walked out of regimental headquarters, it was early evening and the stars were out. I skipped across the parade ground of the regiment in the dark. There was no pain in my legs now. I was buzzing.

I hadn't made it through selection because I was the best soldier. I wasn't. I'd faced some really dark moments: alone, wounded, weeping, and totally unsure of myself. But I had persevered. When all my defences were down, I was still determined to stick it out, knowing that a rising sun would bring a new day, another opportunity, a new start.

In some ways it was a bittersweet moment; I wished Mum were alive to see that I had made it. But more than anything I was glad: I knew that what came next would determine the course of my life.

10

DOWN THE RABBIT HOLE

Baghdad, August 2006

A CAR BOMB IRONED THE CREASES OUT OF MY UNIFORM AS I stepped from the pathway leading out of the Baghdad international airport terminal towards our waiting Black Hawk. I flinched visibly in front of the US Army personnel who had been lining the way. It was the first time I had heard a bomb used in anger. The car had exploded at a checkpoint about 200 metres away; a column of dark smoke marked its origin.

We were about to fly to the Green Zone, the occupied part of Baghdad. The drive from the airport to the Green Zone – Route Irish – was considered the most dangerous stretch of highway on earth. There were more IEDs – improvised explosive devices, or roadside bombs – than in any other part of the world. Blackened hulks of US armoured vehicles were piled up on the sides of the road, where they had been bulldozed by engineer vehicles and then gutted by insurgent forces. The attacks had increased to an average 26 per day. They had become so frequent, my colleagues and I would be taking a helicopter to the Green Zone to complete a reconnaissance for our next mission.

We actioned our weapons and then climbed aboard the Black Hawk. I strapped myself into a seat by the window.

The helicopter ascended and pitched forward across the landscape. I could feel my mouth dry up and my heart start to thump in my ears as I felt the weight of the ascent, my helmet and body armour pressing me into my seat. I looked out the window to the horizon. The sun was a pink orb against an ochre desert, the dust so thick you could stare directly at the sun without the slightest discomfort. Tens of kilometres away, I saw the soaring minarets of the Great Mosque, one of Saddam's unfinished vanity projects.

The helicopter pitched low and right, taking us across the safety of the Euphrates River. Along the banks of the river there were whole blocks that had been levelled by tomahawk missiles. Cars edged their way around the rubble of the Ba'ath Party houses. This was what remained of the cradle of civilisation.

We cut a few metres above the palm trees as the craft pitched forward and the engines roared higher. The wind was buffeting my rifle and arms as I pointed it from the window, ready to fire alongside the door gunner if needed. The door gunner, with his heavy machine gun, was scanning rooftops for RPGs, rocket-propelled grenades. His eyes were concealed behind a black visor. It was no secret that the insurgency had been planting substantial bombs in the tops of the palms in the hope of blowing a Black Hawk out of the sky. They would plant bombs anywhere: corpses, watermelons, garbage trucks and stolen military vehicles. This was a dirty war.

We pitched in low towards the Green Zone landing point, next to a field hospital with the red crescent on the tarmac. As we shifted into a hover, I saw below us a US soldier in a t-shirt and body armour. He was standing next to a quad bike, hosing down a mesh stretcher mounted across its rear. Whatever he was hosing off the stretcher coloured the tarmac a deep maroon.

At a tin-box terminal, an Aussie movements soldier greeted us and put us straight into an armoured car for the next intelligence briefing.

We were the protective security detachment for General Leahy, Chief of Army, who would visit the troops soon. Our job was to ensure he could move safely through Afghanistan and Iraq. The job was one part soldier, one part executive assistant, with a good dash of worried parent. It was my first mission and it offered a preview of the battlefields in Iraq and Afghanistan. In the aftermath of the 2003 invasion of Iraq, and the withdrawal from Afghanistan in 2002, it was considered a decent operational job.

My small detachment included troops with varying levels of experience. Sando was a junior trooper who had completed a support role in Iraq with General Molan. His claim to fame was that he had 'cropdusted' Colin Powell and his entourage at Saddam's palace in late 2003. A whole gaggle of spies, diplomats, soldiers and Iraqi officials had gathered around the Secretary of State General Powell in the halls of the palace after a special visit. Sando took it upon himself to casually pass wind, or cropdust, as he walked two laps around the entire entourage. Sando briefed us on all the tricks and traps in support roles. Make sure you have an advance party ahead. Make sure you have a liaison at each spot. Don't leave the car's lights on. Ensure the engine is running and the gear in drive – you might need to leave in a hurry.

To see Iraq was a surreal dream. It had been called the Special Ops Olympics. Allied forces had flooded the country. All resources from Afghanistan had been diverted to Iraq. As a US admiral would say in 2007: 'In Afghanistan, we do what we can. In Iraq, we do what we must.' Iraq was the war that had to be won. The unnecessary war, no WMDs found, and the broken state had to be rebuilt.

There was no mistaking the fact that the US was in seriously deep shit. Car bombs rocked the daytime air, the attacks often simultaneous. Small arms fire rattled off the checkpoints. Rockets and mortar barrages crumped into the car parks outside the US embassy and 4-metre-high concrete barriers ran for kilometres. Apache gunships rained cannon shells down on the Muqtada al-Sadr's Shia militia a few blocks away in Sadr City. It was our generation's Saigon, and I hoped it would not end with helicopters on rooftops. Through it all, though, the Islamic call to prayer would echo through the land five times a day, a practice dating back to the time of Mohammed. I felt a long way from home.

We took an armoured car out to one of Saddam's palaces, now called Camp Victory. It resembled a European castle, and rumour had it that the moats surrounding the castle concealed the bodies of Saddam's rivals who had been killed during his reign in Iraq. An SAS warrant officer greeted us at the door. It was the bearded warrant officer who had returned my antenna to me two years before on selection. He shook my hand, clearly glad to see soldiers from his own unit.

We stood together in the shadow of a minaret and he lit a Camel cigarette.

'What a shit show,' he said. 'The US is talking about bombing Syria. It's like the bloody end of days. They reckon 3000 bodies a month are showing up in the Tigris. It's a civil war all right.'

Stubbing out his cigarette, he invited us to the mess hall of the camp, a huge tent-like structure with armed guards and metal detectors.

'A few months ago a suicide bomber got in here with a backpack. Killed nineteen.' He mentioned it as casually as if he were talking about a spell of bad weather.

The whole joint was under continuous attack. The twelve checkpoints around the zone were attacked multiple times a day, and mortars and indirect fire were lobbed into the Green Zone incessantly, killing diplomats, aid workers and soldiers.

My whole life I had waited to be a part of a war, and here it was.

*

If Iraq was prime time, then Afghanistan was the late-night infomercial. It had been neglected when things heated up in Iraq and was now spiralling out of control. Afghanistan was a problem child for the world. In the aftermath of September 11, al-Qaeda had been pulverised by US special forces and air power. They'd regrouped in the mountains of Shah-i-Kot Valley, joining the Taliban forces, before, in March 2002, Allied forces pushed the last of them across the border into Pakistan. An SAS patrol had maintained overwatch on the whole battle, staying in place for nine days calling in air strikes – hypothermic, out of food – until they were forced to withdraw from the area. The patrol commander that led the team had shown me his map of the valley, with long black lines for the air strike routes, blue boundaries for Delta force units running up valleys and red diamonds for the enemy sightings. There were a lot of red diamonds. He held the corners of the map delicately, like it was the Shroud of Turin. 'Don't touch it, or the marker will run off.'

While the world turned to Iraq, the Taliban slowly rebuilt in Pakistan. Bin Laden was still at large. I first realised something was amiss in 2005, during Operation Red Wings, when a team of US Navy SEALs was overrun in the hills of Afghanistan's Kunar Province. The rescue team – an entire Chinook's worth of SEALs – was shot down. The war in Afghanistan was not over; it was just beginning.

Prime Minister John Howard wanted to support our American allies, so Aussie forces were recommitted. The SAS was going back, their mission to destroy and degrade the enemy formations in Oruzgan province, between Kabul and Kandahar city – the birthplace of the Taliban. This would be our once-in-a-generation war, like the war our forebears had fought in the jungles of South-East Asia. All I had to do was be decent at my job and I had a shot of making my way to Afghanistan and leading a troop of men into combat. How hard could it be?

Camp Russell, Afghanistan, August 2006

We clicked our helmet chinstraps on as the loadmaster did the round and made hand signals to us over the din of the Hercules aircraft. We sat on red mesh seats, and I leaned forward to keep my head away from the wall of the plane. A US defence contractor had been hit in the back of the head by a bullet that had penetrated the aircraft wall as they took off from Baghdad. He died of his injuries.

As we made a steep descent towards the runway, I could feel my stomach drop. I looked out the port window – rock beds that stretched for miles, ochre deserts like something from the 1984 film *Dune*. I half expected to see a dune worm at any moment. Snow-capped mountains surrounded the valleys. It was easily the most stunning vista I had ever seen. Stark, unforgiving, raw – an ancient land.

Final approach to the airfield, and the aircraft was jockeying. I saw a flash of red and heard explosions. My heart leaped and I felt a surge of adrenaline, even though I knew it was aircraft flares being fired for protection.

As the wheels hit the tarmac, the aircraft rattled and vibrated on the dirt airstrip.

My eyes met those of Lieutenant Colonel Mark Smethurst. He was a special forces commander, and I remembered his piercing blue eyes and cutting intellect from the selection board. This was a regular trip for him, and he was enjoying my obvious trepidation with a wry smile.

We walked from the back of the aircraft ramp with our M4s slung, wearing body armour and helmets, the baking dry heat already drying the sweat from our armpits. The dust was fine, like walking over a carpet of brown flour. The ridge line of the Baluchi Valley dominated the horizon ahead.

There was a touch of Mad Max about the place. A man rode past standing on the wheel pegs of a quad bike. He had a red beard and a tactical pistol at his hip. An M4 with a telescopic sight was mounted across the handlebars. He stared at us from behind Oakley ballistic glasses, expressionless, as he chugged past.

We got in the back of a battered Hilux ute and were driven to the guarded gate towers of the Special Ops compound, Camp Russell, which had been named for SAS Sergeant Andrew Russell, who had died five years earlier, in 2002, when his car drove over an anti-tank mine.

As we drove in the front gate, I saw my mate Mark come past in running gear with a pistol on his waist.

'Mark!' I shouted. I jumped down from the ute and shook his hand. He had an outstanding black beard going, and looked trim, rugged and handsome. 'Mate – how's it going?' I knew Mark had recently fought in Operation Perth, a substantial battle in which a few guys had been badly wounded.

'Yeah, it was big,' he told me when I asked. 'A huge gunfight over a few days. Bill got hit in the face by some RPG frag, and a few Dutchies were killed. We did some strafing runs with an A-10. AC-130 gunships went Winchester a number of times. It was madness. I'll be briefing the Chief of Army about it later on – come join us.'

I nodded. I was trying to act like I could relate to what he was talking about.

I sat in the back of the room as the troop briefed General Leahy on Operation Perth.

Op Perth had been a search-and-destroy mission in the Chora Valley, only 40 kilometres north of the base. There had been a couple of hundred Taliban, up against 3 Squadron SAS, a commando company and some Dutch forces. It turned into a brutal nine-day battle. Australia had not fought a vicious, staged engagement like this since Vietnam. An entire commando company had been cut off, with six men wounded.

Though running low on ammunition, they eventually breached the encirclement and got out. The SAS had called in a number of Spectre gunships, each of which had run out of ammunition in the battle. A trooper had taken a close hit from an RPG and lost a good portion of his jaw. He had since undergone plastic surgery to repair it. *This is super heavy*, I thought. *Real fighting*. Up till then I had only caught rumours and stories from the instructors as we had been training. Now I was seeing the whole report. The stakes had jumped – this was very serious, and we were lucky to have escaped without fatality.

General Leahy was impressed. 'Incredible work,' he said. He thanked the squadron, and emphasised that the report needed to be captured for future reference, as a book or a lessons-learned manual.

One dark-haired soldier spoke up. 'We want our families to know about some of this stuff,' he said. 'We think it would help them to understand what we've been through.' He was solid and confident in his delivery. All movement and noise in the room ceased as he spoke; he clearly commanded the respect of his troop. I later found out his name was Matthew Locke.

His patrol had fought a tough action against a Taliban team that had come to wipe them from their observation post. They had been supporting the battle in the valley below, providing intelligence and calling in air strikes before being discovered in daylight. They had killed the attackers and resumed their support.

The general accepted Matt's suggestion. He thanked the teams again, took a few more questions, then left.

I spoke to a mate as we filed out of the briefing. He had trained me in close-quarter battle the year before and had been present for Op Perth. He told me it had been 'carnage'. These were not part-time soldiers; they were tough, resilient, hardened fighters, and still they had been taken aback by the ferocity of the engagement.

'Mate, if I ever have a mental breakdown, I tell you what, it'll be the clearance after the C-130s had been on target. Dudes with their guts blown out the night before still rollin' around in the dirt. Moaning and shit.' His face screwed up at the memory. A fast-air targeteer that had worked the AC-130s all night told me that in the early morning he had seen a human brain on the ground, alone, in a small grass field, the body that hosted it nowhere to be seen.

I had a foreboding about the war. In my imaginings, I always saw the Aussies telling wry jokes as we hammered away at enemy with heavy guns. The reality was a far cry from this rather benign image; it was bloody, vicious, terrifying and lethal.

Still, despite the danger, I envied a mate who had joined at the same time as me and had already got a run as a troop commander while I was babysitting generals. I flew back to Perth after an exhausting trip and awaited my turn in the squadrons.

It would be another year before I landed back in Afghanistan. This time, I was headed to the Chora Valley.

11

OPERATION SPIN GHAR

THE BASE IN TARIN KOWT HUMMED LIKE A FILM SET. IT HAD grown, now sprawling across the desert floor. Helicopters flew across the base with slung loads, some landing at the hospital. Artillery rounds barked from the main guns on the high ground. An occasional enemy rocket flew into the complex. Sandbags, pillboxes, concrete tunnels and Conexes dotted the complex. Bearded men sauntered across the bases holding giant rifles. The dust coated anything that didn't move, turned it white or grey. A flat ridge line hovered to the east; through the thick dust, it looked like an ocean rising up to the sky. I arrived with my troop in the cool autumn of 2007.

The group under my command was called 'E Troop'. It was a composite troop, a new team of soldiers pulled from across the regiment's various squadrons – part homeless pack, part dirty dozen. I had four teams of six men. The team leaders were sergeants: experienced, battle-hardened leaders. My team leaders included Matthew Locke, who had fought in the hills of Chora the year before. Tough, intelligent and revered by his men, Matt was the most senior of the four patrol commanders I would be leading.

My squadron commander was a major, Nick, and he also had a tour of Afghanistan under his belt from the early days.

A hyper-intelligent giant of a man, he was prone to issuing the most timeless insults. He once referred to a nasty boss as an 'arch fuckwit'. But his earlier tours gave him better strategic context than most officers: he understood more about the unique skills our soldiers had, and where they could be best applied to support strategy. His right-hand man was Buzz – a distinctly different character from the more senior Buzz Lightyear on my selection course. This Buzz was one of the most experienced soldiers in the unit. Unflappable and sturdy, his exploits in the early tours of Afghanistan were legendary. He was invested in the success of the squadron, and that made him an outstanding mentor to new soldiers and officers.

We had formed as a composite troop, pulling spare men from around the regiment to form E Troop. We were a mongrel team taking the unwanted back of the summer fighting season of 2007 and plugging the gap before the snows fell in the northern winter. I feared the fighting was going to be over by the time we landed in country.

Despite my impatience, I had in fact advanced quickly. I had finished selection only two and a half years before, and now, at the age of 26, I was leading this mongrel mob as a captain. It was a coveted position for any officer in the regiment, to be trusted to lead a troop into combat. It was also an extremely demanding role. I was responsible for planning, leading and executing operations. Most of the men in the teams were older than me. Most had done one or two combat tours already. As a new boss, you had to earn the trust of the team, demonstrating both capability and a willingness to learn. If you showed that, teams would fight to support you. Your success would be theirs too. If you lost the trust of the team, were rejected by them, you could suffer a career-ending removal in combat. There were precedents. Men from earlier rotations had joked about the 'sack-evac' helicopter coming to collect troop commanders from the field when they had lost their team's or boss's trust.

So far, that hadn't happened to me. A month into tour, we were chalking up some wins.

The boss would be happy about the latest contact – but it confirmed what we already knew. Operation Spin Ghar would not be easy. We would be covering the same terrain as Operation Perth. The Taliban once again held the area after Afghan forces were expelled shortly after Op Perth.

The place had flared again in the Battle of Chora, which raged from 15–19 June 2007. Dutch, US and 3 Squadron SAS had attempted to recapture the Baluchi Valley. It was savage fighting, with 3 Squadron clearing enemy targets and destroying large groups of Taliban in close combat.

The war effort was not going smoothly. Most major NATO resources had been diverted to the surge in Iraq. Helicopters, drones and fire support – major 'enablers' in combat – were lacking. Worse, the strategy in Afghanistan was far from clear. The Dutch were protecting population centres while US and Aussie forces were trying to decimate Taliban resistance in Oruzgan Province, in the country's south. US command and political attention was a world away in Iraq.

Op Spin Ghar fell under the remit of the British general who controlled the southern province. He was keen to recapture the Chora Valley, which allowed the Taliban from unsecured Gizab in the north to gain access to Tarin Kowt. He was throwing his reserve force at it, a whole Gurkha regiment, replete with their fearsome kukri fighting knives. Nick fought hard to ensure our team would provide reconnaissance support to the commander's efforts. He was smart enough to understand that we needed to align our efforts to support the broader Allied strategy. We could do the work we are best at: close target reconnaissance to enable a 'Main Effort' – to recapture the critical valley. In other words, find out how many enemy there were and where they were based, and confirm if they had heavy weapons that could shoot down helicopters. We would be in the deep thick vegetation and crops of the valleys. The green belt: opium, corn, olives, apricots – it was all there. And the Taliban controlled most of it with impunity.

Chora Valley, 21 October 2007

I swam up out of a deep sleep. A black silhouette loomed over my stretcher in the darkness.

'Waler, wake up. Kaz's patrol has been compromised – they just killed three blokes.'

Buzz released my arm and I heard the crunch of gravel as he strode off towards the command post of FOB Ego, or Forward Operating Base Ego – Ego being the nickname for E Troop, who were also reputed to have healthy egos.

Oh shit. I felt the nausea of deep fatigue as I pulled my boots on, but I was wide awake now.

When I staggered into the command post, Buzz was standing next the radio set, holding the black handset. A single yellow bulb lit the room's maps, plastic boxes and static radio sets. Dust hung in the freezing night air. We had been doing close target reconnaissance of enemy positions each night for a week, and it looked like a patrol had encountered enemy.

'Read back, three KIA, one RPG, one PKM and one AK-47 recovered.'

Buzz was writing in a notebook as Kaz, my patrol commander, recited the details of the confrontation over the radio. The patrol had killed three men and recovered their weapons: a rocket launcher, a PK belt-fed machine gun and an AK-47 assault rifle. That was a serious line-up of weapons for just three enemy.

'What's the location of the bodies?' I asked.

'Bodies. Are. On. The. Trail,' came the whisper from the speaker on the desk. It was common to speak at a whisper, but I sensed the tension in his voice.

Buzz turned to me, handset in hand, expression neutral. 'Looks like Kaz ran into a few blokes during the recce and shot 'em. The bodies are still there. They're watching from a corn-field. They're buggin' out soon.'

'Right,' I said. I was absorbing the gravity of their situation. My team of six were 7 kilometres into enemy territory and had just killed a roving team of three Taliban soldiers. They had to get out, and fast. It was 1 am. If we had them extract on foot, they would have five hours left of darkness as they travelled through enemy-controlled villages, across rivers, through crops, avoiding mined roads and paths, all while dodging giant Afghan hounds, early-rising farmers and Taliban patrols seeking retri-bution. We had been watching the Taliban all week, and they were on edge, waiting for the Allied clearance force.

If we left them there, they would be in serious trouble come daylight. There were over 100 Taliban in the valley, and our men could be cut off. Being cut off is a nightmare scenario for a soldier. It meant you had enemy all around and no real avenue of escape. Two years earlier a Navy SEAL patrol had found them-selves in the same situation, and they were wiped out wholesale, apart from one man who managed to crawl to safety. His story was later immortalised in the film *Lone Survivor*.

'Let's get the blokes ready,' I said. 'We might need to launch a recovery option.' The guys were aware of this, and slept in anticipation of putting their gear on and heading out at a moment's notice. That was one thing about the SAS: the teams were always prepared and moved bloody quickly when given the word. No long orders or lead times, just a quick update, grab the kit, and more orders via radio as you headed out the door. It was called 'bias to action'.

I radioed a contact report back to the Special Ops Task Group, 40 kilometres away on the Tarin Kowt base, Camp Russell.

The squadron commander, Nick, jumped on the radio. 'Send,' he said.

I explained the situation to him.

'Copy all.' The boss started the process of activating aviation support and quick reaction forces. This was parallel planning, so that if things really went bad for Kaz, we had forces ready to launch immediately to assist him.

Meanwhile, we kept in touch with Kaz. As he was preparing to leave the site, a small child walked down the path, spotted the bodies, and bolted home to safety. The patrol was now compromised. They would have to leave the area quickly. On their way out of the valley, they strayed through a known Russian minefield, recognised because it was near a bunker. They patrolled out of it immediately. No mine drills needed here.

They eventually made it home at dawn. The whole troop was lined up, waiting to hear the story. Men handled and inspected the weapons with great interest. The RPG had a bullet hole through the rocket round. The PKM had several bullet holes through the ammo casing. The belt-fed machine gun had a red silk bandana tied around the stock; it smelled of a mild perfume. 'This is the wife's headscarf from the wedding night,' our Afghan interpreter explained. There was dried blood all over the cloth sling of the AK-47.

I asked one of Kaz's patrol members, Westy, to describe the incident.

'Mate, I was on the path as they walked towards us from out of nowhere. They had their weapons slung. I think they must have heard us in the cornfield.'

He waited until they were about 2 metres away, then fired a bunch of rounds. Sparks flew off the men as their weapons were struck. One man's beard caught fire as the RPG propellant was ignited and caught fire on his back. He was struck down in a hail of rounds. As the team swept through to clear them of their weapons, Westy saw a Taliban hiding at the edge of an aqueduct and shot him again.

The team had acquitted themselves well in this battle and they were thrilled to have survived.

Kaz's patrol lined up along the back wall, shirtless, in flip-flops, with their bounty. They struck a number of poses as the rest of the troop took photos and cheered. It was a small win for us, but it was also an ominous sign of what was waiting in the valley.

I looked over at Matthew Locke as he stood shirtless in the morning sun. He was sucking hard on a cigarette. He took a last drag then stomped his cigarette into the earth. 'We're getting out there,' he said to no-one in particular as he walked off towards the tent lines.

I knew Matt loved a fight and was pissed that his team did not have the opening credits of the tour. He had approached me because I was his boss and had planned the recon schedule for the teams. He was annoyed that his team had one less night patrol than the others. He wanted to join the action without delay.

That day I added some green paint to my weapon and helmet. We would be operating in the lush green belt, so green would be the order of camouflage. Matt walked past as I was rattling the spray can and said, 'Fuck knows why you're painting that – you'll be in the office while we run the clearance.' He said it deadpan, but I knew he was ribbing me. He was continuing the traditional sparring between officers and soldiers.

Matt went out the following night for a close-target recon. I put my gear on and went with him and the last man in his patrol. It was important for us all to see the ground. I always felt honoured if a patrol commander was happy to have me latch on to his team; it meant he was confident that I knew the tactics and could fight alongside them. As the patrol was out alone, he was in charge. When he was in the troop, and all four teams were out, I was in charge.

I was still quite new to all this. I had no combat experience and, secretly, I doubted my own abilities. While trepidation felt pretty normal, I was selected to overcome it and lead anyway. Self-doubt is not a bad thing in small doses, with so many lives at stake, that fear is there for a reason. I wanted to be known as the best officer. To just 'be there' in the field was not enough.

Matt, on the other hand, was 33 years old and a proven combat leader. He had been awarded a Medal for Gallantry the year before in this very valley. This combat action had propelled him into the ranks of the regiment's finest soldiers. He became a patrol commander, leading a team of six. Official recognition for brave conduct in battle was the like the Holy Grail. It made you a legend, cementing your name in the history of the regiment. It was good to have a respected fighter like Matt on my side. I knew it would make for a harrowing trip, but with his guidance, I could learn quickly.

0700 hours, 23 October

Matt had just returned from a night close-target recon and was writing up his report. I strolled into the command post in flip-flops and shorts, mug of instant coffee in hand. 'How'd you go?'

'Good,' said Matt. 'Take a look at this.' He still had green camouflage paint around his forehead and neck. He smelled like wet vegetation. He turned the ruggedised laptop towards me. On it was a slide titled 'Enemy Fighting Position', with a top-down wire diagram drawing of an enemy fighting bunker, including the depth, length and width measurements and with added commentary using arrows and text boxes.

'Whoa,' I said. This was impressive intelligence. It meant they were ready for a clearance.

'We found it, so I jumped in and took a look,' Matt explained, eyes fixed on his work.

'How the fuck did you measure it?' I asked.

'I used my rifle, just held it up the walls.'

'No shit.' I was impressed. Normally we would be happy with sighting enemy in various positions from a distance. This was accurate to 1 metre.

The SAS had developed a reputation for daring and cunning in the jungles of Vietnam, and we were now doing close-target reconnaissance into enemy positions, undetected. This was our mainstay – we were good at this hard, dangerous, grinding work. But this was ballsy: jumping into an enemy pit in enemy territory, knowing that at any moment a stray Taliban could come back to his pit and find a couple of Aussies taking measurements of his foxhole.

We sent the sketch off to the Royal Gurkha Regiment and the aviation unit that was committing to the assault.

When they saw Matt's sketch in an intelligence report, the commanding officer of 1 Aviation group exclaimed, 'They are either lying or they are fucking crazy.'

We were not lying.

The patrol had seen plenty. Matt had spent twelve hours creeping around in the dark in enemy territory, and upon returning to base he'd typed up his entire patrol report rather than catching some sleep first. I appreciated it, because it meant I could send the patrol reports off right away. He was also adept with his laptop and software. Aussie soldiers are typically not cerebral men. Most are very far from white collar IT professionals when it comes to driving a laptop. Matt was an exception. I once listened to him as he sat for an hour showing his second-in-command how to use PowerPoint. No matter how much his 2IC fumbled, Matt never showed any sign of impatience. He was the best kind of leader.

0800 hours, 24 October

Since I was so flat out planning, I was often the last to pack my gear. I found this pretty convenient as I would go around to five or six guys and ask them what they had packed so I could copy their shopping list. That day it was food, water, cold gear ammo and body armour.

I walked over to the brew point to join Westy and Matt Locke.

'What are your fellas doing? Are you running plates?' I asked, referring to bullet-stopping Kevlar body armour.

'No, mate, green roles, no requirement,' said Matt, referring to the lush green terrain we would patrol through. He paused, then added, 'I say that now, but you'll probably have to drag my dead body off the battlefield.'

'Yeah, you'll get hit right here!' Westy quipped. He pointed at the base of his sternum. A couple of guys chuckled and Matt raised his eyebrows.

I walked around to the rest of the guys prepping kit, asking them for their load list.

'What are you taking for water?' I asked Eddie.

'Only 4 litres for us, mate. I'm storing two in a bladder and the other two will be in my chest rig.'

'Cold gear?' I asked.

'Take your puffer jacket,' he advised. 'It's bloody zero degrees out there.'

'Ammo?'

'Yeah, I'll throw in a few more mags and maybe a couple of 40-mil bombs. That's weight worth carrying.'

'Food?'

'Just an MRE hot pack.' MREs were the US rations.

Armed with this intel, I went and packed a single thermal shirt, neck tube and beanie made from merino wool. 'Go light, freeze at night' is the army maxim. I added a couple of MRE hot packs. I explained to a few soldiers the chemistry of exothermic reactions in the hot pack and why hydrogen peroxide releases heat and hydrogen when mixed with water. They didn't look impressed.

For extra ammo I packed five 40 mm high explosive detonating points. We called them 'gold tops' because the swollen

110

bullet was a yellow gold. The first time I'd ever seen one was watching *Terminator 2*, when Arnold fires one into a liquid metal terminator.

I also packed a spare battery for my personal radio: 'No comms, no bombs' was the saying. The personal radio was secure and you could talk to all your mates, and even to aircraft overhead if you had to. If you got lost, it had a beacon function you could activate to tell people where to get you.

Finally, I packed two army muesli bars and power gels, adding a few sachets of dried fruit cubes out of the Australian ration packs. All the rations were sealed in green wrappers.

I secured my pack straps and made sure none were loose. In close country, a loose, swinging strap might be enough movement to give away your position.

Around my neck I wore a small hexagonal disc and I had another on my boot, the laces threaded between the holes. These dog tags would enable people to identify me if I was killed or badly maimed. I checked my M4 assault rifle, adding a little extra weapon oil on the bolt and moving the working parts back and forth to distribute the oil. Weapons can get 'thirsty' when you fire a lot of rounds, slowing their operation as they heat up. I checked my maps. Matt had printed out a good A4-sized map with the colourful British report lines and objectives. They were all named for British war poets such as Sassoon, Brooke and Owen. One of the British objective locations marked the Kala Kala graveyard area. That was where my mate had seen the dead Taliban soldier gutted from the AC-130s. I used an orange highlighter on the small numbers on the map lines that indicate the eastings and northings of a military grid system.

Meanwhile, the soldiers were busy cutting lengths of thin green tubing. This was fuse wire for delayed explosive charges, or Claymore mines: a shaped charge the size of a large shoe with 700 ball bearings on the face of it. These could be very handy where we were going.

What is actually going to happen tonight? I wrote in my field message notebook, something I knew would be returned to my family if I was killed. *DON'T WORRY!* I added, hoping to reassure them should the worst happen. *This is the top of the hill for me – I can go no further – and if something happens, I will be in good company, the best in the world.*

It was 1930 hours. I pulled a lock of my girlfriend Michelle's dark hair from my bag, and I taped it onto the inside of my body armour, against my heart. She was part Maori, so she had dark hair. She had also given me a shell tiki, like a Buddha, and I wore it around my neck for luck. We had been dating for a year before I deployed to Afghanistan.

A full moon rose and threw shadows from the tall pine trees. We had 96 per cent illumination – good for pilots, not so good for us guys going out on the ground; it meant the enemy could see us.

It was to be a troop move on foot, about 6 kilometres, onto the helicopter landing sites. We would mark the landing sites with infrared lamps, and pull down some wires that were in the way. We would receive the first helicopters of clearance troops.

Boys were crowded around the rear of one of our assault jeeps, music playing from the vehicle's speakers: 'Hells Bells' and 'The Unforgiven'. The mood was upbeat; men were laughing as they worked. I had camouflaged my face, hands, ears and neck with brown and green paint. I was wearing my body armour and backpack. My rifle was an M4, with an M203 grenade launcher below. I had an ACOG magnified scope and my night vision goggles were on.

'Troop photo, fellas?' I suggested as we were kitting up. I controlled the troop, but I also had my own team, with the troop sergeant and a handful of comms and aircraft control operators. We stood in front of a table set up with a coffee urn and cookies on it.

'No, we can't get one in front of the brew area, that's gay,' said Pez. 'LRPVs are the go.' Our long-range patrol vehicles were Mad-Max style jeep rovers – much more warrior-like. The photo was taken by Nick the signaller. 'Good snap,' he said. 'That's a keeper.'

I shook hands with Buzz as we walked out of the gate. He would be manning the base while we were gone; I knew he would prefer to be coming with us.

'See ya, Waler,' he said, but his handshake was firm. He had patrolled the green belt before and he knew what could be awaiting us.

12

THE 22ND EASTING

0213 hours, 25 October 2007

WE PATROLLED THE LANDSCAPE IN NEAR SILENCE: 26 MEN AND one dog wandering through a field of marijuana, sweet and pungent, growing so high it obscured the night sky. We walked in four teams of six men, with Matt's team in the lead. My team came next: me; Jimbo, the signaller; Horse, with Rischa the dog; Pez, an operator who called in drones and aircraft; and Doogs, the troop sergeant. Then came the sniper team, packing heavy weapons. They would take up position on a ridge to protect us from the open river flank. The fourth team brought up the rear. We were sticking to the shadows as much as possible; that way we didn't cast shadows of our own, and we'd be hard to detect with the naked eye.

We crossed a small aqueduct, chest deep and just wide enough to step over. The man in front of me pointed at the river and held two fingers up before pointing at the aqueduct. I knew that it marked the 22nd Easting. Everything west of here was controlled by our enemy.

I flopped to the soft earth on my backside in the landing zone, or LZ. We were in enemy territory now, so I was trying to be quiet. I pulled out my map. I was also wearing a GPS on my right arm like a watch. The whole valley was bathed in ghostly white moonlight, so bright I could actually read both map and GPS without a torch and confirm our position.

While Horse and I kept to the edge of the LZ, my troop sergeant, Doogs, used his huge frame to push over some rotting power lines to clear the site. This was the third tour for Doogs. He had been blown out of his car twice by roadside bombs on his last tour. Pez had witnessed it and said he was tottering around with his pistol drawn, thinking he had been ambushed.

The night was freezing. I shoved my hand in the hot pack I'd slipped in my crotch, looking for more heat. I looked at Horse in his oversized puffer jacket; he looked toasty. He was standing with his hands in his pockets, and Rischa, his Belgian Malinois princess, was sitting on her haunches at his side. He was wearing a US Army camouflage bandana to cover his bald head. At 6 foot 3 inches, he was easy to spot at the best of times. It was a stunning night, crystal clear. We could have been in a Margaret River vineyard except for the soft hum overhead of an MQ-9 Reaper drone armed with Hellfire missiles, its unblinking eye checking our surrounds for enemy.

0430 hours, 25 October

I paused as a light thumping breached the calm. The first two Chinooks thundered through the valley on final approach, 40-foot beasts with twin rotors and packed with Gurkha troops. They pulled in hard to the landing zones, and through my night vision I could see the troop sergeant standing in the field as a circle of sand, dust and tree branches whipped around him. Men were almost blown off their feet as the helicopters swooped down with their lights off. Everyone shielded their eyes and necks from the sandblasting. The rear ramp dropped, and 30 Gurkha soldiers – compact, strong Nepalese men – ran off the back of the helo ramp. With their combat packs on, they were as wide as they were tall. The helos took off again immediately;

I saw a double flash of their infrared lights through the dust to warn other helicopters of an ascending platform.

The Gurkhas were all heavy breaths and shouted whispers. 'ARE YOU TF 66?' hissed a kneeling British officer at full volume. He must have been the company commander.

Horse sauntered over, hands in pockets with carbine hanging off the front of his chest, Rischa at his side. He bent down to the officer and whispered, 'Form-up point is 200 metres to the south. Area is secure, you can head over now.'

They picked up and headed to the form-up point which would start the clearance.

0600 hours, 25 October

We met in the creek bed once Kaz had returned from his task of marking a support by fire location. As we sat, guys began removing their cold weather gear in preparation for a foot move. The night had been icy and we were wet from the legs down. The patrol commanders walked towards me, hands on their carbines, scanning the fields ahead of them for enemy.

'Eight Oscar, this is Echo Charlie, marry up complete, continuing task in accordance with phase three plan,' Jimbo rattled off to our headquarters back in Tarin Kowt.

The patrol commanders sat down with me. It was early dawn, and we now faced a dilemma over our next step. On one side of the valley were 150 Allied troops, and there was a ton of attack helicopters and drones overhead. That was a very complex battlefield, more dangerous to me than the Taliban. Working with inexperienced soldiers, and with little direct communications, there was always a chance of being shot at by the Gurkhas. To our south-west, we had open battlespace, but likely Taliban formations moving towards us. Daylight was now a serious issue; we no longer had the advantage of night vision. Both options were dangerous, but I preferred the idea of tackling enemy rather than friendlies.

The patrol commanders realised the sticky situation we were in. Kaz's brow was furrowed. Matt's usual relaxed demeanour was serious. The thrum of two Apache helicopters sounded overhead as they circled a thousand feet above us.

'We've married up and task is complete for the reception phase,' I confirmed. 'We have a couple of options, I think. One is we continue to push south-east to our blocking location, although it's a bit later than what we would have liked. The other option is to wait in location: we have a bit of observation onto the river here.'

The patrol commanders looked at each other. I could sense tension in the group.

I continued. 'I reckon we go have a look. We're in strength so we should be all right. Move down to blocks and pull up on the interdiction spot.'

A few nods but they were tight-lipped. I couldn't tell if it was due to the danger, or because it was a bad plan, or both. I wasn't sure what they were thinking.

'I reckon our job here is done,' Taff, my British patrol commander, offered. He was an exchange sergeant from the Special Boat Service and like Matt had a lot of combat experience. 'We could go back to base and reset for another task.'

'But seeing as we're already here, we might as well go take a look,' I countered.

'Yeah,' Matt agreed. 'Let's push down and have a look – there's not much going on here at the moment, but there might be movement down that way.'

'Righto,' I said. 'Move at six thirty.'

I drafted a note for the HQ.

Troop HQ, Echo 1, Echo 3 and Echo 4 all in location. Reception complete. Phase 2 about to begin.

Commander's intent. Push south-west 1000 metres, begin Phase 3. Due to timings, Echo 21 will remain with troop minus for Phase 3, Echo 2 minus will remain in observation post.

    Comments: Deception and marking went well, almost nil incident. Air deconfliction a concern (Echo 3 lased by Reaper drone). Nil enemy force activity. Icom indicated there was disunity in enemy forces.

I checked my watch.

It was 0609.

13

MAN DOWN

0630 hours, 25 October 2007

TROOPS BEGAN TO STAND, ONE PERSON AT A TIME, SCANNING in all directions. Weapons were up and parallel to the ground. We were in the enemy's backyard now, boxed up against a shallow river, an obstacle. Hard to cross, easy to cover with machine-gun fire, and easy to traverse. A highway on a battlefield.

'This is a shit area, isn't it?' I said to Taff.

He grimaced, showing the gap where his two front teeth were missing, and whispered in his northern English accent, 'Yeah, this is shite – too open.'

I reassured myself by checking the area for a good tactical path. We had some covered approaches in these irrigation ditches. I could see that the tree line ahead had a small trench running alongside it. A trench was good cover. There was a cornfield in front of us. The whole area we were walking through was farm land. Freshly ploughed fields with rich, dark soil. Water rushed through the small aqueducts, their sides still bearing the scars of hoes and shovels. The place was pristine, carefully tended – which was why the large, dry, scruffy corn-field in front of me looked so out of place. By now, it should have been harvested, reduced to stubs, and the remaining plant matter ploughed back into the soil for the next crop.

I had an uneasy feeling, but I couldn't tell if that was just nerves getting the better of me. The air seemed to hum almost imperceptibly. I felt as if I were being compelled forward rather than moving of my own volition. This land did not feel welcoming. My scalp prickled as I scanned the corn and the line of trees that ran alongside it. My trigger finger was beside the guard, my thumb resting on the metal post of my safety catch. Every few steps I applied the slightest tension to it, to check it sat horizontal and safe. My weapon was at my waist, parallel to the ground; the barrel protruded from the bottom of my view and followed my eyes. I stopped, my ears straining towards the trees to capture any stray soundwaves.

Nothing.

My earpiece crackled to life.

'*All call signs, E45, male in black walking away from us, south edge of the cornfield.*'

Another call: '*Female walking away, with a kid.*'

I realised something that, until now, my ego hadn't allowed me to recognise. *This situation is slipping out of my control.*

CRACK CRACK CRACK CRACK.

Pause. *That can't be.*

CRACK CRACK CRACK CRACK CRACK CRACK.

Fuck! FUCK! Enemy!

This was what it sounded like to be shot at.

We were in contact. They were in the corn, less than 50 metres away. It sounded more like 10 metres.

My heart rate jumped to maximum, my legs turning to hot jelly, my mouth, sandpaper-dry.

I pushed forward and dropped to my knees in a shallow irrigation ditch facing the cornfield. Small eucalypts lined the forward edge of the ditch. I peered into the withered corn stalks. More shots – heaps of shots coming in. Green leaves fluttered around me. Green leaves – I'd heard of this. You know when you're getting shot at, I'd been told, because leaves start falling all around you. Leaves were whirling around me now. There was a whipping in the air; it felt close to my head but I couldn't quite tell.

I kept my eyes locked on the cornfield.

'*Man down, there's a man down*,' came a trembling voice over the radio.

Great, I thought. *It must be one of theirs. Good shooting.*

I was hunched forward, trying to keep my head down, half expecting a bullet to cleave the side of my face off at any second. I shuffled right to a tree stump on the edge of the corn. My right foot was shaking. *Helmet!* I thought, then remembered it was in my backpack; I wouldn't be getting that out. My breath was ragged. I could inhale, but exhaling required a conscious effort.

Pez was on the radio to the Apaches that were cutting race-track circuits in the sky above us. '*64, this is Echo Delta, we are receiving small arms fire from our north-east from a cornfield directly in front of us. I will mark our position – stand by.*'

Fuck, he sounds really calm, I thought, *considering the amount of fire we are taking.*

I was going to fire back, I decided. I wanted to launch grenades to kill or supress the jihadis shooting at us.

'Is anyone in the cornfield?' I yelled, wanting to know if all our guys were out.

A hail of bullets whispered and cracked into the vegetation around me. I ducked my head beneath the parapet. That was the first time I had shouted in a battle, and it was almost my last. The bark of a river willow next to my head was shredded with bullets.

I took a knee and aimed my rifle into the cornfield. I was carrying a 40 mm grenade launcher under my carbine, and there was a high-explosive round loaded. I held it up to my shoulder and aimed it level with the ground. I knew it would travel about

30 metres at that trajectory. I tensed my shoulder and levelled the weapon at the corn.

Thoomp . . . BOOM!

Time of flight was too long on that one; I wanted to bring it in closer. I pushed a release button lever on the left side of the grenade tube, and the whole tube slid forward to expose the metal breech. A shell the size of a shot glass tumbled out, smoke pouring from it. A blue cloud of acrid cordite settled in the trench, a familiar smell. I pulled up a Velcro latch on my chest plate and took a grenade from it. My left hand was shaking as I placed it in the tube. My right hand stayed on the pistol grip of the rifle. I didn't even bother with the safety catch as I reloaded, normally considered a safety breach in training, but we were too close to the enemy.

I stood up a little higher, depressing the barrel height.

Thonk . . . BOOM!

That was better. Closer.

Firing felt very good: a familiar action in an unfamiliar situation. We had done it so often that it required no conscious thought. I knew that, as team leader, I was meant to be leading the troop, but we were caught out and needed to regain the initiative. 'Use explosives to win back the initiative if you need to,' I remembered an instructor telling us.

I pulled the weapon tube open again and reloaded, slipping another round into the breech. Closed it, and fired.

Horse and Pez, beside me in the trench, were similarly busy. Every time I fired a grenade, Horse's dog yelped and jerked on her lead. Horse had his hands well and truly full as he tried to fire and hold the dog back on her lead at the same time.

Aaron ran down the trench from the left, where Matt's team had been when the enemy started firing. He had his helmet on.

'Matt's down, Pri 1. He's unconscious; he's not breathing.' His voice was shaky. Aaron never gets rattled, so I knew it was bad. Pri 1 signals a serious casualty – it means 'dead within the hour' if medical aid is not forthcoming.

I pushed left a few steps down the trench, which by now was knee-deep in foaming sludge. I held my weapon up; the safety catch on my carbine was off. I never ran with my safety catch off. On training cycle, it was an offence that would get you kicked out of the unit. But I knew that if I didn't have it up and a Taliban soldier came through that corn, I'd miss him, and then I'd be fighting hand-to-hand.

When I cornered the creek line, I saw a whole team of men scrambling. One was lying prone and shooting on the corn side of the trench, while another climbed over him to fire at an enemy. It was gritty, desperate fighting. Matt's second in command, Clay Watts, put his foot on the parapet, shouldered his M4 and fired twenty rounds to cover me as I moved to them. I saw three more men hunched low over a man lying on his back on the left side of the corn. It was Matt. They were using scissors to cut away his combat shirt. Aaron was directing them. 'He's not getting enough air – he needs a tracheotomy,' he said. His voice was back to steady now, no shaking.

I took stock of Matt's condition. I knew he was seriously injured, and we had to evacuate him. I knew we were in strife. As all these facts registered, I felt present but detached. I was working, fighting, but I had turned off most rational thought. It was an odd feeling of being alive but knowing your whole existence could be taken in a moment.

Another soldier knelt next to Clay, firing his weapon. The legs and back of his uniform were wet. He had been shot through the backpack at the start of the battle and his water bladder had ruptured. He was kneeling low and returning fire. *Bloody brave*, I thought.

'FRAG OUT!' Clay bawled.

Everyone stopped firing and turned to look as he threw his grenade . . . but the moment lost some of its urgency as he grappled with the pin; Aussie grenades had a reputation for being shit.

Got it! He braced to throw from his kneeling position. He heaved the grenade over the parapet in a full-armed throw and we all ducked our heads . . . BOOM!

Debris rained over the ditch.

Good one! Shit, that was louder than I remember. Fuck, they must be close if we can throw grenades at them.

'Fuck, yeah!' shouted Clay down the line, smiling, satisfied with the throw.

I was now shitting myself at the realisation that, if we were throwing grenades at them, they were less than 30 metres away. To make matters worse, we had a casualty, which meant we couldn't move. We had three guys working on him, and we would need four to move him. The enemy had the advantage.

Bang, bang, bang, bang, bang.

Sticks and bark flew off another tree barely a foot from my head.

I knew when I'd been spotted by a Talib, because he did not fire one bullet, he fired twenty rounds in about two seconds. It was brutal. They were clearly intent on making the most of the fact that they had us pinned down.

I shuffled a metre to the left and pulled my rifle up. I shot at everything that could possibly house a soldier. Both sides of a wood pile, the flanks of the corn, the gunfire noise in front of me. My rifle clacked away as I fired, looking down the ACOG scope, the red chevron on the sight bucking and jumping as I pulled the trigger. As Clay turned and moved past me, I saw his suppressor shimmer with heat, felt its radiant temperature on my face and smelled the cooked metal and cordite.

I look over my shoulder and saw Kerr doing compressions on Matt's chest and Johnny waiting for a pause so he could blow air through the tube inserted in Matt's neck. His condition was deteriorating fast; we needed to evacuate him ASAP.

'Where are they?' I heard from behind me.

I looked up and saw Kaz kneeling in open ground behind me, scanning the cornfield ahead. He was fully exposed to enemy fire and had covered about 50 metres to get to us. I was bloody glad to see him.

'Mate, bring some guys up, and get some fire down,' I rasped. My mouth was still dry. I had not yet settled into the battle; this was really my first instruction since the shooting started five minutes before.

'What's happening? What have we got?' Kaz asked, shouting over the sound of gunfire. The rounds were thundering around us.

'Matt's down over there, and we are putting fire in from here. I need you guys to come up and carry Matt out of here. We'll provide covering fire.'

The signaller was lying down with his radio set against his ear, and I could see he was already sending a nine-liner – a standard casualty template – back to base. This would cue the US medevac helicopters and their Apache escorts to come and get Matt.

He finished and sat up. 'Want your helmet?' he asked.

'Yes,' I said gratefully, and he pulled it from my pack for me as I returned fire.

'*We're in contact too*,' came the voice of another soldier over the radio.

'You will act as rear passage of lines,' I shouted into the radio in response. 'We will move the casualty through you.' Rear passage of lines meant every team would hold its position, creating a corridor of men facing outwards and shooting. You moved the vulnerable casualty down the tunnel while you had all-round protection. This tactic would buy us about 100 metres of distance from the enemy, hopefully allowing room for the helicopters to land so they could evacuate Matt.

Finally we had some sort of plan. A plan is essential, even if it's a crap plan; the important thing is just to do something.

I ran over to Matt and dropped to a knee beside him. Johnny knelt near his head, leaning forward to blow into the small tube inserted into Matt's throat. The man doing compressions on Matt's chest and the man blowing in the tube both looked grim. I knew that Matt's life hung in the balance. He was critical, but giving up was not an option. We had to get him out to the medical facility in Tarin Kowt; we could deal with the rest later.

Two Gurkha soldiers ran up the aqueduct towards us. One was carrying a belt-fed machine gun with brass rounds and link hanging from it. A British doctor in uniform, weaponless, was right behind them. I leaned forward to one of the men and shouted, 'COVER!' while pointing at Matt. Lengthy explanations were not needed. The soldier nodded and went to help the team that was shifting Matt onto a small tarp. Four men helped drag Matt up the line: three of ours and one Gurkha. The Gurkha with the machine gun had left it on the parapet as he helped us. When I heard a machine gun open up a few seconds later, I looked over and saw that Kaz had acquired it and was raking across the cornfield with heavy rounds, firing from the waist in a very non-regulation stance. The belt ran out and he threw the hefty gun to the earth, disgusted that the Ghurkas had left a good weapon unused.

While the rest of us fired, the team transporting Matt pulled him up out of the ditch and started crossing the field beside it. The sun had risen now and they were exposed.

'They're gonna get shot,' warned Taff.

It was chaos. Utter chaos.

I fired my M4 into mounds of grass and low through the cornfields. My rifle was clacking away, and I could see the air shimmering over the top of my suppressor.

The return fire was building. Leaves and branches continued to flutter down, and as I looked up at the wall of trees above us, I knew it would be a perfect RPG target.

I saw a bald man kneeling right near me, returning fire with his M4. That was strange; I couldn't remember anyone in the team who was bald besides Horse. Then I realised it was Sean McCarthy, one of the comms soldiers. His job had been to monitor the enemy radios, but here he was, slinging lead. I registered that as impressive. We were trained to do this all day; he was trained to listen to radios. Sean was planning to attempt SAS selection one day, but he never got the chance; he would be killed by an IED blast in July 2008.

Meanwhile, the snipers had watched the melee unfold from 500 metres away and high on our left flank, and they were keen to get to work. It was hard for them to see where our front line ended and the enemy's began, so they'd held fire while we got our bearings in the opening minutes of the battle.

Eventually someone threw Sean a bright orange panel marker to pin to a tree. This would signal to the snipers up on our left flank where our forward lines of troops stopped. This was key, because anything further down the valley from that orange panel would be dead meat once the snipers went to work.

Sean took the orange panel and stood up from the ditch to tie it off to a tree. I saw the bushes to his front tremble from the bullets passing through them.

'DOWN!' I yelled. 'You'll get shot.' I motioned with my hand. No sooner had I said the words than the orange panel was shot from his hands and fluttered to the ground. Sean stooped over to pick it up and resumed tying. I could not tear my eyes away, I was so certain I was about to see another man shot. Finally he tied off the corner of the panel and crouched down again. He peered up at his handiwork, satisfied. He looked over his shoulder to see me watching; clocking my frozen face, he gave me a thumbs-up.

The snipers came over the radio: *'Panel marker spotted. Stand by, engaging now.'*

I knew what was coming. The first .50-calibre round thundered through the valley into the bushes on our flank. There was a booming explosion.

The sniper team had spotted enemy moving up the dry river bed around our flank and had unleashed semi-armour-piercing, high-explosive rounds. The first rounds clipped a fighter with an AK-47 and he collapsed into the river bed. Another man in sandals and a prayer cap ran over to help him. As he reached his comrade, one of my snipers shot him through the side. He too collapsed in a heap. A pair of fighters ran out to get the two men. They were felled in place by more heavy-calibre rounds. Enemy fighters were being killed in droves by the snipers; it was carnage.

The Apaches started firing cannon shells along the river where the fighters were flanking us. The noise was a physical presence, more a feeling than a sound. A Hellfire missile hit the treetops nearby. The top half of a tree was shredded into kindling. I flinched, and felt the loose parts of my uniform rattle in the concussion. Years earlier, I had stood third row back from the front of a Rolling Stones concert at the Voodoo Lounge with Dad. My jeans had rattled in the same way; the ringing in my ears had stayed with me for days.

We were living in small packets of time, maybe five seconds apiece. Each new five seconds was a chance to live or die, kill or be killed. There were multiple choices to make in those five-second increments: Shoot or not? Call out or not? Look this way or that way? Throw a grenade, or don't risk it? To lower my weapon might mean death if a fighter emerged from the corn in front of me. Troubles went away; employment, bills, partners, politics, car troubles, personal injuries, fears. Surviving and helping my mates became everything. The universe had contracted to a square kilometre of Afghan soil.

My leg had stopped shaking by now. Speaking, moving, shooting back, looking for work, covering each other was a good feeling. *We are actually trained for this*, I realised at one point. My signaller, Jimbo, was lying flat to the ground, hexagonal antenna near him, pointing south to FOB, a finger stuck in one ear, handset pushed up to the other ear, shouting out the casualty evacuation report. 'Do not approach from the south-west: enemy,' he was shouting.

'Medevac inbound, ten minutes.' Jimbo looked at me, nodded, and began packing away his handset.

We needed to move a bound back to cover the stretcher team. I put Kaz to our flank, protecting Matt's team and giving them space to work.

As we ran back, I saw the antenna trailing behind Jimbo on the ground, so I scooped it up. I was certain we would be shot in the back making this bound. I looked right and saw Taff making quick steps left and right, like a rugby player feinting his tacklers. He was dodging the aim of a Taliban rifle. I was running beside my mate, Westy, a Maori fella whose helmet was tilting across his head as he ran. 'Why you doing that for? It means you have to run twice as far.' We both started giggling as we ran.

We paused from the new position and heard the approaching medevac helicopter, coming in low and fast. They were approaching from the south, and I could hear the revs dropping as they approached the LZ. They were late; it'd been 30 minutes since we first called in the contact. I wasn't mad – we had been in such deep shit, it would have been more dangerous if they'd arrived earlier. The helicopter swooped in low, the trees bowing in the rotor wash; I could see the red cross on its side. I heard enemy fire ratcheting up. The helo was flying directly over the enemy position now, about 80 metres above.

Too low! Not from the south! FUCK!

I saw yellow sparks jump from the tail boom, heard the ticking of metal being punctured. Bullet strike.

That helicopter will go down. We're going to be here all day! I wasn't laughing anymore.

It fell out of the sky more than landed. We ran over. The door gunner pointed his twin guns downwards as we crossed between the enemy and him. I saw the back of the pilot's head as we ran over, a brown ponytail protruding from under her helmet. An IV bag cable hung from the roof. Matt was hauled onto the metal deck where a red-haired Aussie nurse in desert uniform was kneeling to receive him. We later found out it was her second day in country.

The revs picked up and the ground swirled around us as the helicopter began to rise.

We now had full mobility. 'Break contact,' I ordered.

We formed a troop line and started firing down the line as the troops peeled back. I waited my turn, covering the corn. As the man next to me fired off half a mag, he turned and tapped my shoulder. 'Last man,' he informed me. I turned and fired a grenade, blowing up a low eucalypt branch further down the aqueduct. I fired a dozen rounds, turned and ran down the line, reloading. I hit Clay and said, 'Last man. Good hustle!'

'Not that good,' Clay corrected me, a reminder that we had one badly wounded team leader.

I reloaded as I ran down the aqueduct to a dirt-walled compound nestled among the green. I could see a British soldier standing in the doorway, waving us in. There was a whole British platoon inside.

The fighting raged around us. I looked up at the sniper nest on the rocky ridge and saw gouts of white dirt and dust flying up. An Apache was completing a missile run, white streaks reaching towards the ground and thumping in. Mortar shells whined above us and crumped onto the hillside. I had no idea which side they belonged to. It was a 360-degree battle, raging in every direction. What a bloody morning. We were all glad to be alive, but we knew Matt was in dire straits.

I asked the team sergeant to come with me and stormed into the living area of the building. We found ourselves in a kitchen with ornamental pots, tea kettles and folded maroon blankets. It was the first time I had stood in an Afghan home. It felt strangely intimate.

I took my helmet off and put my rifle on a stack of blankets. I could feel everything I had contained in me right behind my face. Before I knew it, I was crying.

'We should never have gone down there. That was my fault.' My face contorted with sobs. I couldn't hold them back. The tears were the first real release of emotion since arriving in Afghanistan. It felt like the fabric holding my sanity together was tearing at the seams. I wiped my eyes and the camouflage paint mixed with tears, and formed a brown sludge on the back of my glove.

My troop sergeant, Doogs, concerned for me, put his hand on my shoulder. 'No, it's not your fault – we were doing the right thing. You're a great boss: everyone thinks so.'

I appreciated his comforting words, but I was shattered. I walked out into the courtyard to find Jimbo, who had set up the radio.

I jumped on to speak with the boss.

'How's Matt?' I asked.

'*E11 has passed. He's dead.*' My boss let that sink in.

'Roger,' I whispered.

I was shattered – I had never seen a life stolen like that. Only moments earlier, there had been fire in his eyes and the determination that had saved whole teams. I felt awful, deflated. It's hammered into an officer that everything that happened on a mission was your responsibility; I knew I would feel the weight of this for a long time to come.

Not only that: accepting Matt was dead would mean accepting our own mortality as well. If the best could die here, so could we. I knew his wife and son would be at home, blissfully unaware, and that notification teams would be putting their dress uniforms on so they could visit Matt's home to deliver the worst news a family could get: *Your husband, your father, has been taken from you, way before his time.*

14

THE GOOD DIE YOUNG

MATT WAS DEAD. THE MAN WHO'D TALKED ME THROUGH ROUTE planning in enemy territory after I had made a terrible error. Who, despite not having slept in 24 hours, took the time to show his 2IC how to change fonts and border colours on a PowerPoint presentation. The man who drank dirty Jim Beam and Cokes at the bar. Who had scaled a cliff to fight off the Taliban only last summer.

I was numb, apart from a tingling in my fingers and toes. My head throbbed. I leaned back against the mud wall of the compound, M4 on my lap, and felt a stillness wash over me. My spirit, normally buoyant, was crushed. Something in me had died with Matt. I knew life was going to be different after this.

I looked at my watch: 0900. We had been in combat for almost an hour and a half. It had felt like a lifetime.

'Complete cas and ammo,' I told Kaz and Clay, who had taken over Matt's team.

They checked if anyone else was injured. No-one was. Men swapped ammunition clips, making sure everyone had ammo. Your ammo did not belong to you; it was the team's.

I knew my boss would be waiting on the detail. It would be excruciating for him back at base, organising assets, helping where possible and waiting for word. He had not yet pushed me for it, and I knew he would be under pressure from every general in the country for more information. He was protecting us from that crap at the moment, so we could do our jobs well. I knew the whole bloody country would be waiting. It was the first loss of an Australian soldier to enemy fire since Vietnam.

I drafted up a short report. It explained the whole situation, devoid of the obvious terror we faced at the time. It ended with:

Assessment: enemy demonstrated determination and resilience despite significant return fire and close air support. Determination and flanking speeds indicative of fighting positions.

As I worked on the report, a young Gurkha platoon commander came over to me. He had red hair and looked a lot like a certain member of the British royal family who was secretly on tour in Afghanistan at the time. 'I'm terribly sorry about your lad.'

I just nodded. I was too upset to talk about Matt. Instead, the platoon commander and I discussed how we could support him and his men as they broke into the next series of compounds. 'We can give you some support by fire,' I offered. 'We'll put our snipers up and a patrol to give you a hand.'

After writing the sitrep, I scrawled a short entry in my notebook about the battle and what I had thought. *First contact. Brutal. There are a few things I will never leave home without: 40 mm, helmet, good radio.*

The rest of the team was slumped against the interior walls of the compound, our first rest in twelve hours. The battle still rang and rattled around us, but we were happy to steal some sleep. We all watched a trooper walk gingerly across the roof of the mud hut in front of us. The rooftop was lined with straw. As he walked, a stream of machine-gun fire zipped past him.

He collapsed face first into the straw, having ducked in front of the entire troop. Everyone laughed, happy it was a miss.

I walked up to the rooftop where the first team was covering across.

'How are ya?' I asked, trying to sound positive.

'Good boss, good.' I knew they were trying to act as if they were fine too.

Steve, an experienced patrol 2IC and air traffic controller, turned to me. 'Steep learning curve for you today.'

I nodded. I was happy we'd made the best of a bad situation, but I knew I had made a mistake. I'd had no idea just how vulnerable you were in the green belt in daylight; we had lost the element of surprise, and it had cost us.

We decided to wait until nightfall to get out.

'We can't go back through that battlespace now – it's too busy,' I said to Doogs. I was more worried about being killed by our own forces at that point.

'Yeah,' he agreed. 'Let's move tonight under cover.'

We would have to wait it out in the compound, then head to a pick-up. It would be an 8-kilometre move on foot, most of it through enemy territory, the rest through a battlefield with foreign troops and poor comms. We were tired and it was going to be hectic, but we had trained for this type of scenario.

As the day drew to a close, I stood with Steve looking across the valley as the sun dropped behind the ridge line. I was thinking about the battle.

'Did your ears shut down?' I asked. 'I swear my ears blocked out all the noise.'

'Yeah, they did.' Steve nodded. 'The human body is built for combat.' He turned away from me and trudged back to the compound walls.

I stood for a moment, gazing at the foreign landscape. We were so far from home. Then I went back inside to continue planning our extraction.

We passed our plan to the boss. Buzz was going to pick us up at a vehicle drop point in the Bushmasters, giant troop carriers with a V-shaped hull for deflecting mine blasts. That would save us a few kilometres and enable us to pull the whole team out together. I briefed the patrol commanders and we started our walk out. We put our night vision goggles on our helmets and the PCs briefed their teams over the radios.

The battlefield had calmed, there was only sporadic fire now, and night was falling. The green of the valley faded into grey. As we approached the river, I felt certain that I would be shot while crossing it. It was 30 metres wide, waist deep with dark brown water. I was sure it would be covered by the enemy – you could fire 100 metres each way up the river: north, towards the folded mountains around Chora, and south, to the narrow Baluchi Pass. We positioned cover teams as we waded across. They were our 'foot on the ground', stationary, watching, while the other foot moved. We crossed with our weapons held up above the water, tense and silent, waiting for the burst of fire. *I'll just drop under the water and do my best*, I thought. But they either did not see us, or were not game to fire.

On the other side of the river we slumped to the marshy ground and waited. I felt like I could stay there forever, in the dark, in the warm mud, thick trees all around us. The fatigue was soaking me up.

Twenty minutes later Buzz sent me the grid for the pick-up point. I wrote it down and entered the numbers into my GPS. I called the team leaders over and shared the grid with them. I had to repeat the eight digits no less than five times. We were so exhausted we could not retain information long enough to write it down.

The moon shone bright across the fields as we made our way to the pick-up. It was deadly bright, shadows everywhere. I started seeing men kneeling in the shadows, only for them to dissipate when I focused; my mind was playing tricks on me.

Clouds passed over a full moon and we made a break for it, running across the open turf.

We were picked up by the Bushmasters right on schedule. As we rolled back towards the FOB I was tense, waiting for an IED blast, but none came. When we arrived at the compound, Buzz and some signallers were waiting for us. The signaller took my weapon off me and helped me down from the vehicle; I was too tired to move myself. Buzz shook my hand. I said to him, 'Mate, I'm sorry.' I was looking down, playing with the stock of my M4. 'This place isn't worth it,' I said.

He replied, 'Tell me what place is.'

I was weeping again, silently.

Buzz said, 'Do you think if Matt was standing here after you stopped a bullet he would be blaming himself? He wouldn't.'

I nodded. His words helped a little. At a really vulnerable moment, they allowed me to forgive myself a little.

One of the patrol 2ICs came past and put his hand on my shoulder, and said nothing. It was the same man who had told me to stop walking when I was on the Happy Wanderer phase of selection. This was a place where you had to go way beyond what you felt capable of doing, and today had been the biggest stretch of all. We had walked in a tiny area where death and life overlapped. A lot of enemy had died that morning. They had stolen one of ours. It felt like an unfair swap.

I climbed into my swag, and slept. I don't think any dreams came, but when I unzipped my swag and sat up in the daylight, I wanted to believe that was all it had been. But the aches in my body and my filthy face and cut hands told me it wasn't.

A padre from the SAS parked his government car outside a house in a leafy suburb in Perth. He triple-checked the address and the number on the letterbox. Satisfied he was in the right spot, he steeled himself for a moment. He checked his dress uniform, then walked to the front door and knocked three times. Matt's teenage son, Keegan, opened it. He was only thirteen years old, but he already had the broad shoulders and dark eyebrows of his father.

'My dad's dead, isn't he?' Keegan asked.

The padre nodded.

Keegan watched him for a long time.

'Is your mother here?' the padre asked.

'She's at the shops. She'll be back soon,' said Keegan.

The padre waited with Keegan in their lounge room for Leigh Locke to return home and find out that her husband had been killed in a valley half a world away, fighting the Taliban.

That night, the team sat around a fire at the back of the compound. Each man stared into the dancing orange flames. For an hour we all just sat and stared. The silence said it all. Matt – a very, very good man. We all thought of him, of what we had done, and what we would do next.

We were flying home to Camp Russell to farewell Matt on the ramp at Tarin Kowt, and then would continue our missions.

After Mum died, Dad had told me: 'The good die young.'

Now I knew it to be true.

15

OBJECTIVE RAPIER

BACK AT THE BASE, MY BOSS – NICK – GREETED ME WARMLY.

I sat down on the large sofa with tacky green fabric. I had not taken off my body armour and I was clutching my rifle. I knew we had to go back and finish the clearance of the valley.

'Mate, you guys did a really good job,' Nick said. 'Most importantly, though, how are you?'

Jesus Christ, if that happens again, I'll lose my mind. I think I'm already losing my mind. I got one of my guys killed and we're only five minutes into the tour.

'I'm okay,' I said aloud. 'It was pretty intense, but I'm okay.' I was lying. I was so 'okay' I wouldn't let go of my rifle even in a secure base. 'I think everyone did a good job.'

'Bloody oath. Good – it's important you're okay; I know it's been a lot to handle.' Nick was a hard boss, but compassionate, and he could read a room better than anyone. I think he knew I was rattled.

'I know that the casevac was late. There was confusion over whether he was priority one or priority two. Either way, once the crews took off, they flew through the Baluchi Pass to get there quickly.'

'Yeah, it was low – I thought they were gonna get shot down,' I said.

We talked about how the guys had handled it, though I knew we had not even had time to process the loss at that point.

'I think we're right,' I said. I believed it for the most part. No-one had broken down.

'Do you want to pause for a day or do you want to keep going?' the boss asked.

We still had to support the mopping up of the clearance. He had given me an out if we needed it.

'Nah, I think we're okay,' I repeated.

At the base, we held a small ceremony for Matt out the back of the compound. We set Matt's tan boots down with his rifle and beret at a small shrine. Behind it was a Land Rover with an Aussie flag and the boxing kangaroo hanging from it. We crowded around to listen to tributes from Matt's mates.

Kaz stepped up to speak. He had lost three close mates in the Swan Island car crash in Victoria a few months earlier. Now Lockie was gone too. Reading from notes, Kaz spoke not to the group, but to Matthew. He talked about what a character he was and what he'd meant to him. He looked up from his notes and gazed up at the sky.

'I love you, mate . . . I love you.'

To hear a battle-hardened soldier openly proclaim his love for his mate was heart-wrenching. We all loved each other, but we rarely said it aloud.

We stood there in the dust with the sunset behind us, 30 bearded men and a dog, and stared at the boots that Matt had so recently worn.

Buzz spoke next and talked about shaking Matt's hand as we'd stepped through the gates the night prior. He wished he had known it would be the last time he would see him alive. Buzz had received Matt's body on the tarmac when the bullet-riddled evacuation helicopter landed and he had escorted him to the medical facility.

I stepped forward reluctantly; I had not planned to talk, since I did not want to be centre stage, but it felt like the right thing to do. My words were halting, and I mumbled – I was uncomfortable in the spotlight and had not planned a speech. I spoke about Matt's firm handshake the first time we'd met; how I'd come to know him as a taciturn but capable man. Most of all, I knew him as a good bloke. I ended by quoting a lyric from the Snow Patrol song 'Eyes Open' that had always held meaning for me.

A bugler played the Last Post. We stood to attention. Large men with wild eyes and beards all absorbed the notes we had heard more than a dozen times before, in a safer land. This tribute was for a mate, not an obscure army lost a generation ago. As the last note sounded, a droning helicopter lifted above the building behind us, and as we looked up, a black Apache bathed in the setting sunlight climbed out of a dust cloud and slowly tracked over us.

It was the British Apache crew from the battle, and they were farewelling one of the bravest soldiers from the Commonwealth.

Sergeant Matthew Locke was flown home to RAAF Base Pearce. His grief-stricken family stood on the tarmac as a team of soldiers in dress uniforms hoisted a silver casket to their shoulders. An Australian flag and Matt's sandy beret adorned it. The lead pallbearer was Ben Roberts-Smith, a distinctive figure at 6 foot 7 inches. He cried openly as he held his mate's coffin on his shoulders.

Matthew was farewelled at a memorial service that drew 1000 mourners, including Prime Minister John Howard, Governor-General Michael Jeffery and all Matthew's mates standing at the rear. The mourners told stories of him as a child, husband, soldier and father. John Williamson, an Aussie folk singer, walked to the stage with a guitar, sat on a lone stool and played 'True Blue'. The crowd was still during the tribute. Matt's wife, Leigh, had asked for 'Travelin' Soldier', a Dixie Chicks song, to be played as a final farewell; it was a song she had played to him as he left on his multiple deployments.

After our own ceremony at the base in Tarin Kowt, we piled into a Chinook helicopter, and headed back to FOB Ego. When we arrived back at the base, the British held a service for Matthew. The commander of the British Gurkha regiment came and shook my hand. I thanked him for the assistance his Gurkhas and the British doctor had offered us.

That evening, we prepared to head out to finish the clearance. This time, we attached two LAV assault vehicles for the trip; we were not going to be caught out without adequate fire power.

The clearance was quiet, however. The fighters had either been killed or had left the valley.

Chora was back in Allied hands, for the third time in eighteen months. We packed up the forward operating base and prepared to head back to Camp Russell. We were all happy to be alive, to have survived a battle.

That evening, we piled into the Fat Lady's Arms. The tin-and-timber hut had filthy green carpet and four years worth of captured enemy weapons bolted to the walls, including shotguns, AK-47s and sniper rifles decorated with pink and white polka dots and coloured electrical tape. We had recently added Kaz's haul of weapons: the belt-fed machine gun with the perfumed headscarf and the RPG with bullet holes. The machine gun still had live rounds hanging off it.

The night started with cold beers from the bar. The renowned Q-Master acted as host. He was an entertainer, one of the best in the military. He'd gained his experience emceeing boxing nights in the battalions, sledging the crowds.

'Good to see you all here and we are starting on time, but I just need to check that on the new G-Shock watch I stole from you cunts!' He made a show of checking his wrist.

The crowd booed and jeered him.

'Minimum dress is undies and thongs. No fuckin' nudity, thanks!'

The room roared. A moment later Horse walked in, wearing the precise minimum dress.

A slideshow of Matthew's best photographs played in the background to a soundtrack of Aerosmith's 'Livin' on the Edge'. The mood was high, as the stress of a heavy mission was lifted from us all. Cigar smoke filled the room and most blokes had their shirts off within the hour.

At one point someone showed the footage of the British Apache attack helicopters that had supported us. Men howled as the black-and-white thermal images showed Taliban fighters in groups of five running to the target only to evaporate in a Hellfire blast. The only fighter remaining was an old man at the back with a machine gun hefted over his shoulder. He lagged behind the group, so he had been spared when the all the agile youngsters in front of him were hit. Another clip showed a fighter emerge from a bunker in a cornfield to shoot directly at the Apache with a rifle. He turned and went back in the bunker as a Hellfire hit it and the structure collapsed. One man stood in a creek, hiding behind a large tree so the helicopter would not spot him. The water was swirling around his legs as the Apache optics zoomed in and out on him, looking for positive ID. The tree and the fighter were obliterated with 30 mm explosive cannon shells. I cheered too. I loved seeing the enemy get their arses handed to them.

Later the team medic stood with both hands on the bar and talked me through what he had done to help Matt. I put my hand on the back of his neck. I knew he was trying to work out what else he could have done, but there was nothing. He gave it everything, and he'd done it under fire.

Two days after the wake for Matt, we went after our next target: a bomb maker with the call sign Rapier. All the human targets in Afghanistan were compiled on a Joint Prioritised Effects List, or JPEL – a hit list, in other words. It included Taliban governors, money men, bomb makers, team leaders and all the other nasty people who were influential enemy, or targeting Aussie soldiers. Rapier was right near the top of the list. He was an effective IED maker and we believed he was responsible for the roadside bomb that had killed David 'Poppy' Pearce in early October.

This was a totally new style of operation: 'targeting'. Reconnaissance was a traditional mission profile. Relying on concealment, the primary aim was to collect intelligence to support strategy. It was hard, shitty work.

Targeting was quite different. Aggressive, short duration and focused on killing or capturing an influential combatant. It was high adrenaline, a very different style. This type of work would eventually supplant our traditional reconnaissance role in Afghanistan.

We came up with a plan. We headed into the desert for a few nights to run the diversion. By day we ran the checkpoint, and by night small teams roved through the enemy villages unseen, looking for a tiny electronic signature of the man, to identify him. It was rumoured he had been trained by Pakistani intelligence. His operational security measures were excellent. He rarely used a phone and he changed home locations each night.

One night, we confirmed his location and decided to commit to the attack. We loaded our patrol jeeps and drove to a drop point a few kilometres from the target. We cross-loaded again, this time adding more men into each car to reduce the noise signature.

I was sitting on the edge of my car, looking through night vision goggles, when the car in front disappeared. The landscape lit up in bright green under the NVGs, and car parts were flung 100 metres into the air.

'FUCK! Fuckin' IED!' shouted a trooper. As we ran the cars off the road, I had the hot jelly feeling in my legs again. I expected to hit another IED at any minute.

Three men were carried up the hill to me with various levels of injuries, including Westy and Kaz. Between them they had facial burns from motor oil, a shattered leg and a smashed face from being hit by a heavy machine gun. The mine had sheared the car in half. I could have sworn I saw a limb go flying in the mess, but everyone had their legs. It was a horrendous sight: the casualties, the debris, the jeep on fire. We evacuated the wounded. Westy sucked on painkillers as he was evacuated. 'Sweet bro,' he said from his stretcher as we ran him out to the evacuation helicopter. All three of the wounded were sent back to Australia, including Kaz, my most senior team leader. I was now down two out of four team commanders.

We held the position overnight, and in the morning we awaited pick-up for the damaged car. The enemy were chatting on the radio, saying they would rocket us soon. I believed them. We were alone in the desert, sitting targets.

A van drove past with about a dozen men, women and children inside. We pulled them out and made them sit in the baking morning sun. The three males were swabbed for military-grade explosive, and all three came up positive. We immediately detained them; they were cuffed, and photographed in front of their families. I was sitting on a small foldout chair, smoking a cigarette, carbine on my lap, staring at the locals.

As we processed the Afghan men, I looked at the terrified women and children. I felt nothing. For the first time ever, there was no love in my heart at all.

My moral compass had shifted a lot in a short time.

An hour later an army recovery team arrived and loaded the decimated jeep onto a truck bed. I stood at the front of the car with an infantry company commander as he admired the damage. The front half of the jeep was sheared off and leaking black oil.

That was the end of this targeting mission; we would have to get back to Rapier. We later found out he fled to Pakistan to avoid us. A partial win, but not an efficient method of targeting.

Stano, the squadron XO and my best mate in the army, came into my troop office. 'Hey, do you want to draft up a CONOPS for the next Rapier job? Boss is keen to see something.'

I could feel my jaw tighten as I stared holes into Stano. Was he serious, asking for a concept of operations now? 'I just lost four blokes,' I snapped. 'Give us a fuckin' break, we're down a whole patrol.'

Stano looked taken aback. I had overreacted, and that was rare for me. He knew me well – as classmates at ADFA, we had battled opponents on the footy field together. The year before, we had both hunted for the fugitive Alfredo Reinado in the jungles of East Timor. With his mop of ginger hair, he was a proud redhead and charged people with giving him an original nickname. *I've heard 'em all, cocksuckers*, he would declare.

Stano moved to stand beside me and gripped both my shoulders. *It's all right, it's okay*, his touch said. I was reassured; he understood what I was feeling.

That evening the team wanted to have a drink in the Fat Lady's Arms. The boss said no. I didn't bother to enforce his order. I couldn't care less; I was out of bandwidth and needed rest. I went to bed early and could hear the music and noise coming from the bar. I slept, waking when I saw a green flash that blew my mates away.

The next day, the boss and the squadron sergeant major pulled Doogs and me into their office. I leaned against the plywood wall, arms folded, legs crossed, staring at the dirty tiles on the floor as they dressed us both down.

'We told you no drinks and you ignored us, and the blokes ignored you,' the boss said. He was pissed off.

'Doogs, get your blokes to cut their fuckin' hair. I'm not asking you, I'm telling you. They're in the army. Think they're fuckin' rock stars.' The SSM spoke quietly, but you could tell he meant it. I had figured out that the quieter an SAS warrant officer gets, the greater the danger you're in. He was testing Doogs with barracks discipline.

My mind was elsewhere, though. After seeing one guy killed and three more wounded on my watch, rogue hairstyles were not on my priority list.

'Your blokes are not listening. This is an issue. You need to get control of them.' I was still looking down at the tiles, but my vision had blurred. I panicked. Tears. I was crying – and I didn't think I could stop.

The boss was speaking forcefully as he looked between Doogs and me, asking what the punishment for the team should be. By now, the tears were running down my face. I heard the boss's voice drop a few octaves as he noticed. He was as surprised as I was; he could see now that I had not been ignoring them. I wasn't being insolent; I was just a bit fucked up. I continued to stand there, staring at the floor and crying, watched by three SAS men I respected. I felt like a lost teenager.

Everyone went quiet, recognising that I was in pain – and embarrassed, too. I had been durable and rugged for most of my life, but these cracks were now appearing: irrational anger at Stano, tears when getting told off. Bad dreams had finally arrived too. Most nights I was either kneeling at the edge of the cornfield with Matt, or I was stumbling around the hilltop at night with my shattered mates and a blown-up car.

The nightmare I had been heading towards my whole life had finally arrived.

16

MAXIMUS

0500 hours, 1 December 2007

'FIRST WE WILL WASH IN THE RIVER, THEN WE WILL PRAY, THEN we will kill them.'

My interpreter was translating the words being spoken over an open channel walkie-talkie.

Fuck. This is bad, I thought. I could sense trouble now, and all my dials were flashing red.

We were perched in assault cars atop a low cliff at the edge of the Helmand River. An opposed crossing of a river in Deh Rawood – enemy territory. This was a bad area: the British were making a push on Musa Qala, a famed Taliban city only a few valleys away, and we were tackling their rear to tie up their reinforcements. The area had layered, coordinated defences spanning many valleys, and a bunch of heavy weapons and artillery. This would be a real fight. The intelligence reports, and the stories of teams who had visited this place, were just plain scary.

We were attempting to make a push from Tarin Kowt and cross the Helmand in one period of darkness – a bold move. If we were late, we would be caught crossing in daylight. After Chora, I knew what daylight would mean: a close battle and likely fatalities. If we cleared the other side of the river, we would be running full disruption and targeting operations to pummel the enemy reserve forces while the British went to work. The whole squadron was in on this one – we had a platoon of Afghan troops in Hilux trucks, and squadron headquarters had come out for the op as well.

So far, the worst-case scenario was unfolding. One patrol car was stranded, drowned, in the middle of the river. The first glimmers of light were on the horizon to the east. We had about 30 minutes of darkness left. When the grey dawn emerged, the enemy on the other side of the banks would see our car stranded in waist-deep, freezing water in the middle of the 150-metre-wide river. It would be such an obvious target, I knew they would be anticipating a trap. But there was no trap. We had just fucked up the river crossing.

The walkie-talkie chatter had spiked since our vehicles drove through the village of Cheksai in the black December morning. The intelligence reporting indicated up to 100 fighters, and possibly a contingent of foreign fighters from Chechnya, Bosnia and Pakistan.

I pulled a checked *shemagh* – a Middle Eastern scarf – tighter around my neck in the biting dawn chill and stared along the length of the river through NVGs. I spotted three figures in the water on the far banks, standing in ankle deep water, throwing water on themselves and rubbing their forearms. I could see a long object hanging from the side of the washing males.

Jesus. Oh shit. My blood went cold. This was the first time I had seen men actively preparing their bodies for martyrdom. I sat up in my seat and swung the mounted machine gun towards the enemy. 'We have PID on three fighting age males, 400 metres south, far bank. Possible AK-47.' That meant we had positive identification of enemy. We could shoot them.

Next to me, Steve was casually guiding a Reaper drone pilot to target the males. 'Reaper call sign can see seven males in that cluster,' he said. The pilot he was talking to was stationed in an air-conditioned hut in Las Vegas, linked to him via satellite comms.

I passed this on to the squadron commander, Nick, who was a tactical bound along the river with men from the Afghan police force. 'We are going to initiate on these guys,' I said. I could feel everything spiking in me: heart rate, respiration, adrenaline.

'*Give us five more minutes to get the car out*,' came the troop sergeant over the radio. He was manoeuvring an armoured truck through the water towards the stalled vehicle. I could see Doogs in waist-deep water reaching under the back of the car to attach a tow chain. '*Five minutes*,' he repeated as he waded back to the driver's side. We pre-hooked tow ropes to the front and rear of the vehicles for exactly this scenario.

'Hurry. Hurry, Bravo. Best speed. We're gonna open up soon.'

I looked right. At 100 metres I could see our bogged car start to move. I looked left, and at 300 metres I saw the enemy fighters walking towards the car in a loose formation. They did not know we were covering them from our spot, elevated two storeys above them on a cliff edge. Through the night vision goggles, I saw each man was holding a long, dark object in both hands. A bright spotlight flickered on top of the enemy position, bathing the first man in an invisible green light.

'That's Reaper spotting the first man,' called Steve.

Ten minutes until first light. At the rate they were walking, they would be in range of us in less than five minutes.

Hurry, Doogs. Hurry. Hurry. I could feel my body starting to shake, part from the freezing air, part anticipation. I took an anti-tank rocket tube from the side of the car, pulled the tube covers off and extended the weapon, the sight mechanism popping up. Then I jumped back in my command seat behind my machine gun. I looked at the .50-calibre barrel next to my head, manned by Jimbo, my radio operator. All I could hear was the dull diesel motor of the truck whining and a chain clanking as it towed our car out of the mud and a muted drone thrumming overhead.

Two jeeps were either side of me. The drivers dismounted and pulled the heavy rocket launchers from the side of their cars. The drivers loaded their tubes from a kneeling position. I could see one man dialling the nose cone on a rocket the size of a champagne magnum, entering the range to target so its fuse would explode over the heads of the Taliban. The crew men were in the turret of the car with a belt-fed 40 mm grenade launcher ready to go. This was a rare two-minute window to prepare heavy weapons in advance of a controlled initiation on the enemy. *When you strike at the king, you must kill him.* This would be the opening salvo of the mission, so it had to count.

My machine gun was trained on the first enemy man, with safety off. I had activated my infrared laser and it made a faint dot on the far side of the river. The sky to the east was orange now. The truck was still 30 metres from the bank.

Hurry. Hurry, Doogs! I checked the safety on my gun again.

Five minutes until first light.

I keyed the radio to the troop. Five cars would receive my transmission at once.

'This is Echo Alpha. Fire control orders: controlled troop initiation. Fire mission: two rounds HE, 20 rounds 40-mil, 100 rounds .50-cal, on my command – stand by.'

The rocket men crept forward with their tubes to the edge of the small cliff, crouching behind shrubs for camouflage. Horse had pushed forward with a heavy rocket launcher, and Sean McCarthy was running behind him like a caddy, carrying two heavy rockets. They were unsealing the rockets for fast reloading.

One minute left.

The truck was hitting the bank now, the car 20 metres behind on the tow rope. The night vision was barely needed at this point.

Enemy troops 200 metres and closing.

We had a clear shot.

We're shooting – we can't hold any longer. I could feel a ball of dread rising in my stomach.

A call came in from Squadron HQ: '*Do you have positive ID?*' They were double-checking that the men we'd sighted were armed.

'Yes, they've got weapons!' I hissed into the handset. My voice was shrill; I was trying to steady myself, and failing.

There were four men in the river now, walking through the ankle-deep water in formation.

I pulled the crew weapon hard into my shoulder and clicked the aiming laser on again. Through my night vision, I could see green dots swerving across the enemy formations as men dialled their weapons in. I spotted mine, and settled it at the feet of the lead man, knowing my shots would climb as I fired. I would walk the rounds on by watching the tracers. The towed car was hitting the riverbank now. We were clear.

I prepared everyone to fire. 'All call signs – standby. Ready ready, ready ready, standby, go go go.'

Three rockets exploded from their tubes and ripped towards the enemy positions. The dawn calm erupted into rocket engines and dust clouds, and a battery of red trace rounds sailing towards the enemy. Each trace was followed by five more bullets.

I pulled the trigger on my crew gun. Clack. The bolt rammed forward and stopped.

'*Stoppage!*' I shouted.

'Can I shoot?' Jimbo yelled from atop my car on the .50-calibre.

'SHOOT!' I yelled as I pulled open the feed tray on my gun.

I lifted the tray up and wiped the rounds clear. When I looked up again, I caught a little slice of hell through my night vision.

Streams of red and green tracers flew down into the enemy positions, wobbling and flicking and tumbling into the morning sky as they skipped off trees and people. A geyser of water erupted into the air beside the fighters as Horse's first rocket fell short into the Helmand.

My vision rattled as the .50-calibre opened up next to my head. I replaced the ammo link rounds on my gun tray and pulled the cocking lever back to action the weapon. Our car was bathed in bright yellow muzzle flash; my head was pummelled from the overpressure. In the car beside me, a heavy bolt chugged back and forth as it cycled 40 mm rounds through its breech and launched them towards the battered enemy. The trees on the far side of the river jumped and flashed. My hearing dissolved and muted into a low whine. Perhaps I should have worn ear protection.

I pulled the weapon back into my shoulder and loosed a couple of 20-round bursts into the enemy position. The weapon bucked in my shoulder, and the rounds rattled on my feed tray as bullets sailed towards the enemy formations. I had seen the spits of water and dirt around the soldiers. There were no standing figures now. I knew they were either struck down or digging into the bank with their eyelids. It was a carnival land-scape of bullets and rockets, and a thin belt of smoke drifted downstream on the Helmand. We were shooting from eleva-tion, and we had more firepower lined up than Napoleon in Red Square. It was vicious, an unfair fight.

'Prepare to move!' I shouted into the radio. We were exposed in our position, now we had lit it up.

Horse was already racking the rocket launcher back to the side of the car and jumping in the driver's seat. As he started the engine, I flicked my gun to our flanks and began firing into the vegetation and alongside the compound wall to our left. I was certain someone had snuck up on us and was about to gun us down at close range. The shrubs were shredded, and chunks of rock masonry flew off the walls. Shells collected at my feet in the bottom of the car.

Raking the gearbox into reverse, we felt the ripping engine of a rocket-propelled grenade as it flew overhead. It sounded like tearing fabric. Horse and I turned to each other, question marks in our eyes. An explosion 20 metres behind us and a gout of dirt told us what that was. 'RPG!' shouted Horse as he reversed. Thumps of rounds were coming over our heads. It seemed they had been on the verge of initiating themselves; we had beat them to it by mere seconds. It had given us the advantage while they were trying to set up on us.

I fired a few more bursts of rounds into the shrubs and trees to our left. I was wild by now, shooting at anything that moved; I knew I had the ammo to do so. As we reversed backwards, I saw the SSM standing right next to the dust from the rocket explosion. Helmet on and rifle slung, he was directing our car to an exit point with his arms like a guide in a car park. He wasn't even stooping. I had seen him more stressed when the troop refused his directive to cut our hair.

'Down here,' he mouthed and pointed at a dirt path as we drove forward.

As we paused off the edge of the hill, a quad bike zipped up next to us, the driver with a handset next to his ear. It was Steve, talking to Las Vegas.

'Clear hot – Reaper inbound, 500-pounder. Time on target: twenty seconds.'

We were dropping bombs from the Reaper drone to allow us to break from the area.

I stared back towards the riverbank where the men had gone down. Smoke and dust hovered near the thick river reeds that lined the river. 'Ten seconds,' said Steve. 'Five seconds.'

There was a whining noise in the sky above us. A roiling ball of yellow and black, the size of a truck, erupted from trees lining the river. It was dead silent for a second, then the rattling shockwave punched us. It was a bullseye drop, right on top of the enemy formation. I was stunned by the force of the explosion.

Steve was on the radio to offer congratulations back to Vegas. 'That was *devastating*, directly on target,' he said, his admiration palpable. He listened to Vegas for a few seconds, then turned to me. 'They can see body parts and weapons in the blast crater – there are men moving in there now, picking up weapons. We're going to drop again.' I appreciated his quick thinking.

Thirty seconds later, there was another eruption in the tree line. We were stomping them while they were hurt. It was not fair, not even remotely, and that's how we liked it. It had been six weeks since Matt had died; we wanted them gone, and we would use any tool at our disposal to punish them.

In combat, there are no rules: always cheat; always win. The only unfair fight is the one you lose. This maxim had stuck in my mind, and as bad as it felt, I would rather feel bad than be killed or have my team killed. After Matt, I would never fight fair again.

I pulled up to the squadron formation 200 metres away and met Stano and Nick in the centre. We had pulled out of small arms range, but we knew they had heavy weapons in the area that could reach out and touch us.

Everyone was wild-eyed and debriefing. We checked in on each other. We were all okay. That had been so, so close to a catastrophe. If the enemy had opened up and destroyed the car in the river, it would have been death. If we had succeeded, and crossed the river, we could have been split across the river, one half trapped within an enemy formation and not able to use air cover. We had been moments away from a very bad day. It had been averted with some skill, and a lot of luck. And it was only the first morning of a two-week mission.

Nick told us we had run into an enemy formation that was armed up and getting ready to take on the British company that was clearing the Musa Qala nearby. Now that we had surprised them, we would be holding and atritting them to support the assault. We took time to repair the car and re-arm. Stano stood by my car as I swept brass shell casings from the floor and resealed my rocket launcher.

'Holy shit,' he said. 'That was hectic.' He had been manning a 40 mm launcher and had fired 30 rounds at the enemy.

An hour later a heavy machine gun opened up on us from the mountains on the other side of the river. Single, probing rounds to get the range dialled in. Horse was standing exposed in the middle of the formation, arguing that the rounds would be subsonic from that range, until one zipped past his feet and scattered him off the hill.

Stano and I stood on the hillside and got a photo together. Then I collapsed and slept in my driver's seat for an hour, snoring my head off. It had been an intense day.

That night, I thought about how that contact had felt compared to others. I wrote in my diary: *It felt good to PUNISH THOSE CUNTS from a distance.*

The next morning, I told Sean McCarthy to go to the truck, refill all our 84 mm rocket rounds, and get me twenty more 40 mm rounds and two more rockets for the car. The element of surprise was gone, so I knew it would be a busy day.

We drove carefully; there were IEDs everywhere. As I looked out the window, I saw an ancient fort looming over the river. It was from the time of Alexander the Great. Stano had said in the intel briefing that Alexander had abandoned the valley when his chariot drove over a pressure-plate IED. The image of an ancient chariot and soldiers being catapulted into the air made the whole troop laugh.

We were moving up to the riverbank again to close with the enemy. Intelligence had them preparing their defences and their weapons for the assault. They were chatty and excited on the radio, calling out to all the usual suspects. They spoke of potatoes and grapes and watermelons and olives – all call signs for their weapons. Occasionally the Taliban would argue over the radio because they were confused about what fruit and veg stood for what weapons. The result would be a heated argument between two insurgents over what type of fruit and vegetables were being moved around the valley that day. It was usually settled by a mullah coming on air to inform everyone of the official combination of produce. That morning, the mullah admonished his fighters not to make mistakes again like they had the day before. We laughed; we knew we had smashed them hard.

They brought plenty of fruit and vegetables on day two – enough for a near conventional battle.

We pushed up to overwatch positions on the river, and spotted a man calling range on us from a graveyard atop a bare hill. My car was positioned at the leading edge of the engagement with another patrol. Horse walked out of the car with Sean in tow, carrying the rockets. Horse wore a black ten-gallon hat as he loaded the rocket launcher. I was frowning at Horse and Sean. I had put my helmet on and was scanning the field with laser rangefinders. Horse looked like an apocalyptic cowboy. Sean was now his eager right-hand man, and he turned the silver cone of the rocket to dial the range in. I stood by. We decided we would shoot the man in the graveyard; there was too much activity coming from that area. Two cars fired rockets at once, and a sniper took shots at the same time. Twin orange bursts went off over the grave site and fragments threw gouts of dust across the hill. After a moment, the man emerged from behind a gravestone and wandered around aimlessly in his turban and black robes as though inebriated. The sniper took a second shot and hit a gravestone at his feet. He turned to us and held his hands up, as though to criticise the accuracy of our shot. These

George McEwin – Mum's father – fought the Japanese in the jungles of Morotai in World War II. It was from Grandad that I learned my first lessons of war.

Six-year-old me in the arms of my mother, Jane, a tall, strong farm girl from Western Australia. Here we are, with my brothers Steve and baby Dan, in the new family home in Leeming, Perth, 1985.

Family dinner with (from left) me, Mum, Dad, Dan and Steve. My dad, Rob, went from being a truck driver in Newman to a customs job in Perth. The move introduced me to the first love of my life: the coast.

Getting three boys to the beach was the only hope Mum had of wearing us down. The Western Australian coast was our playground. I would find out in the years to come that this was not a standard of living that all families around the world had. We were a lucky few.

In school I joined cadets for the experience, on the path to my SAS dream. I was the only kid in my high school to go on work experience at the SAS base in Swanbourne. Here I am ready for a cadet camp in 1994, set for a good night's rest with my non-camouflaged blue 'wimp mat'.

With Mum and Dad after the marching out parade at the Royal Military College, Duntroon, December 2000. I was an occasional disaster as a cadet, but I built on my errors and graduated to 2 RAR, an infantry unit that was soon headed to East Timor.

Posing for a photo with my first command, 5 Platoon, B Company, in Balibo Fort, East Timor. There was danger in East Timor, but by 2002 it was a stretch to call it a war zone.

The villagers in the highlands of East Timor wanted the same things we did: safety for their kids, peace, and the chance to make a living. It was a good feeling to help with the security of the province. Here I'm with a villager in the highlands, on the border of Indonesia, March 2002.

Boxing was a great leveller in the army. I thought I was pretty decent, but ended up getting flogged a few times, mostly by the same opponent at 2 RAR. It would be many years before I came out of retirement. I'm in the back row, third from left.

The Solomon Islands was a surprise deployment to help disarm local militia and to establish police control on surrounding islands. I was a senior platoon commander and planning my upcoming attempt to join the SAS. Unfortunately, I made that path harder for myself due to a lack of discipline and some bad ideas on this deployment. July 2003.

SAS selection in Bindoon, September 2004. This was taken on the third day of the three-week course, when we were still in good shape. The dream had finally arrived, after eleven years of waiting, in all its grim glory.

We spent most of a three-hour period in a push-up position on pea gravel, working together to move a rope to the end of the court. Three ambulances were parked nearby, their doors open and cannulation bags ready. We were rated on our willpower more than the physical aspects, and even on our sense of humour.

Chowing down during selection after three days of no food and hauling equipment. By the end of the course, I had lost 16 kilograms. It took six months for sensation in my extremities to return. But, despite all the rigours, I made it to the end.

After passing selection, I entered the reinforcement cycle for specialised training. As a probationary soldier, I could be removed at any time, so I lived in a constant state of exertion and concentration. I loved the pressure. It was a dream come true – we were trained by the best soldiers in the military.

A night jump into water. I never loved these. In training we were guaranteed to do many things we were sure had a high probability of injury or death. The SAS has lost 48 men in training over the years and roughly a tenth of that number in combat. We train to replicate combat conditions – necessary, but risky.

The beret parade at Campbell Barracks, August 2005. This marked the end of my probationary period and the true beginning of my membership in the Special Air Service Regiment. I had waited my whole life for the day, but it felt like another step in a very long journey.

Celebrating my new sandy beret with my paternal grandfather Harry Wales, Dad, my grandmother June Wales and my younger brother Dan. My parents knew I wanted to do this, but my new job kept them awake with worry on occasion – especially over where it would take me next.

I'm looking grizzly inside Forward Operating Base Ego, Afghanistan, 2007. It was my first combat tour as a troop commander, and I was excited for the battles ahead. I had studied military history and thought I knew what I was in for. I was wrong.

Dusk in the graveyard of empires. Here a team from E Troop, my troop, takes a break after a long day and enjoys a sunset while the crew gunners maintain overwatch on a ridgeline.

Matthew Locke had helped me in the early stages of my first Afghanistan deployment, sharing stories of his previous missions. Strong, capable, intelligent, aggressive – he was good at his job and a capable leader, a worthy recipient of the Medal for Gallantry. He was soon to be tragically lost in a firefight that would change my life, and many others', forever.

The weapons seized by one of my teams after a face-to-face with an enemy patrol in the dark: an AK-47 assault rifle, an RPG and a PKM 7.62 mm machine gun. Collecting intelligence in enemy terrain is difficult, grinding, unglamorous work, but the SAS excel at this more than any other unit.

Horse with his dog, Rischa. Rischa was a 'working dog' that considered our troop to be its pack. Dogs were used extensively in Afghanistan because they could outrun, out-smell and out-bite a human. We treated them like one of us.

Overwatch. All-round protection is drummed into you as a fundamental from the earliest point of training. Enemy can come from any direction, any time. This sniper is maintaining overwatch with an SR 25, a 7.62 mm sniper rifle. His spotter can be seen to the left of him.

Patrol photographs before combat missions are a tradition, such as this night photo with my troop headquarters team on 24 October 2007. We were headed for the thick green belt, hence the camouflage and green uniforms. This valley was controlled by the Taliban. Matthew Locke was killed in action the next morning.

The wake for Matthew Locke, late October 2007, in the Fat Lady's Arms. We had fought hard and it felt good to relax in the pine hut with a dirty carpet.

Ready to roll out from Camp Russell to kill or capture an enemy bomb maker in Oruzgan Province. The cars were heavily armed. Here I have a 7.62 mm MAG 58, and the crewman has a .50-calibre Browning with semi-armour-piercing, high-explosive rounds. The row of tubes mounted to the car are 84 mm rockets.

One of my soldiers does a battle damage assessment after dropping multiple 500-pound bombs on enemy positons, to the backdrop of a stunning sunset. Afghanistan is a beautiful country whose hardened people have a history of outlasting foreign invaders. This image was taken in Deh Rahwood, early December 2007.

Friendly faces or enemy spotters? These young children would watch and talk with us during our mission in Deh Rawood. Our shift to counterinsurgency was a difficult coalition strategy – the Afghan people did not want what we were offering, and pacifying the Taliban was proving challenging.

A 500-pound airstrike lands on an enemy cave position while two SAS soldiers keep a low profile in the foreground. The ridgeline has scorch marks from an airstrike the hour before. We were maintaining pressure on an enemy formation that was looking to move on the British presence in Musa Qala.

Taking a moment to pose for a photo with Stano on the first morning of a two-week operation near the Helmand River. We had been in a heavy contact earlier that day and I knew we were in for a long stretch.

Sean McCarthy was a signaller who went outside the wire with us. He hadn't received our level of training but pulled his weight nonetheless. He intended to attempt SAS selection one day, but was tragically killed by an IED blast before he got the chance.

By the end of my first Afghanistan deployment, the troop was running on very little; I was decimated from the stress of combat.

E Troop. I'm one of the few holding a weapon, standing fifth from the right. We lined up the cars and got this troop photo in the setting sun before we left the scorched valley of Deh Rawood behind us. It was the end of the tour, but it was the start of a reckoning.

I visited the old FOB Ego in the fall of 2008, renamed as a tribute to the fallen Sergeant Matthew Locke MG. I was on my second tour of Afghanistan and still feeling the effects of the sustained combat from my first tour. I was terrified to head back out to the Chora Valley, but it was far from the end of my days in combat.

people were hard. We complained about overpriced coffee in Western Australia; here they complained about not getting shot at accurately enough.

As I scanned the graveyard, a distant whining made me pause. The sound was really soft. I could not pinpoint where it was coming from. I looked at Horse, still packing his black cowboy hat, my eyes asking the question. He'd heard it too. I scanned the barren horizon again. 'It can't be a rocket; it would have hit us by now,' said Horse. But there was a definite whining, and it was getting louder. I put my binos down and looked at Horse again, just as the ground erupted into a geyser of dirt only 40 metres away, throwing debris across the hillside.

'Fuck!' I ducked low into the car seat.

It was a mortar round; it had been hanging in the air for 30 seconds before it landed on us.

The mortar had missed by as much as a gust of wind hitting the shell at its apex. That meant they had us ranged.

'FUCK! Reverse off!' I shouted, knowing that more rounds would be loaded into their mortar tubes. All they had to do was fire a salvo and we could be vaporised.

Horse was already grinding the gears into place and reversing out. More rounds exploded in the saddle to our left, crumping into the earth and throwing dirt and rocks and hot metal in all directions. The car team on our left flank opened up on the mortar position. It had been fired from behind a small hill, concealing it from direct fire. That was textbook tactics; we were probably using the same terrain the Soviets had fought in twenty years earlier.

We parked behind the saddle and pointed our vehicles into the green belt. It was too much excitement, and it was barely 9 am.

I was rattled by the encounter. 'Fuck me, that was close,' I said to Horse.

As usual, Horse was about as stressed as you get driving along a quiet country road.

That exchange got the day started, and it just escalated from there. The enemy brought out all their tools. The entire valley was energised to take on the infidels. Airburst RPGs exploded above us in orange and black clouds. A heavy machine gun scattered rounds across our fire position as we repositioned our cars. All day I heard the enemy chatter in the back of my car as the interpreter listened to the walkie-talkie channel the enemy was using. I learned that they shouted '*Allahu Akbar!*' – God is great! – just as they fired their weapons; sometimes this gave you a split second to respond or take cover before heavy rounds landed. I also learned the various code words: potatoes and pumpkins were bad, generally rockets and mortars. The grapes and dates were smaller machine guns.

The boss would sometimes be on a satellite phone back to Canberra, getting real-time intelligence. He would pass this on through the radio: '*Look at this grid now. If you see enemy then let's drop on them.*' We knew it was accurate intelligence. If a commander of some sort had used communications, we would know where he was. They were popping up on the grid as they coordinated their fighters. We had reports there were seriously capable bosses in the fight, men on our JPEL, and we were keen to drop bombs directly on them.

An RPG team was spotted pushing up the valley and our merry sniper had the idea to call in some 155 mm artillery rounds. Fired from a tank called Maximus, 9 kilometres away, the rounds were accurate to within an arm's length. We just called the fire mission, added the grid and a target description, and they flew in a minute later.

As I looked up the valley, I could hear the familiar ripping of the air as a projectile forced its way to the target, spinning along its axis for stability. The enemy below disappeared in dust and twigs and branches as they fled through the valley. More rounds were called in on their position. It was a battering. If this was precision firing, I would hate to see unrestrained bombing.

During an engagement a French Mirage fighter came 'on station' and offered to drop bombs on enemy positions across the river. We obliged, Pez sent a grid target of bunkers to the fighter bomber. I watched through binoculars, waiting for the blast. An orange flash kilometres up the valley caught my eye. The bomb was 2 kilometres off target – the pilot had entered the wrong grid. It had landed in a village on the banks of the Helmand. *Jesus, what a mess*, I thought. I hoped it hadn't killed anyone.

Late that afternoon, we witnessed four men on motor-bikes meeting on a hillside. They were 1500 metres away and reasonably safe from direct fire. They stood there conferring, occasionally pointing towards us, rifles slung over their shoulders. They seemed to be debating their next move. We called in an F-16 jet to drop a 500-pound bomb on the group at dusk, setting the range to burst 10 metres over their heads. The team was enveloped in a fireball of plasma gas and searing shell fragments. They appeared to evaporate. As the explosion sent up a column of dust and ash, the setting sun bathed the clouds in rose, crimson and red. It felt like a warning from some other being watching the gross spectacle.

I sat in my car and typed out a contact report from the day. Normally you typed a report for an engagement that lasted an hour or two and had a defined end. I didn't know where to start with this one. We had started fighting at first light, and it was still going as of sunset. We had seen an array of heavy weapons. A lot of enemy had died that day.

Afterwards, I stood at the edge of our position and looked over the limestone lands. Alexander's fort still loomed over the river's edge. Farmers used pitchforks to clear the opium stalks in the fields. The call to prayer sounded, and the farmers came together in the field with mats in front of them. Ten of them lined up abreast and faced the setting sun. They knelt and bowed, straightened and bowed, touching their foreheads to the earth while the battle raged on the hilltops around them. This was another universe, another time. The world I came from was a memory I would push out of my head. We would survive here, no matter what it took.

That evening I pulled the team back out of mortar range to a hill so we could set up for the evening. I was exhausted. I pulled my gloves off and stood at the rear of our assault car in the dying light. I started unstrapping my bed mat.

Unfortunately, a Taliban team had not got the memo that the day's fight was over, and they had ranged us with a recoil-less rifle, a giant rocket launcher. They fired a football-sized explosive round at our huddle on the hilltop. Someone bawled, 'Incoming!' as I heard the air ripping overhead. It was a bigger sound than the RPG that morning.

I dived to the ground and felt adrenaline flooding through my limbs and lungs. I had leapt into a thornbush with bare hands. I stood up and peeled the large spikes from my palms. It was almost too much – I had already been mentally unwinding and they'd got me without my gloves on. I was exasperated. *Fuckin' leave us alone! It's bedtime.*

After the first volley subsided, we repacked the cars and moved our position. By the time we pulled up at a new feature half an hour later, the Taliban were whispering on the radio that they were extremely close to us and that they would fire their rockets at us soon. Did they really know our new spot, or were they bluffing? I decided to move the entire troop again. It was a shit idea. I was jumping at shadows, and my team knew it. I argued with one team member over the radio as we shifted a second time. I was losing my grip on tactics and losing confidence too. I was dodging risk as much as I could.

I knew we were near the end of the trip and that we were going home soon, and this was starting to feel less like special operations and more like a conventional battle: moving troops and heavy weapons and tackling foot soldiers. This sort of job was perfect for a cavalry squadron and an infantry company, not an SAS squadron at the end of a long rotation. But since we were there at the pointy end, we would fight and win, inflicting as much damage as possible in the process.

That night in Deh Rawood, I slept on the dirt beside my car wheel, with my rifle next to me pointing towards the enemy positions. All I had to do was roll over and start shooting. The night was punctuated by shots, the sentry shooting a man trying to lay an IED in the road on our approach out. My nerves were shredded. To make matters worse, Sean, the panel marker man, had put a few rocks under my bed when I was writing orders as a practical joke. I was too tired to move them and in the end just curled up between them.

We stood by our cars in the rising dawn light. There was a bitter chill which crept down our collars and up our sleeves. The car seat felt like ice. We were entering one of the coldest winters on record. I licked the broad split in my bottom lip that had formed in the last three months. Our faces were bone dry and peeling from the sun and wind.

As the morning passed, there was more movement in the valley as fighters were sent forward across the river to harass us. We spotted one Taliban soldier walking along the bottom of a cliff face 1500 metres away. We set up cameras as we called in air support. Someone was playing 'Welcome to the Jungle'. We dropped one 500-pound directly onto the man; I saw the black dot start to run in his last two seconds of life before he disappeared in the yellow blast. Everyone cheered, me included. The smoke plume was carried away in seconds by the winds thundering up the valley from the south.

A man leading seven camels out of the valley walked past our position looking sour. We directed him behind the cars as we engaged fighters; the camels never flinched amid the gunfire. Even the animals were hardened to war.

By midday, a man brought his teenage son to our position, holding his son's arm. His village had been hit by the errant Mirage bomb the day before. The kid's bicep had been split open by a bomb fragment. We treated the boy with stitches, plaster and antibiotics while the battle raged on. It was the least we could do after bombing him by mistake.

As we drove to another position along the river, the troop passed a small building that was a community refuelling point. Several dozen Afghan families stopped and stared at our vehicles as we passed. We had been killing their sons all week. One small girl raised her hand to wave at me, but her father grabbed her hand and lowered it. A hundred or so people, and every one of them wanted to tear our limbs off, I could feel it. I stared at them from behind dusty sunglasses.

I leaned out the side of my open car and spat on the ground as we passed. I wasn't sorry for the damage – yet. That would come later. For now, we wanted to do our jobs, and to survive.

How are we ever going to explain this when we get home? I wondered. If we ever got home . . .

The next morning, the enemy were feisty. They were still excited and babbling on the walkie-talkie. I had figured out the pre-battle windows and built a routine around it. We referred to 4 pm as 'rocket o'clock', as the enemy had had lunch, rested, prayed and were ready for the late afternoon session. To prepare, I would oil my crew machine gun, using a bottle to spray oil in the working parts as I pulled the bolt back and forth. I would urinate, pull up my pants and tuck my shirt in, retie my bootlaces. Then I would brush the dust off my weapon sights and optics, and check all the ammunition holdings. Lastly, I would eat an American MRE – poppyseed pound cake was my favourite – and then I would drink a whole bottle of water. My routine took me less than ten minutes, and I was ready to go.

When things were out of control, I discovered, that tiny bit of control helped to calm my mind.

I was dreaming more and more. In one dream, I was sitting with my mum on the porch of a log cabin I had never seen before. She was beautiful and blonde and strong-jawed, just as I remembered her. I asked her about what she had loved during her time with us. She talked about looking after us kids in Newman when Dad was at work, and all the times we ate together as a family. She was not smiling or engaging with me much. She knew it was me, but she was not warm or welcoming. I understood that she was not yet ready to accept me wherever she resided; it was not my time. When I sat up in the black dawn, I knew I wasn't going to die in Deh Rawood. Mum was not ready for me.

We were running on very little; I was decimated from the stress of combat. The way I saw it, we could attrit the enemy in the valley and still achieve our objective. A few guys had complained about this being a conventional task, and I agreed. I think Nick did too. But the truth was I had lost my nerve.

Nick pulled me aside one night. The squadron sergeant was with him, and I could see they were trying to understand my behaviour. They asked me if I was okay, if anything was wrong. I said I didn't feel right, and we had taken a lot of hits as a team. I was down two patrol commanders and working hard. The real reason I was being difficult, though, was that I was scared to lose another man and scared of being killed myself. I had become selfish. The mission must always be the first priority. Instead, I was putting myself first, then my team, then the mission.

Nick nodded as I spoke. He could read me well. Still, I knew I was on the cusp of being fired in the middle of a tour. That would spell the end of me, professionally and even personally. Stano would have been a good replacement – fresh, aggressive and excited to do the work. It was the hardest time. I was bloody lucky to keep my job in the end.

We lined up the cars and got a troop photo in the setting sun before we left that river and the scorched valley behind us. We were heading home. We drove all night through a long pass under the streaking white stars; I never took my eyes off the ridge lines above me.

In the early dawn, the perimeter lights of Camp Russell came into view. We had made it, against long odds. It was the end of the tour, but it was the start of a reckoning.

How are we ever going to explain this?

ACT II

THE ROAD HOME

Was it possible they were there and not haunted? No, not possible, not a chance, I know I wasn't the only one. Where are they now? (Where am I now?)

Michael Herr, *Dispatches*

17

THERE'S NO PLACE LIKE HOME

TEN DAYS LATER, WE PREPARED TO HEAD HOME TO AUSTRALIA. The boss and I sat in his plywood office in Tarin Kowt and debriefed each soldier, reviewing their performance. Everyone looked different – some slouched with shoulders hunched, expressionless, as though the energy had been sucked from them. The only thing that mattered to the men was to know they had acquitted themselves well when it mattered most.

The trip home took us through Kuwait, and then on to a giant strategic aircraft for the final leg to Perth. We stopped at Diego Garcia – a British island in the Indian Ocean – for a refuel, and everyone disembarked to stretch their legs in the terminals. One of the signals officers had taken a handful of sleeping pills for the journey home, and he was slumped across a terminal lounge, face waxen, only barely conscious. He had to be carried back to the aircraft.

We boarded a bus at the Pearce air base to drive back to Campbell Barracks, where our families waited. Everyone was silent on the bus. I wore a blue collared shirt with a Little Creatures logo on front – it was my favourite beer, and it reminded me of Fremantle's salt air.

The families cheered and clapped a bit as we walked into

the sergeants' mess at Swanbourne. Matthew Locke's widow, Leigh, stood alongside her son Keegan. I saw that her excitement at welcoming a familiar crew home was tinged with the sadness of knowing Matt was not with us.

I shook hands with my dad and hugged him, and my girlfriend Michelle, too. I was amazed by how unfamiliar she felt and smelled. The whole return seemed a bit of an anticlimax. I had dreamed of that trip my whole life, and it had nearly finished me.

From the base I went back to my small beachside apartment. There was my red Ford in the driveway. It was a relic from a past life, all covered in dust and ocean salt. I spent that night drinking wine with Michelle and trying to explain where I had been: the terrain, some of the fighting, the aircraft. It was like I was describing another dimension; it was so different to the life we lived at home. Trying to describe it felt like a waste of time.

I pulled a bottle of duty-free bourbon from my bag and walked along Marine Parade holding the bottle by the neck, listening to the sound of my flip-flops on the footpath. People stared at the bottle as I walked past. I stopped at a park bench and watched the sun sink into a rippling Indian Ocean. A lone paddleboarder stood paused to watch it recede. This was my dream place – Cottesloe Beach and a still December sunset. But it felt very different now. The austere mountains and mud huts and clear rivers on the other side of the planet felt like the real world.

I walked to Westy's apartment, and greeted him with a big smile. His leg was still braced up. We sat in his garage drinking his home brew and talking about the trip.

'Want to see my leg?' Westy's foot had been resting on the blast plate of the car when it hit the mine.

'Hell, yeah.'

He stripped the Velcro boot from his leg and showed it to me. It looked like a twisted purple pretzel. 'Doc said the force transferred straight into my left foot and shattered all the bones. He reckons if there are more infections, I might lose it.' He wasn't sorry, he was proud.

'No shit.' I looked at Westy for a reaction. He just took another sip of his beer.

We sat up late watching troop videos in his lounge room, enjoying the replays and talking through each engagement. We drank a lot.

I woke up on Westy's couch the next morning, mouth dry and skin burning up. I walked home with a stunning headache.

This became routine over the summer.

In order to sleep, I had to push boxes of books against my doors – it made me feel safer. I missed hearing the crunch of a sentry's footsteps close to my swag. Ironically, I had slept more easily behind enemy territory, knowing there were soldiers watching over me. I knew those soldiers would never sleep, never rest, while they guarded their mates. Now, safe in Perth, I felt like I was in danger, even though I knew there was none. In my dreams, I would find myself back in the cornfield, trying to burn it down or carry Matt out, trying to somehow change the outcome. It was difficult to separate the dreams from real life. When I woke up, I swore my palms were sweaty from holding the checked plastic grip on my rifle.

Everyone struggled with the hangover. One of Matt's mates would dial his number every night after drinking, waiting for an answer that was never going to come. Stano and I would drink at the beachfront bars then head home to my balcony and continue drinking until sunrise. As the morning runners came past, we took to pelting them with fruit and vegetables. I found myself eating a raw onion for no reason at all. We were wild, feral. I looked down on all civilians and resented their comfortable lives. I felt like I had lost a lot of faith in humanity.

The next weekend I had a few mates over for drinks then we headed out to Subiaco. At the end of the night, I became separated from my mates and stood by the side of the main road waiting for a cab. When it approached, I hailed it, but as it pulled over a brash South African youth in a crisp white shirt ushered two teenage girls into the car ahead of me.

I stormed over to him. 'I fuckin' ordered that. I ordered that.'

'You were too slow, brother. We were waiting.' As I got closer I heard him say, 'Fuck off,' under his breath.

I could feel the venom rising in me. '*You* fuck off, cunt.'

The blonde girl getting into the car froze, fear in her eyes.

I stood by the side of the car, fuming. I pointed at the young guy, thumb and forefinger cocked like a gun. 'I wish I had my M4 – I'd put one in your *fuckin'* head.' I dropped the thumb hammer on my handgun and mimicked the recoil of a weapon.

Wide-eyed, he jumped in the passenger seat of the cab and pulled the door shut. The car took off.

I felt ashamed of myself. I stood on Stirling Highway under a single yellow streetlight, and I felt like I had a broken chest. I stood on the street for a long time, as six months of grief came out of me. The loss of my mates, my old life, my sense of hope. I had the feeling mine was going to be a short life. I would keep going back until the war ended, or it finished me.

I went back to work. I had been assigned to a new squadron. It had airlock entry, swipe cards, entry logs and vaults. There wasn't a single window in the whole building. I would enter in the dark of the Perth winter, and I would exit in the night. My boss and Buzz had brought me across to this new squadron. It was a vote of confidence in me. I needed a very high clearance to work there, and it had taken many months of forms and interviews to secure it.

But I was struggling at work. Before my tour, I was able to focus on one task for hours on end, and could endure eighteen-hour days of heavy mental work. Now I would read a document and have to pause after only a page. Reading tired me. I would lose my ID pass, my car keys. I couldn't decide what to do for dinner when I got home. It was easier for me to sit and stare out the window.

Michelle and I argued non-stop. She had no clue what I had been through overseas, and I gave up trying to explain it. We fought in the car driving home from a work function. 'You hate me!' she shouted. She was right. I hated her and every other person in this half-asleep town. I only cared about the men I had fought with, and my family.

After we arrived home, I walked across the road to the beach and listened to the waves crashing unseen. I put the small tiki she had given me in my mouth and shattered it with my teeth. She later saw the single shard of it on my neck, and when I explained what I had done, she just said to me: 'Your spirit is broken.' The next time we argued I threw her bag out of my apartment into the driveway, smashing all her cosmetics and perfume bottles. I told her to leave.

Matthew's dad Norm came to Perth to visit the SAS. He wanted to meet the men who were with his son when he died. Welcomed as a dignitary, he was taken to my boss's office to talk about Matt. I was out at the time so I didn't get the chance to shake Norm's hand. The boss gave me his phone number to call. I stared at the number written on a scrap of paper. The thought of calling a parent whose son was killed under my leadership was not appealing.

At the time I was doing a special course in techniques for reconnaissance. It was a hard course to get into, and I found myself struggling from the outset. I was slow to comprehend the lectures, and in the field I was a disaster. I could not pick directions effectively and was slow on the radio. I also didn't care. By week two of the course, the boss had pulled me into his office with Buzz and the course director to warn me that I was going to fail. I was not surprised.

The boss was constructive and curious about it. At one point he said: 'You're not likely to complete the course, but you'll be able to stay in the squadron and still help out in different roles.'

'I just think my mind has been elsewhere,' I said, voice trembling. It was an understatement. I could feel the tears building just as they had when I was getting reprimanded in Afghanistan. Buzz and the other NCO were looking at me with sympathy in their eyes. It was rare for soldiers from the unit to reveal emotion like that. I could see they felt for me, but it was difficult for them to help. The onus was really on me to pull myself together. There would be no lowering of standards just because we had a rough battle on operations.

They let me go before I really broke up – I was bloody grateful for that. I left the building in darkness and drizzle, and sat in my car in the empty parking lot. I pulled out the slip of paper with Norm Locke's number on it and dialled. He answered.

'Hello, Norm speaking.'

'Hi, Norm, it's Mark Wales here. I was Matt's troop commander.'

'Oh, hi, mate. How are you?'

Silence.

'Mate, are you there?'

'I'm sorry,' I said. I could barely get the words out. 'I'm sorry about Matt.' By now I was really crying.

'No, mate, it's okay, it's all right. Take it easy.'

I looked out the rain-streaked window of my car across the deserted car park I had skipped across the night I was accepted into the SAS. That was three years earlier, and a lifetime ago.

'Mate, you have to take care of yourself, okay? Make sure you look after yourself. Maybe get some help, okay?'

Here was a man who had lost his son on a foreign battlefield, now trying to console me.

After the call ended I sat in the car for a while and listened to the sheets of rain belting across the base.

In the days that followed, I finally admitted to myself that something was going to give: my sanity, my health, my job, or all of the above. I knew I was in trouble. It was clearly mental illness that was afflicting me. I visited the base doctor and told him I wanted to see a psych. He looked at me, alarmed.

'Okay, for sure. Are you thinking about hurting yourself?' he asked.

'No, no. I'm not suicidal,' I assured him.

'Okay, phew,' he chuckled. He made a quick phone call, then handed me a note. It was a referral to a psychiatrist.

'This man can diagnose you and we can go from there. You don't have to tell us if you want to keep it private.'

I did.

I checked my flanks and the streets, and parked as close to the psychiatrist as I could. His office was plush and clean, and he spoke in a very mild voice, which made me feel more crazy. He asked me a series of questions about my deployment. When he asked whether I felt a lot of guilt over what had happened, it struck me dumb. I could not quite get around the question. It was a clear sticking point.

He told me, 'You have a moderate level of post-traumatic stress disorder and depression, I'm afraid.'

I was not surprised.

We talked through treatment options. I did not have to take medication if I didn't want to, he said, and I was glad to hear it, since I wanted to make sure I could keep working. I did opt to see a psych for treatment, though.

At least it was a step in the right direction, as unpleasant as all that feelings business was for a tough soldier.

I was determined to patch myself up, lest I be relegated from the unit. I had to keep going back, deploying where I could. There were only a few paths I could see to escape it: death, injury or the sanatorium. Giving up was not an option, after all the work I had put in.

Although I was determined to keep my diagnosis quiet, I did tell a few trusted friends, including three of my mates from the regiment. I had completed selection with all of them, and we had seen each other at our best and our worst. I decided to tell them what I had been through one night when we had come together to check out Billy's new two-bedroom bachelor pad.

We were at Fast Eddie's burger bar, and I had ordered a beer. It tasted cold and fresh. I put down my glass and looked around the table at the guys.

'Hey, I wanted to let you guys know that I have some PTSD and depression from the trip last year,' I said.

In the silence that followed, I inspected my beer label.

Rob was the first to respond. 'It's okay, mate. I can't say we're too surprised.' The others nodded. 'It's all right, mate.'

It was what I needed to hear. I was not being disowned by my mates. I'd never really feared I would, but all the same it was good to hear that I had their support.

I had told my boss and a few people in the squadron whom it would affect, but for the most part I kept it a secret. I was too embarrassed, and too scared of losing all I had worked for. There were legends in the regiment of guys who had folded under the pressure. One had hidden in the roof alcove in regiment head-quarters, disorientated and mad. Another became partial to a shot of heroin before running close-quarter combat drills.

I was determined to stay sane, but I knew there was no way I could do it alone.

18

BEIRUT

May 2008

I SLUMPED ON MY COUCH AT HOME. IT WAS FRIDAY, A WEEK OF long days at the barracks was over and I was looking forward to switching off. My work phone rang with an unidentified number. I answered immediately.

'Mate, can you come back into work? Come straight to headquarters.'

I was out the door before he'd even hung up.

When I got to HQ, the operations warrant officer was standing in the ops room. Three large-screen TVs were all streaming new footage from Lebanon. It looked like there were rebels fighting in the streets of a major city.

'Can you be in Lebanon in 24 hours?' he asked.

I met Nick in the office at my squadron and talked through the job.

'Not totally clear yet,' the boss said, 'but possibly recon for an NEO.' That was a national evacuation operation. Defence liked to have special ops soldiers there early since they could operate independently, report back to Australia, and organise evacuations of civilians or recovery of Australian hostages. Since Beirut seemed on the verge of civil collapse, they wanted a defence planner in there as soon as possible.

Nick looked at me. 'Are you alright to go, Waler? You don't have to if it's not the right time.' To his eternal credit, he was giving me an honourable 'out' from the mission. I had revealed my PTSD diagnosis to him recently, and he had offered me leave if I needed it. I declined. Now I wanted to show I was still capable by doing this mission.

'Nah, I'll be right,' I said. 'I'm fine.'

'Okay. Good luck. Let's chat on secure when you land.'

Sydney, 12 hours later

The sun was rising to the east as I touched down in Sydney. I took a cab directly to the Special Ops national headquarters at Garden Island. I had four hours before my flight to Damascus, Syria departed from Sydney Airport. Pete Winnall met me at the front. Now aide to the Special Ops commander, he was on his way up. Decorated for leading a troop in Oruzgan in 2006, he was a capable, intense man, with a razor-sharp intellect and a woeful sense of humour. He signed me in, and we hurried to the meeting with the head of operations.

'Did they brief you in Perth?' Pete asked.

'Yeah, Ops just gave me timelines and a point of contact for the embassy when we arrive.'

Pete went on to expand on the Perth briefing and added an important point: that there was an imperative for the SAS to demonstrate that we could do more than just kinetic operations in Afghanistan and Iraq. He said he was glad I was given the job. It was a good feeling to have earned that faith from Nick after a tough year when we lost Matt.

'Don't worry about Darth Vader,' he continued. 'He's pretty good. Just listen to his questions closely.' He was talking about Brigadier Jeff Sengelman, the Special Ops head of operations who was about to brief me – a formidable figure. General Petraeus, the US military commander, had personally requested Sengelman for his staff during the 2007 surge in Iraq. Stano had told me a story about how Sengelman had explained the surge strategy to a recalcitrant junior planner. He drew a line on a piece of paper and, pointing to it, said, 'This is the train we're on: the winning train.' He then sketched a line underneath that ran parallel before plummeting off the edge of the page. 'And you're on this train. This is the dickhead train.'

As we walked into a compact office, a tall silver-haired man rose from behind his desk and extended his hand. 'G'day.' He had an unflinching stare, but was genial and upbeat. He talked us through the situation.

'So, Hezbollah have taken over parts of Beirut, the Lebanese army have the rest of the city. We have no idea where all the Aussie nationals are arrayed in Lebanon. Most are in Beirut, though.'

I was nodding, trying to keep up. As he talked, I wrote notes in a small notebook. I was brought up to speed that fighting had broken out between Fatah al-Islam, a Sunni Islamist militant organisation, and the Lebanese Armed Forces. The Australian government, concerned about the high number of Australians in country, decided they needed some eyes and ears on the ground, or in the worst case an extraction plan for them.

'We might have to pull citizens out. I think at last count there were 10,000 Aussies. Is that right?' He looked at Pete, who nodded. 'So, we might need to plan an evacuation for that many. The airport is closed, so rule that out for now, but look at ports and the roads out.' I was still nodding, writing quickly. This was the most informal but effective mission brief ever.

'We don't know exactly what we need from you yet – just get over there and we'll see. The situation's pretty fluid, as you know.'

'So, most of this will be irrelevant by the time you land, Waler,' said Pete, deadpan.

I wasn't sure if I should laugh, but Darth Vader was smiling, so I chuckled to make it clear I was keeping up.

It was loose. Vague information and volatile parties; it could become a big war in a small place.

'No authority for weapons,' the brigadier went on. 'No rules of engagement at all. I don't think we have UN chapters to cover that. Use a blue passport. Head straight to the embassy. Where are you landing?'

'Damascus, and then road move to Lebanon.'

'Okay. Good. Any questions?'

I had about a million.

This approach was a long way from the intense three-hour planning sessions where we went through every detail, down to what pocket the encryption codes would be carried in.

Afterwards, I walked down the corridor with Pete. 'I think you passed,' he said. 'He smiled. Must be in a good mood.' Deadpan again.

As he showed me out, Pete shook my hand. 'Good luck. Don't get killed.'

'Thanks, mate.'

Damascus, Syria

The border checkpoint was the only spot where we could safely transit from Syria into Lebanon. At the checkpoint office, an officious man, all sweat patches and epaulets, peered at our passports. I glanced inside the border post and counted no fewer than eleven framed pictures of President Bashar al-Assad.

The border guard stamped our passports, and as I walked back to the van I got a quick look at the plates of the three cars behind ours. One stood out: a green van with dark windows. I made a mental note of the last three digits: 03X.

I got back into our van and we continued along an unsealed road, chalk-white rocks and apricot trees dotting the landscape as we traversed the Syrian plains. The Mediterranean Sea shimmered in the distance and our driver pointed out the coastal city of Tripoli. He made shooting noises and smiled; it was obvious that dental clinics were rare in Syria. Three columns of black smoke billowed from the city. One of the largest Palestinian refugee camps in the world extended from the edge of the city into the desert. A small explosion rolled silently from the side of an office building as we watched. Hezbollah and the Lebanese government were battling for control and al-Qaeda had a known presence. We would not be shopping for carpets in Tripoli.

I was jetlagged and skittish, scanning for danger ahead, looking at the cars behind us.

As we drove further into Lebanon, Beirut came into view. The famed Corniche, regarded as one of the most beautiful promenades in the world, ran alongside the green sea. The cars were a mix of late-model Mercedes-Benzes and BMWs. Beirut was a known port for smuggled vehicles. Women with striking dark looks drove convertibles. A young man on a scooter kept pace with us for several blocks, roostering in a wheelie the whole way. This was a modern, developed city and it was incredible. You didn't have to look hard to see reminders of the civil war that had racked the city through the 1980s, though; it looked like a tank round had probed every level of the Holiday Inn building.

We drove down the street where Prime Minister Rafic Hariri was assassinated only three years earlier. His motorcade had driven past 1000 kilograms of high explosive in a parked van. Our toothless driver gave us the hand signal for car bomb and threw his hands up to mimic the explosion. As we looked at the gutted buildings, I could see the balconies ten storeys up had been peeled upwards by the blast wave. This was a place with a history of violence.

On day two, we drove into the Shia-held parts of the city, and the tension was palpable. Piles of dirt with Hezbollah flags on them had been placed in the main streets to block vehicle movement. Lebanese army tanks with quad-barrelled machine guns, each as big as a cannon, sat at the checkpoints. We were there to find out as much as we could about the layout of the Hezbollah and government forces. I had taken a ton of classified imagery; if it was discovered in a search, I would be in serious shit.

We cornered one point, and three Hezbollah soldiers walked towards our van. I felt my heart straining as I tried to keep calm. A university-aged man with a soft beard, an AR-15 and a chest rack of magazines walked to my side of the vehicle. He was wearing a blue terry-towelling hat. The young man spoke to the driver in an even tone. He was civil, polite, professional. I was impressed. These were no insurgents; they were a formed, trained army. The man waved to the driver as we passed through the checkpoint.

I can't put into writing the details of what happened next, for operational security reasons. Suffice to say, I completed the mission, and it was some of the best work I had done. There was no rule book, no clear mission, but I took a few risks and was able to deliver information of value to the government.

Pete told me later that the information we obtained and the quality of the reporting helped shape the perception that the SAS could be trusted to gather intelligence in high threat environments. It was important validation that I had managed to recover from 2007 and repay the faith shown in me by many.

It was a good lesson. I could have passed on the mission, but the choice to step forward let me gain control of fears that had gripped me for too long.

19

SAND PIT

By 2008, I was spending more time in Afghanistan than Australia. I even had a girlfriend there. I'd met the attractive brunette at a British embassy function while on my second posting, when I was a liaison officer in Kabul. She told me she worked with the British Treasury. I told her I was a liaison officer in the Australian Army. We were both circling each other with these half-truths. I knew she was something more, and vice versa. I never asked. That was the etiquette.

I would ride a mountain bike through the secure Green Zone at night, a Glock pistol tucked in my jeans, hoping I didn't get stopped or kidnapped as I pumped the pedals as hard as I could. She had her own quarters – a shipping container converted to a room with a carpeted floor, a pine desk and a single bed – a rare luxury in Afghanistan.

One night, as we lay squeezed together in her single bed in her Conex, I saw a stack of books in the corner of her room. They had titles like *My Life in the Taliban* and *Tactics of the Red Crescent*. I asked her if she found them interesting.

'Yeah, I do.' She was looking at me, clearly wanting to say more. 'You know what I really do, don't you?'

I frowned, playing dumb. 'No.'

'I work for British intelligence.' She rubbed the bedspread with her hand.

'What, MI6?' I asked at low volume.

She nodded.

Over the next hour, she explained about how she'd been recruited, the training she'd undergone in former Soviet Bloc countries, what her role was in Afghanistan and how the British were reorganising for counterinsurgency. The Queen had spoken with her graduating class. I was intrigued. She was not glamorous, like a movie spy, with a thigh holster concealed beneath a tight red dress. She was fit and good-looking, but she played it down, tying her long hair back in a ponytail, eschewing make-up and favouring loose clothes. She would pass as a typical diplomat. But she was sensitive, honest and intelligent.

Since she had confided in me, I repaid her trust, explaining that I was in the Aussie SAS. She told me she had guessed that because of my muscular build and facial hair.

We continued to see each other when we could, meeting either at her place or in my small apartment. Before long, we were planning a trip to New York, with a stop-off in Hawaii to attend a mate's wedding.

By the time I had finished my second deployment in Afghanistan, I knew I was in love.

I went back to the squadron in Perth. We were working incredibly long hours and suffering from it. I went and visited the doc – the same one who had referred me to the psychiatrist the year before – with a really itchy patch on my flank.

'Whoa,' he said, when I showed him the rash. 'These are shingles, mate – you gotta take it easy.' He must have thought I was a nervous wreck. Another mate who I had trained with during selection had his facial hair start falling out, leaving big bald patches on his face. It was stress-induced alopecia.

I knew it wouldn't be long before I was sent back to Afghanistan – or the Sand Pit, as we called it. There was more work in the Middle East theatre than there were officers to fill the slots. I had completed two full-length tours: the first in 2007, and the second six months later in 2008.

The rotations in combat squadrons went for six months, after which, instead of a much-needed rest, the teams came home and went straight into intense counterterrorism duties. The training for counterterror roles was arguably more dangerous than war – the fatality rates were high. During counterterrorism duties, patrols would sometimes be pulled off duty to head over to Iraq and Afghanistan to spend two to four weeks in protective security detachments. Spare officers were allocated to fill liaison roles in all the Middle East battlefields. They needed liaison officers in Baghdad. Staff officers in Kabul. Combat operations leaders in Tarin Kowt. Protective security detachment leaders. The barracks back in Swanbourne was a ghost town. Two of the three squadrons were fully deployed at once, and the third squadron was always away training somewhere. When a job popped up, the operations staff would ask two questions: Are you in Perth? Are you beret-qualified? If it was a yes to both: Good – go do this job. And off we went. We were flat out.

After the Vietnam War, Australia had experienced twenty years of peace. During that period, it was unusual to see a soldier with campaign medals. Now there were more small wars and deployments than we could attend. I had joined at likely the highest operational tempo Australia had experienced since World War II in terms of duration and intensity. I never forgot those who had overseen the regiment in the two and half decades from the end of Vietnam to the violent liberation of East Timor, though. With our equipment, training, tactics and the confidence of the government, we were the beneficiaries of 50 years of hard work.

But it seemed that very few Australians either knew or cared about the conflict. One morning, I sat in a cafe in Cottesloe and listened as a table of locals in Ralph Lauren polo shirts and white boat shoes complained about their superannuation losses from the recent global financial crisis.

I sat there seething. There was a fuckin' war going on. People were being decimated and here they were talking about their dollars. I felt like Neo taking a trip back through his old neighbourhood in *The Matrix*, now recognising the whole thing was a facade designed to keep the human race compliant. It seemed to me as if all this – the footpaths, the cafes, the polo shirts – was nothing more than make-believe.

I had lost all respect for ordinary Australians. I believed I was better than them: more virtuous, braver, faster, smarter. They were the sheep and we were the wolves. *Leave the fighting to us*, I thought, *so you can fret about your super losses*. I was starting to believe in myself and our mission like it was the only thing worth living for.

I wanted to keep going back to Afghanistan. It was all I could think about. I had meaning there. People relied on me. The war was a spectacle unlike any other, all helicopters and artillery and carbines and beards. We were kings in Afghanistan, whereas in Australia we felt like a necessary evil. I would be tolerated as long as I didn't become crippled or homeless, at which point I would become a cost centre. I knew that people appreciated the fact that we would do dirty work on their behalf, though their appreciation felt patronising at the time. After all, who would knowingly go to war? We would, I often thought, and it's the only thing worth doing. I was certain that facing the likely damage – possible death, even – was preferable to the regret I would feel if I stopped or quit.

*

In 2009 I went back to Afghanistan in another liaison role; this would be my third long trip. Again, I would be in Kabul, where my girlfriend was still posted, but I had the freedom to travel to Tarin Kowt and visit the fighting SAS squadron that was rotating through. During one of my liaison trips, I visited Tarin Kowt and got to spend a rare day in the accommodation huts with the teams that were in place.

I visited one of the team rooms. There were four bunks, containers of protein powder, Aussie flags and pictures of women on the walls.

'Waler, get in 'ere, cunt,' one of the soldiers said when he saw me. I was an officer, but in country we were more than a little informal, and I enjoyed the camaraderie of the teams. As I shook his hand, I could have sworn I smelled whisky. It was midday. I loved a drink – encouraged it even, on operations – but something here wasn't right.

I walked into the room and shook hands with the other soldiers. One of them opened a laptop. 'Check out the photos of this fuckin' ambush. Epic. Want a drink?' He held up a bottle of Johnnie Walker.

'Sure,' I said. I was helpless in the face of peer pressure.

He half filled a red cup with Johnnie then added a dash of dry ginger ale. I took a sip and suppressed a wince – it was strong.

A page of thumbnails popped up on the laptop screen. 'Check this out – we smashed these cunts.' He showed me a picture of a bullet-riddled Hilux ute with bodies slumped in a pile in the tray and bodies hanging out the side of the vehicle doors. There was a crimson and foaming white pool of blood under the man hanging out the passenger side. 'I hit these blokes from the side with a .338.'

He scrolled on through the pictures. Images from the inside of the car looked like a scene from a low-budget horror film. Red spray patterns and drips crossed the dark dashboard and flecks of grey matter were sprayed across the steering wheel and dash.

Three men in the back of the car were slumped against each other as though asleep. Another slide showed a human brain, vascular and covered in clear fluid, plopped into a centre console recess. It had tipped out of the head of a man in the back seat.

'Fuck!' I responded. I felt ill, but I tried to sound professionally curious. It looked like a very serious ambush.

'Yeah. Pretty sure this guy got hit with a .338 round that had gone through the head of his mate sitting next to him.' The bodies were destroyed, all misshapen and swollen and missing parts of limbs. One male was missing the top half of his head.

'So I reckon the round deformed a bit when it hit his mate. It knocked his block off.'

Next was another man, lying prone in the tray, with eyes wide open, shocked. The only giveaway that he was dead was the translucent glazing of his eyes.

'We couldn't see what happened to this bloke, but then we lifted up his kameez and saw a fuckin' huge hole in him.'

He clicked on to a soldier standing at the front of the vehicle, now bathed in flames.

It was dark. It was a rare part of soldiering, but contacts like this one were the part I feared the most: it's hard to unsee sights like that. I thought about my grandad trying to survive in Morotai. The combatants had hated each other with a passion. You have to summon some dark emotions as a soldier – a bit of anger; hatred, even – to survive.

I knew that this ambush had also precipitated a savage battle in which multiple soldiers were wounded. Incidentally, that battle was the one in which the bravery and heroism of troops under pressure was clearly on display, with Mark Donaldson carrying an interpreter to safety, earning the first Victoria Cross since Vietnam.

The soldier closed the laptop and sat back in his chair.

'Yeah. It was carnage.' He sipped his drink.

Despite its grim nature, we were doing great work in

Afghanistan. The missions were difficult. We had progressed our skills tremendously and never really lost a battle. In fact, we handed their arses to them on most occasions. While we were never being defeated tactically, the wins were becoming irrelevant. They were not al-Qaeda with an apocalyptic agenda. They were the Taliban. Arseholes, yes. Dangerous and brutal, yes. Their goal was to eject the foreigners from Afghanistan, and they were not running against an Excel-generated timetable for victory. Their sanctuary in Pakistan meant we could win every battle we wanted, and it would make very little differ-ence. Their strategy had no runway. They had all the time and all the people in the world to see it through. Victory – a stable government, a secure region free of the Taliban – was getting harder and harder to see.

This wasn't without precedent – I couldn't believe how short our memories were. In 1972 the Nixon government had pounded a sanctuary for the North Vietnamese Army harder than all the targets in World War II other than the atomic bombings. Laos, the bordering sanctuary, was bombed so much the water was poisoned, but to no avail. The Soviets had killed almost a million combatants and civilians during their decade-long occu-pation of Afghanistan, yet here we were going down the same path. Kill/capture missions were the 21st-century version of the same thing – industrialised killing in the hope of weakening an enemy – while the real question went unanswered: is this mission, this war, even relevant anymore?

This was known by the military and by our political leader-ship – the carnival would go on, more people would die, more proclamations about 'difficult, fragile' progress would be made. Meanwhile the moral injuries piled up behind the casualty lists – especially in special forces. We were being flogged with operational tempo, which we loved, at least initially. Selected and trained to generate high-tempo operations, we were the willing workhorses of the Aussie task group. But the cost was high. Death, injury and burnout was boiling to the surface. I had seen all three of them as far back as 2007. Two years later, it was more of the same.

The use of special forces had a political and military expediency: we were warriors, and a dead warrior is more palatable than a kid from a rifle company. So we were used, and used, and used. And we loved it. Promoted it even. That's what a war is – you go and fight, and the unions don't get involved, you work your arse off. But as I had mentally fractured on my 2007 tour, I could see the same leading indicators in 2009. Brutality in good soldiers, depression and the promise of an early death. It was ever present.

I never had the courage to try to stop the train, though. I was going to ride it, first class, to the end of the line.

I was still intrigued to see the war unfolding. It was getting more violent every year I had returned. The IEDs were more advanced, for example. In 2007, we only had to worry about car bombs. Now you had to watch for booby traps wherever you stepped. The legs, arms and genitals of Allied soldiers were often blown off in horrific bomb attacks in villages and compounds. Meanwhile, the living conditions were improving as we set in for the long war.

We were now proficient at moving booze around the war zone. The teams were pretty thirsty and it was always a good op to organise drinks. A cold beer in the centre of Afghanistan was a hundred times more special than a beer back home. It was hard to get, hard to hold onto, and a very naughty offence. It was far from a daily occurrence, particularly as we were outside the wire so much. But whenever senior ranks caught wind that we'd got away with it and enjoyed a few, they usually weren't too happy. For us going out in the field, the chance to drink together after working so hard was a treat. The process involved shipping an order in from Dubai and flying it in a UN aircraft into Tarin Kowt. We would give it an innocuous label, so it wouldn't be fucked with by over-zealous army transport inspectors. We would move the pallet from the airstrip to our compound. One of my colleagues was sometimes seen in the black of night, driving a forklift with a shrink-wrapped pallet on the front. Men would be waiting to open the gates of the compound as the merchandise arrived. The booze was unpacked. Cases of Johnnie Walker, Captain Morgan Spiced Rum by the pallet, and a ton of European beer in pint-sized cans. We had developed a network of transportation modes . . . 101st Airborne Chinook pilots could fly the packages from the Kandahar base. Teams of guys would fill trunks with booze at the Kabul PX and pack it with foam. I even bought a bottle of 2008 Dom Pérignon once. The booze would be hauled across the country. Sometimes one of us would fly with the cargo, fending off the army transport dangerous goods inspectors, telling them it was classified materials. One time I was carrying a full trunk of booze across the road from Kandahar airport in the dead of night and was nearly pancaked by an armoured recon vehicle that did not see me in the dark. American MPs prowled the Kandahar base roads, doing alcohol tests on drivers.

Booze was a currency in Afghanistan. A lot of deals were done over drinks. One evening, we commiserated with a CIA head of base after the bombing in Khost that saw seven CIA personnel killed. Commiseration turned into dark plotting. 'Some very bad people are gonna have a very bad day soon,' she said over the top of a crystal tumbler of Macallan twelve-year-old Scotch. I believed her.

The neighbouring squadron of British SBS soldiers would visit the base, bringing the entry fee of a case of beer. The Brits had an unusual penchant for nudity and would be stripped and cheering within the hour. British nudity was a disturbing trend across all units. Men would climb on their mates' shoulders, beers aloft and dancing, testicles stuck to the back of their mate's neck. They later agreed to support our operations in emergencies.

There were a few times when the drinking was authorised. Australian officers would visit and have dinner and a beer with us, thanking us for our hard work and sharing information on the tactical scenes. In that sense, it was very much a release mechanism, and there was method in the madness. But sometimes, the method *was* madness.

The drinking habits of the Special Operations Task Group were arguably the worst-kept secret in Afghanistan, and I was one of the worst-offending officers when it came to promoting the habit. If I knew a drinks session was planned, I would change my flight schedules to make sure I made it. I would be one of the first blokes at the bar we had crafted in Kandahar. We played Vietnam-era tracks on those nights off. My drinking came with consequences. I missed meetings, range training and even some flights. I got good at lying to superiors with cover stories. A mate and I got a hold of an air rifle in one of the facilities, and after a night of drinking we went on rampage and shot the troop TV with it, punching a hole through the plasma display – a mistake that cost us US$600 each. We had a full *Guitar Hero* kit and after drinks we would be trying our hand at every 90s alternative track there was. I became the drummer, and I was pretty handy at most Smashing Pumpkins tracks, even when very drunk. I'd even had an 808 electronic drum kit shipped over and set it up in my room so I could improve.

As the war dragged on, the stresses increased at a slow boil. A senior officer explained his view to me: 'The fighting has been a good thing, mostly. We're like metal – being shoved into the fire can temper you. Too much heat, though, can make you brittle.' With my carrying on and drinking overseas, I was making a bad situation worse. At a time when I was still suffering a degree of mental illness, and I'm sure others were too, the drinking culture may have been exacerbating our conditions. I was more interested in being popular than in being a leader who did the right thing. A leader sets the tone for the rest of the organisation. The message I was sending to my teams was loud and clear: 'The rules do not apply to us.'

20

FOREVER WAR

By the end of 2009, I was preparing for what I knew would be my final trip to Afghanistan with 1 Squadron. Pete Winnall had asked me to join as the Squadron XO for Rotation 13, in the northern summer of 2010. I was burned out, but I knew this would be my last tour in the regiment – and probably my last tour ever. After five years in the unit, I was due to rotate out into the wider army.

The war was not going well. Obama's team would be deciding on its future very soon. The strategy had tipped into counterinsurgency, protecting the population centres. This seemed interminable. It did not pass a sense check: the resource and time needs would be too great.

I wanted to understand whether the Allied mission to bring stability to Afghanistan was achievable. I got hold of every new book published by every top think tank I could find. Doing the rounds of Washington were two books about the Vietnam War strategy. *A Better War* was a revisionist history on Vietnam, arguing that if the political leadership had listened to General Abrams, the war may have ended on US terms. Creighton Abrams was offering the options of a retaliatory push into neighbouring Cambodia – retribution for the attacks emanating from the safe haven adjoining South Vietnam. He recognised the implications of Cambodia for the entire war strategy, emphasising the importance of the enemy's base area and lines of communication across South Vietnam's borders: 'That's the interminable part of this war,' he observed. 'Unless you can solve that, you *are* here forever.'

This highlighted the intractable issue of Pakistan. We were dealing with exactly the same problem, 40 years later: a sanctuary sharing a land border with Afghanistan that provided a training, resupply, manufacturing and planning base, coupled with an almost endless supply of fighting-age males who could enter the fray in Afghanistan. This was a regional war, and although the Allies were exerting influence in Pakistan, it was negligible compared to the focus on Afghanistan.

The second book to influence me was *Counterinsurgency in Afghanistan* by Seth Jones, which analysed counterinsurgency wars since World War II and the factors that resulted in a loss or a win. His core argument was that the US needed to focus on 'improving the capacity of the indigenous government and its security forces to wage counterinsurgency warfare'.

He determined that there were three variables correlated with the success (and failure) of insurgencies:

1. Capability of indigenous security forces, especially police
2. Local governance
3. External support for insurgents, including sanctuary

The moment I read this, I realised the coalition effort was in serious trouble. We had only really turned the strategy towards this in the latter part of the war. Further, each one of these criterion would require a substantial effort on its own. And the question of nullifying the third criterion was moot. There was no stopping external support and sanctuary for the Taliban from Pakistan. This came in the form of state support, from

Pakistan and its intelligence service, ISI, and in the form of a sanctuary for recruiting and re-arming. As for the first two points, the government was hated, irrelevant in most tribal areas, corrupt, and provided worse levels of institutional service than the Taliban did. The indigenous forces were hopeless at best and dangerous at worst, beset with tribal divisions, desertion and drug use. We were incorporating local troops into our raids, but this was too little, too late.

To make matters worse, in 2010 a book was published that revealed divergent objectives between the military and the US government. *Obama's Wars*, by the renowned journalist Bob Woodward, revealed a military and political leadership at loggerheads over strategy. John Brennan, the future director of the CIA, said: 'It will take a generation to develop an Afghanistan that can achieve modest governmental goals and consolidate these goals.' According to security adviser Thomas Donilon: 'We are not accepting . . . that to defeat Al-Qaeda means that we would have to do a long-term counterinsurgency strategy to defeat the Taliban . . . a strategy that would take six to eight years and a trillion dollars.' I felt sick when I read it. A high school student of history knows that to win any war as a democracy, military and political leadership need to be closely aligned on national objectives and strategy. This book told us that they were not only rowing in opposite directions, but one side was trying to scuttle the craft.

But to me the biggest red flag of all was watching Obama deliver his 'surge' speech. It was clear that he did not believe in the war he had inherited or his own government's strategy.

I watched the surge speech in late 2009, and realised that Obama was clearly not enthused about the war. There was no rousing call to action. No determined belief that we could finish. Just a troop surge and a timeline. It looked like he was only half committing to a war. Churchill's all-or-nothing approach came to mind. When discussing the failed Suez Crisis he declared:

'I would never have started the war, and if I had, I would not have stopped until it was done.' War is a runaway train, very hard to stop or even steer once the boilers are hot, the pistons are firing and the carriages are racing along the rails. The lesson for me was: do not fire that train up unless you have every intention of seeing it to the end of the line.

Afghanistan was no different.

Enter the Australian contribution, now in its eighth year. Our strategy had meandered badly over the years. In 2001, we were killing al-Qaeda. In 2006, it had been special reconnaissance and combat missions. In 2007 it was counter-leadership. (After winning the election against John Howard that year, Prime Minister Kevin Rudd illustrated the impasse when he sat with military leaders and asked about our government's strategy in Afghanistan. 'I was met with crickets,' he said.) In 2008, the commandos were doing counter-narcotics, while the SAS targeted Taliban leadership.

By 2009, it was counterinsurgency. Protect the population, no night-time raids, drive carefully on the roads. This was the new strategy. The brilliant minds of the Iraq counterinsurgency were taking the model of the Iraq surge and the Sunni Awakening that resulted in the degradation of al-Qaeda in Iraq and applying the same strategy in this ungovernable land.

No longer would battle with the enemy be an end in itself; it was determined we had to win the support of the Afghan people, establish a secure and functioning government, and set the conditions for withdrawal. To complete this task, the US president had allocated 30,000 more troops, and a deadline of eighteen months. Immediately, the Taliban knew how long they needed to wait. The intractable problem was the gaping divide between the strategy and the resourcing for it. One estimate said that 500,000 troops, a trillion dollars and twenty years would be needed to succeed in counterinsurgency.

We were only being promised about 6 per cent of what was needed to complete the mission. The military charged ahead regardless.

Before long, directives about population protection landed on operations desks. Air strikes were out; de-escalation was in. Medals for 'courageous restraint' were being considered for troops that actively de-escalated combat situations. You couldn't make this shit up – the satirical novel *Catch-22* was based on the same premise, and it felt like the author's ghost followed us. These directives could not even pass the pub test. I could imagine an Aussie at any pub saying: 'So they send you to war, and ask you to not fight too hard?' It was absurd. Proportionality of response is common sense, and a Law of Armed Conflict. But retarding your troops is dangerous, ineffective and damaging for morale.

The SAS was traditionally a recon force. In the jungles of Vietnam, they had conducted long-range reconnaissance and plenty of ambushes using field craft. It was the distinctive skill of the SAS and it still underpinned our training – the unsexy, difficult, tedious work of long-range reconnaissance. Sitting in observation posts, watching, barely moving, not cooking, not speaking for a week at a time. Gathering information which could provide the military with a strategic advantage. That was our mainstay, but our mission was evolving.

In Afghanistan, we had started in 2007 doing reconnaissance and fighting where needed. There was still a lot we did not know about our area. By 2009, the Special Ops Task Group was in full targeting mode. We had the helicopters needed to undertake the missions. We also had the drones and the signals intelligence to know where to land. That meant we could launch from Tarin Kowt and land surrounding a valley in the space of an hour. The tactics were aggressive. A clearance team would sweep through the target compounds, while teams on the high ground covered them with heavy weapons.

We could surprise the enemy. That was worth a lot in combat. It was a dramatic departure from long-range reconnaissance. The 'Kill/Capture' task verb was becoming common. We ended up being so effective at them, the nomenclature was later changed to Capture/Kill, as though relegating the term 'kill' would make it more likely that troops would kill their target. It showed how little senior leaders understood the reality of close combat. The SAS generally launched against enemy or terrain that was more treacherous than conventional forces were willing to tackle. Unleashing a team on that is like rolling a boulder down a hill. Once it's moving, gravity takes charge. You couldn't stop the teams from killing perceived threats in the field any more than you could stop gravity.

Now the squadrons were arriving in country, and instead of six weeks in the field, living out of patrol vehicles, we would line up drone surveillance, watch a target for days, and then launch on it when we felt we had enough intelligence. By that time, we knew plenty about the target area, how many males were there, how many females and children, cars and difficult terrain.

We would call it something like a 'targeting mission'. In truth, the missions were a state-sanctioned, legally authorised killing or capture of a nominated enemy. By the time we launched on a target, we had reviewed the intelligence in great detail and had legal authorisation for the mission. The decks were signed off at the highest levels of the International Security Assistance Force. I counted an authorisation PowerPoint deck with a total of 82 slides. It contained legal justification for the action, a broad concept of the operation and other details around rules of engagement. This ensured that the ISAF commander was authorising operations that all supported a single aim or mission. If a task was deemed irrelevant to the mission, it was declined. If the threat to civilians was too great, it was not approved. When these were signed off, it was a great check and balance against teams running operations that did not support the coalition goals. I felt confident that what we were doing was both legal and just. The problem was that these missions dragged on in an endless war. The damage that wrought on the moral fabric of troops was immense.

I was now a senior troop commander and had combat experience. I was trusted to make good decisions, and work with the teams when needed. But I was trashed, exhausted from repeated deployments. In 2009, I had spent 300 days on operations around the world. Managing the ongoing symptoms of trauma had been a battle. I still slept badly sometimes. I had been getting counselling in Fremantle when I could. I had taken up surfing and drumming as a way to keep my mind off work. They both helped, but my drinking levels were ruining all the progress.

I bought new equipment to prepare for the trip. I bought weapon parts: a recoil dampener, a 7-inch receiver, a red dot sight and a flip-up magnifier. I bought lightweight plastic magazines. I bought a new body armour vest, and a bandolier for 40 mm grenades. I read widely. I felt ready. After five years in the SAS, I was not new blood anymore. I had fought, made mistakes, had some wins and had been leading troops for years.

A month before I left for my last tour to Afghanistan, I flew over to Thailand to meet my British spy girlfriend, who was now based in Bangkok. I told her I didn't want to see her anymore; I was going back to Afghanistan, and when it was over I might head to the US to study. I knew I couldn't have a relationship in this state, despite the fact she had shifted her posting to South-East Asia – far from her own home – in order to be closer to me. I sat with her in her apartment for a day and we both lamented the situation I had created. It was horrible;

I was putting my personal life on the backburner so I could keep heading off to a questionable war.

I knew this was probably the last trip for me. If I survived, maybe I could do something else with my life.

21

THE HEART OF DARKNESS

June 2010

WE HAD A SMOOTH LANDING ON A BITUMEN AIRSTRIP, NEWLY added in the latest surge. The familiar car drive to Camp Russell showed we had a new hardened facility. It was a Jenga block set-up of Conexes. The headquarters was a tunnel of Conexes about 50 metres long with a door shooting off to another Conex every five metres or so.

The ops room was made up of four Conexes. It had three monitors, each the size of a coffee table, that showed drone feeds from the latest targets. Men with coffee mugs, new camouflage uniforms and baseball caps sat watching the feeds. Some of these soldiers were approaching double-digit tours of duty; by the end of the war, the average SAS soldier had done more than four tours in Afghanistan alone. CNN ran on one of the screens, and the lead story that day was the sacking of the head of ISAF, General Stanley McChrystal, thanks to some ill-advised remarks about US political leaders in a *Rolling Stone* article.

I sat down with the outgoing squadron commander and XO, and talked through the status of the province. The squadron commander, a veteran of the invasion of the Western Desert of Iraq, was a laid-back guy with a slight frame and a baseball cap that he wore day and night. They had seen some wins in Gizab, where the squadron had supported a local uprising against the Taliban. The rebels were known as the 'Gizab Good Guys', or the triple-G. The squadron was touting their efforts as an illustration of how the Taliban could be ousted by civilians, much like the Anbar Awakening in Iraq was seen as a model of effective counterinsurgency.

'Yeah, it was a good trip,' said the squadron commander. 'We got nine off the JPEL.' It was clear we had got better at targeting missions, reflected by taking such a high number of people off the hit list.

A patrol commander talked me through the Battle of Shah Wali Kot, ten days earlier. He was senior and a no-bullshit NCO, very respected. He showed me the slideshow presentation that had been sent to General McChrystal. It was carnage, bodies of enemy fighters stacked like cordwood in the field.

The Shah Wali Kot offensive was a five-day joint operation across different parts of the district involving soldiers from the 2nd Commando Regiment, Special Air Service Regiment and Afghan National Army. On the second day of the battle, in a village called Tizak, Ben Roberts-Smith fought an action that later earned him his Victoria Cross. Despite heavy fighting, only two Australians were wounded.

'We got 100 KIA. Apaches did some of the work – we smashed them, though.'

A signaller held up a ration tin containing a pile of dusty olive material. It was an enemy chest rig. 'We took this off a Talib in Tizak – smell it.' He held it up to my face and I flinched. It smelled like death: sweet and rotten.

Things had escalated considerably since my first deployment in 2007. We were now accomplished targeting teams, thanks to the US surge, which had brought two crucial assets: helicopters and drones. The drones enabled you to watch a target for days. This de-risked the operation. Before launching an operation, you knew how many people were present and what they were doing. Once a raid was planned, the Black Hawk helicopters could move you there quickly, giving you the benefit of surprise. The Apache gunships would offer overhead cover as extra firepower.

I went to the gym that night to train with the teams, a daily ritual. One of the team 2ICs was in a corner, wild-eyed, sweating and throwing weights around. I could hear the music coming through his earphones from across the room. There was a simmering look to the men – they were lean and tanned. A barefoot commando kicked a focus mitt bag with his friend encouraging him, the booms echoing through the gym.

I kept training over the next couple of weeks and in the absence of beers and western food managed to get down to my ideal 'fighting weight', a lean 103 kilos, down from a heavy, doughy 107 kilos – with a crucial difference in body composition and muscle-to-fat ratio. I had been competing in CrossFit games since taking it up a few years ago, and that improved my fitness. In the mountains, mass is often a liability.

1 July

We stood on the apron of the runway in glasses, squinting against the baking sun. The whole outgoing squadron was standing near the airstrip, waiting to board the aircraft that would take them to Kuwait and home to Perth. Ben Roberts-Smith and I chatted about the areas the incoming squadron would likely work in. 'Arghandab,' he told me. 'Get to Arghandab. Badlands.' His gaze was intense. I had to look upwards at his 6 foot 7 inches frame, even though I am 6 foot 3 inches. He was known as aggressive and forward-leaning in battle. RS had worked closely with my mate Matt Locke – his mentor – when he joined the regiment a year ahead of me.

As one squadron exited the back of the Hercules and the outgoing squadron moved towards the aircraft, they stopped on the tarmac to talk. After a decade of deployments, it was rare to see any more than a team of your mates at once – we had all been sailing past each other in the night for five years now – but here was almost half of the combat unit standing in one spot. Everyone shook hands and said g'day. It was a special moment when one team handed over the torch to another.

I shook hands with Pete Winnall, who was looking brisk, glad to be in country after a three-day transit, and we commenced our handover with the outgoing squadron commander. He was pleased with the progress his squadron had made from Tizak. 'Well, hopefully we left some targets for you,' he said.

Pete told him to piss off and stop flattering himself.

Pete held an operational design session with the patrol commanders. We packed into a room and spent a day going over the effects we wanted to have in our area of operation. Pete started with a review of where we had come from to this current point. I was excited to weigh in. I was well informed from all my reading and was keen to show off.

The part that struck me was the difficulty in finding continuity for our actions. Removing an enemy leader was fine, but if it was not capitalised on with security from Afghan forces and a degree of governance (law and order), then we were not improving the situation. In fact, there were occasions when a targeting operation might make it worse. Pete understood this, and was thorough in making sure patrol commanders briefed him on their plans for integration of forces and governance after strike missions.

Intelligence was briefing us on the Taliban. The intelligence leader kicked off with the statement: 'We are engaged in a war of legitimacy.' He went on to explain the current situation on the ground. The surge infrastructure was in place. We had more troops, helicopters and weapons. Humvee trucks had been replaced by MRAPS, giant mine-protected vehicles that US Secretary of Defense Robert Gates had forced through. It felt like the 'turn to home', the last play of the game.

The operations manager spoke next, revealing more of the US counterinsurgency strategy. We had legal authority to expand operations out of Oruzgan Province to support the US push into Kandahar, the spiritual home of the Taliban, where leader Mullah Omar had preached in the 1990s. Part of the push would be the clearance of the Zhari–Panjwai, a patchwork of grape fields, irrigation ducts and mud-walled compounds across two Kandahar Province districts, perfect defensive territory.

It was storied Taliban territory; the Russians had been defeated there in some of their final battles, and they'd feared it so much they called it 'the Heart of Darkness'. The Canadians had fought here in 2006, in vicious fighting to control the ground, resulting in the loss of sixteen Canadians, including the first-ever female combatant commander killed in action. We would be supporting the US-led push into the region to support the safety of the population, which sounded like a contradiction.

At one point I asked: 'What if the population doesn't want what we are offering? Then what?'

No-one spoke. The whole coalition operations centred on the assumption that the Afghan government, in partnership with the coalition, could offer a better standard of living for everyone. But what if the people didn't want that? It would mean we were fighting and dying for naught.

Parsing the strategic environment was enough to make your head hurt. The dynamic between tribes, government figures, external state supporters, non-profit organisations, the allies, the political tribes that commanded each ally – there were simply too many permutations to configure.

As far as I was aware, there had been no serious ques-tioning of the war effort – and there were so many questions we should have been asking: What difference would we make if we continued this mission for five years? Would the outcome be better than if we pulled out in five weeks? If we made progress, would the progress be worth the cost? What was the opportunity cost of the engagement? Why were we here?

It was clear we did not have the answers. I certainly didn't. All I knew was that there would be no line drawn under the JPEL – we would keep killing these leaders for generations and new ones would continue to rise through the ranks.

0200 hours, 23 July

I got the word I could join the team for a morning raid. I spent the whole night preparing my gear. I had a rising sense of dread at going out on the job, like I had a sixth sense that something bad would happen. I had heard that NFL players would sometimes listen to Phil Collins's 'In the Air Tonight' before a big game – it was like a meditation. I sat in the dark on my bunk and listened to the same track through my Bose earphones. It helped a little.

In my XO office, I put on my uniform. It has built-in hard knee and elbow pads. I put a small metal oil bottle into my thigh pocket, along with a flick blade knife. I added a packet of army chocolate to my pants pocket. That would be my only food for 24 hours. I had finally outgrown the Red Rooster diet I'd had since I was a kid. I place a folded satellite image map of the target area in my left leg pocket and zipped the pocket closed.

I pulled on my low-cut hiking shoes, tied the laces then wrapped a length of black tape around the knots and my foot, to ensure my laces stay tied up in the field. Very embarrassing to trip over laces in battle.

Now that I had started the familiar ritual of dressing for combat, my mind was no longer racing. I didn't think of anything. When I stepped out, I would have taken care of the things I could control. On selection, one of the corporals had told me to 'find comfort in chaos'. I knew where each pouch was, every item I carried, and I could reach them at night, without looking, in the middle of a battle.

I pulled my pistol belt off the wall. On the right side of the belt was a USP tactical handgun, with eighteen rounds in the clip. I put the magazine in, racked the slide and applied the safety catch. I tested the small light under the barrel; it bathed my office in white light. The side-arm was a backup. *One is none, two is one.* I had a rolled-up bag on the left side of the belt, the size of a small pouch, that could be unfurled and used to store empty magazines. I felt for the two hand grenades on the left side of my belt.

Next I pulled a tan bandolier from the side of my locker. It held ten 40 mm grenades, all high explosive. The last two rounds were red smoke grenades for marking targets. The bandolier had a smaller circumference so it could sit above my pistol belt, but below my body armour.

My body armour was a vest which hugged the torso and had armoured plates front and rear. I had a radio, six magazines, a fixed blade knife in a holster. We had trimmed the load from previous tours, but ammunition was always number one. I pulled the vest on and checked the magazines on the front. I pulled each one from the chest pouch with one hand to be sure that when I placed it in my weapon, the magazine was pointing the correct way, bullet tips pointing to my left shoulder. Failing that, I would introduce another friction point when reloading – I would have to turn the magazine in my hand – offering more chance for a mistake, or time for an enemy to shoot back. I turned the radio on and placed the microphone and speaker in my ear. I heard the radio beep to interrogate itself. I pressed a switch on my chest and heard the microphone beep in response. I tested that the knife pulled easily from its sheath. I positioned the small one-armed tourniquet on my front so that I could reach it with either arm in the event I lost a limb and need to perform self-aid.

I attached my GPS device to one arm; it had a compass mount next to it. On my other arm was a small plastic fold-up case with a map of the target site. Each building was labelled with a number and letter. I pulled on my gloves with the reinforced knuckles. I'd cut the tips off the gloves' fingers, so I could feel for weapon blockages in the dark, if needed. In a dire situation, it would also be easier to feel for eyeballs, ears and throats in close combat.

I pulled my weapon off the rack mounted on the plywood wall. I'd had the same M4 with a grenade launcher for five years. I'd given it a fresh paint job and a new weapon sight before the trip, all green and tan and brown patches. I pulled the Viking Tactical sling over my head and racked the weapon once, looking down the open chamber at an exposed cartridge to make sure it was seated in the chamber properly. I pushed the bolt-locking mechanism down and closed the dust cap over the bolt. I left the suppressor on the end of the barrel, so I could shoot at night and not give away my position with a muzzle flash. I checked the metal safety post with my thumb. I didn't need to look; I knew that horizontal was safe. I reached for the holographic sight on top and switched it on, then looked through the scope at the wall. I could see a red ring with a tiny red dot in the centre, meaning the sight was activated and working. I dulled the brightness since we would land early dawn.

I opened the underslung grenade launcher with my left hand, reached for a grenade (from my locker rather than my bando-lier, so I still had full pouches of grenades) and placed it in the tube. The red dot sight on the grenade launcher worked, a tiny glass patch with range increments out to 400 metres. I tested the infrared laser pointer.

I smacked the pocket on my right shoulder. That bulge held a shell dressing, an anti-coagulant made from seashell extract, and a 5-milligram tube of morphine which shot a spring-loaded needle through clothing. I tapped my left shoulder and felt for the flat escape and evasion map. It covered the whole country and had grids to every major coalition base. Inside was US$200 and a letter in Pashto with an Aussie and Afghan flag on it, explaining I was with ISAF and offering a reward for safe passage.

Last: my helmet. This one had got a new paint job too. I'd placed both my night vision goggles on it. I turned them on and checked the battery was ready. Then I turned my helmet to check the infrared strobe at the rear worked. I slid the switch to off and pulled a Velcro tab across to stop it turning itself on in battle. I checked the infrared light stick on the back of my helmet, designed to prevent friendly fire. I pulled an olive-coloured buff over my head to cover my neck, the only bit of warm gear I had for the trip.

I reached for my clear ballistic glasses, then stood still for a moment to go back over the checklist in my mind one last time. Pistol: loaded and actioned. Rifle: loaded, actioned. Suppressor: on. Grenade launcher: loaded. Radio: ready. Goggles: ready. Map: check. GPS: check. Morphine, escape map, oil, knife: check. I left my office with my weapon cradled in my right arm, helmet in left hand with NVGs up, and walked to the airstrip.

0400 hours, 23 July

The whole troop walked out to the airstrip apron and waited for the Chinooks to arrive. We would be landing before dawn in a valley that was dominated by high ground, and I knew that before the morning was out, there would likely be a gun battle.

Everyone was quiet but upbeat. These minutes before battle were always surprisingly positive. The hard work of planning was done and we were ready for action. The early morning was crisp and cold. We heard the drone of the helicopters in the distance, and a minute later blinking lights descended from the night and blasted us in rotor air. As we walked up the back ramp of the Chinooks, the burning exhaust of the engines hit me with the burnt-biscuit smell of aviation fuel and bathed my neck and face in warmth. The whining of the rotors was deafening. The aircraft pitched up, and we speared towards the valley in a pitch-black sky dotted with stars. The peaks and boulders rushed past in the green of our night vision.

We landed on the edge of the village and ran towards the targets with weapons to our shoulders. I could see the patrol commander on my right side. We had moved into a flat formation, sweeping towards the target like a broom handle pushed broadside. I was on the far-left flank, trying to keep up. As we neared the compound, I could see a copse of bushes to my left, just large enough for a person to hide in. I ducked under a tree, heard the sound of a branch scraping across my helmet, nails on a blackboard, as we crept towards the target. We moved along the compound wall and I stacked up first at the door. I'd be the one to face whatever was on the other side. The patrol commander asked if I was ready to go in. I wasn't, but I squeezed his arm in the affirmative. The door banged as I entered, turning my laser on and sweeping to the right. There was a sheep pen in the corner and I could see their wild eyes over the top of the fence. I swept the laser back to the middle of the compound and spied a large pile of rags. I saw a head stick out of them and heard a woman yelp. The women and children had gathered in the middle of the compound to avoid being shot. I hadn't seen them; if they had been the enemy, they would have nailed me.

We cleared the compound room by room. Hessian covers hung over each door and every room was dark. Nothing.

We walked back out into the centre of the compound and saw the Apaches circling a few hundred feet above us, menacing the village below.

We pulled back as the first grey shades of dawn turned our goggles too bright. I moved into overwatch on a hill near the compound, and as the sun rose, all I could see were the towering hills around us. We knew the Taliban would have overwatch and fire positions set up in the hills.

We took off our goggles and put our suppressors away. The clearance went on for another hour. I changed my position every five minutes to avoid getting shot. By now the rays of sunlight were reaching lower into the valley, and the sun was on the cusp of clearing the ridge.

We walked to the extraction site, ready to be pulled off target. This was the most dangerous part. It was their last chance to get us. As we halted, I saw a small foot pad that carved through a mound of earth. It was waist deep and as wide as my hips, but I forced myself into it, my head sitting just below ground level. I covered our rear, checking for movement through my rifle sight. I could hear explosions nearby as one of the clearance teams threw grenades into a cave. We were being watched; people in the valley had intentions on our lives. I'd felt it in Chora: the same crackling in my nerves I felt now.

The hilltops barked to life, two heavy guns roaring from a nearby hill. Rounds ricocheted and whizzed off near my head and I realised that in fact it was 'unfriendly fire'. I poked my head up from my hole and saw three men running in three different directions from the gunfire as gouts of dirt erupted in front and behind them. The signaller called out on the radio; he was breathing hard, rattled. He had literally dodged a bullet.

As we waited on the LZ, the Apache gunship rolled in to strafe the targets overhead. It was deafening. For a second I was back in the cornfield in Chora. The Apache flew directly over my hole and fired two missiles, each one exploding on the hilltop, shattering the jagged shale fingers.

That night, back in the command post, ops over for the time being, I tried to calm down by reading. I'd bought a book about life in the Harvard Business School MBA program. I'd originally had the idea of running a microbrewery when I left the army, so I'd completed a brewing diploma while I was deployed to East Timor. Halfway through an assignment on water types used in brewing, I realised that I didn't need to know how to brew; I needed to know how to run a business. The idea of studying for an MBA appealed to me, and the program sounded incredible: diverse, fun and full of opportunity. I tucked that ambition away. Before taking that next step I had to survive this one.

13 August

On a warm night, the team rolled out on another job, this time landing in a green belt in an unknown part of Kandahar. I was in the command post running the ops centre for this one, along with one of the men from the team, his hand swathed in bandages; he had shot himself in the hand with a 40 mm grenade that he'd accidentally fired from his own gun when getting out of a vehicle. 'It's all right,' he assured me. 'I'll be back in the field in a week.' He was just glad he still had his hand.

As the teams cleared up a dry valley, they were engaged at close range by a bunch of Taliban. One of the troopers was gunned down and badly injured. The rest of the team had to fight at close range to both kill the enemy and rescue the injured soldier.

I was in the command post when the call came through the radio. '*Pri 1 casualty, multiple gunshot wounds. Stand by.*' My heart sank.

'Okay, everyone minimise,' said the head signals soldier. That meant no talking unless critical so the airwaves could prioritise the evacuation.

An unnatural quiet had descended over the command post. For once there were no phones ringing, no radio screeching, there was no chatter at all. Pete and I were both standing by the handset, waiting. 'Not good,' said Pete, his voice tense. To the signals soldier he said, 'Activate the AME. Pri 1.' That was the aeromedical evacuation team, and Pri 1, or Priority 1, meant a serious injury.

We started the evacuation process for the casualty. The helicopter crews broke the rules to evacuate Browny during a dust storm and extracted one team. It was too dangerous to extract the rest of the troop so they remained on the ground. We got the word that the injured man was dead on arrival. We learned that it was Trooper Jason Brown, a tall blond soldier with an easy saunter and hunched shoulders, a quiet country boy. That week someone had plastered the walls with A4 printouts of his army ID picture, emblazoned with HAPPY BIRTHDAY. I had shaken his hand and wished him all the best. He had turned 29.

When the teams returned, they were dead quiet. In the courtyard I spoke to Clay Watts, the patrol 2IC. He was one of the guys that was with me when Matt died.

The final report revealed that the close contact had been fought by Clay's team and two other Taliban. The patrol commander had been hit no less than six times on his helmet, trousers and body armour as he tried to save Browny. He also stopped one of his men charging forward to certain death to rescue Browny, determined to take on the job himself. During the melee he killed the two Taliban fighters at close range. They were so close that the 40 mm grenades the men fired at them were not detonating; they had a 16-metre arming distance.

Pete wrote a bravery citation for the man and we sat down and read it together. Pete was recommending him for a Star of Gallantry, the second-highest bravery award, but it read like a Victoria Cross, for which the qualifying criteria was extreme peril. What the patrol commander had attempted was risky in the extreme. He had risked his own life to try to save his dying teammate.

'This reads like a VC,' I said to Pete.

Pete was a step ahead. 'I know – that's what I'll be recommending as well.'

It would be the second recommendation for a VC, after Mark Donaldson's two years before. Unknown to us, there were two more being reviewed: Ben Roberts-Smith for the engagement in Tizak and Dan Keighran for his efforts in the Battle of Derapet. A third VC at the same time might be one too many.

The army padre pulled on his uniform and went to see Jason Brown's parents in Australia. When she saw him at the door, Jason's mother's first thought was that Jason had won an award. Instead she was told he had been killed. She was apologetic, telling the padre, 'You have such a terrible job, telling families about this. Would you like to come in and have a tea or coffee?' The grief came later for Mrs Brown and her husband, who had served in Vietnam.

At the ramp ceremony in Afghanistan, the squadron lined either side of the tunnel at the rear of a Hercules C-130. We wore sandy berets on our filthy dishevelled heads. I had been to six or seven ramp ceremonies this trip, and we were normally somewhere in the middle of the line of troops farewelling the soldier. This time, we had pole position at the rear of the waiting C-130. Its ramp was down, and an Australian flag hung inside the cavernous plane. I could hear the progress of Browny's casket because the bagpiper was walking alongside him.

Browny was walked down the line by his mates. He was in a silver coffin, with the Aussie flag over it, and his patrol carried him on their shoulders. I stood facing one of the dog handlers, and a firing party was positioned off the side of the plane. As the bearer party approached the ramp, we all saluted. The dog jumped when the gun fired, rearing on its back legs and yelping as the handler tried to calm him down. He knew. Dogs know when their tribe has lost one.

I found myself a bit overwhelmed by the bagpipes and the dogs and the firing and the men in berets. I was crying openly, and when Browny was positioned in the aircraft for the ride home, I reminded Chappo, the troop commander, to go and put his hand on Browny's coffin. I had not done that with Matthew, to my regret.

It had been three years since Matt died, and here we were again. It was a grinding, long bitch of a war with no end in sight. In fact, we were at the bottom of a steep curve, and after nine years of war, the violence levels were headed in only one direction: up.

We organised a wake for Browny. There would be an auction of his gear and the money would go to his parents. We planned to hold it in the Fat Lady's Arms. When the base was rebuilt, the bar was shifted from the dodgy hut it had occupied in my 2007 rotation to a full-sized room with a TV and a *lot* more weapons up on the walls. There was a good pie warmer and a beer fridge, and the Aussie flags were up on the wall.

We invited the US helicopter crews to attend, and they drove from the other side of the base. None of them were allowed to drink, and they were shocked at how cavalier we were with the beer. Everyone rolled in wearing boardies and singlets with thongs.

Not your typical-looking wake. No stale sandwiches, black mourning suits or mumbled condolences. Nor was our conduct approved in any official way. But we were working in a war zone, regularly heading out in the same conditions where Browny lost his life. We could be at another ramp ceremony any day now. Nights like this were a necessary stress release. The auction gave it purpose, too. We were doing right by Browny's family.

The auction inspection began, with a running commentary from the auctioneer. 'Step right up, cunts, step right up. Take a look at Browny's gear and pick your target. I'm taking his gloves tonight, people, just so you know.'

I took a look at Browny's pistol belt. It had his pistol holster, wrapped in strapping tape and painted green, and his helicopter bungee hung from the side of it. I loved it. I set a stop-bid price mentally for US$3000.

The auctioneer started with the opening bids. The biggest bids were for his body armour. Pete offered $2000 for two condoms found well-preserved in Browny's gear. Pete was feeling generous and awarded one each to Chappo and me. Chappo demanded to know if they were 'medium-sized' condoms. More laughter. One of Browny's $2 badges went for $500.

The auctioneer pointed at the US helicopter crews, who were lurking at the back, trying to avoid being noticed. 'What about you fuckin' seppos? You've been mighty quiet. Put some of that war money to work. What's your bid?'

The whole room turned to the Yank contingent, jammed in the corner of the room like a terrified school of salmon facing a pack of hungry bears.

'Ah, fuck it, don't worry,' said the auctioneer, letting them off the hook. 'Just don't crash us, you cunts.'

By now the room was firing: it was hot and humid and the crowd was roaring. The atmosphere was energising, an effective form of pain relief, as we continued to cheer at how much we were raising for Browny's parents. The auctioneer opened the bidding for the gloves, and was silly enough to remind the crowd that he was intent on taking them. Just as the bidding was closing at $740 to the auctioneer, one of the snipers put in a dummy bid.

'Okay, cunt, twelve hundred,' said the auctioneer.

'Fifteen hundred,' the sniper retorted.

The auctioneer dropped his hands in exasperation and muttered to himself, looking at the gloves. *'Fuckin'* hell. Fifteen fifty.'

'Sixteen hundred,' the sniper fired back. It was clear he had no interest in the gloves; he was just driving the price up to shit the auctioneer.

'Seventeen hundred – done.' The auctioneer slammed the gavel on the table as the whole room erupted at how he'd been played.

He held up Browny's belt and started the bidding. I was up against one of the snipers. The bidding climbed in $500 increments to $2500. The sniper tried to wipe me out with a jump to $5000. I winced. That was my surf trip money going down the drain. But pride won out. I bid $5200 and the cheers went up. I was committed now. The auctioneer turned to the sniper, who bid $5900. I closed it at $6000 and dropped my head in my hands, the buyer's remorse strong. Still, I was happy the money would be going to Browny's family.

The night was a bender. One visual that stays with me is the two attack dogs in the team putting their paws up at the bar, standing with their handlers. The dogs were wearing pink tutus pulled over their mid-sections, which seemed appropriate in the circumstances.

Before the night was out, we raised US$99,000 in cash for Browny's family.

I withdrew my dollars the next day and rolled it in a ball. I felt the weight of $6000. It felt heavy.

A few days later we held a patrol targeting briefing. I was sitting at the edge of the room, watching the intelligence officers flick through the latest targeting deck, with all the objective names: MACE, Nunchuck, Torpedo. Everyone was paying attention and asking questions about locations, high activity zones. I looked over at the patrol commander who'd rescued Browny. He was sitting with his arms and legs folded, staring at his feet.

I was pretty sure I knew what was on his mind.

22

A WALK IN THE LIGHT GREEN

I WAS SPENDING MY NIGHTS DRIVING ACROSS TO THE US aviation base on the other side of the airstrip. I would jump on a quad bike before sunset to make the evening brief. It was my favourite part of the day, a rare moment of solitude. I cued up my iPod with 'Fortunate Son' by Creedence Clearwater Revival, the premier Vietnam-era song to play when you were near helicopters. In my tan t-shirt, I drove flat out along the airstrip with my rifle slung on my back, helmet on. On the high ground to my left stood the bunker for a self-propelled howitzer called 'Maximus' – he had lived in that cave for four years, trundling out of his dark hole to bark rounds at the enemy.

It was complete freedom. One day I was driving flat out along the dust and gravel road when two Apache gunships hovered and tracked alongside me, barely 15 metres off the ground, and I accelerated to keep up with them as I gave a fist pump in the universal coalition hand signal for 'go get 'em'. The pilot and gunner from each Apache gave me a salute. It was a thrill. It almost made the war worth it.

5 October 2010

I got the word at dawn I could join the team for an assault. Maps were printed and wrist-mounted GPS were handed over in a box so the objectives could be uploaded. An hour later we were walking across the tarmac towards the helicopters. Four Black Hawks in a line, with two Apache gunships running cover. We climbed aboard and clipped our safety strop harnesses onto the airframe, weapon barrels pointing down. The six-helicopter packet lifted off at once and tracked towards the target. The helicopters hugged the valleys, sitting below the ridge lines. I sat on the edge of the open door, looking at my mates in a Black Hawk beside us; we were close enough to see their faces. I admired them as we flew, heavy machine guns, rifles, men's legs and sniper weapons bristling from the sides of the aircraft. Two Apaches pursued us like wasps, their black shadows flitting across the mountains. It was a broad daylight raid: we were heading deep into enemy territory to capture a major commander. He had a team with him and was unlikely to volunteer to be arrested.

I was holding a Maximi machine gun, a belt-fed 7.62 mm gun that the auctioneer had lent me for the mission. 'Take it, fucko, it's a beast!' I had a backpack with 800 rounds in it. It was so heavy that the pack straps squeaked when I stood up, and I could feel the tips of my fingers tingling under the strain. I had a World War I metal gun oil bottle in my trouser pocket; if we saw heavy shooting, I could put plenty of oil in the gun. I was packing for a full day of work.

The helicopters were rolling in for final approach. My stomach turned as the nose of the Black Hawk tilted forward and our speed doubled in a few seconds. Warm wind was buffeting through the open doors. The ground became a blur.

A team leader with headphones on held up two fingers to the team. Everyone mouthed, 'Two minutes,' and unclipped safety strops from the mounted D-rings. I felt my mouth dry up a bit as we popped over the ridge line and the village came into view, a dark green streak of vegetation with a shallow, pebbled river running through it. I still shrank at the sight of rivers and corn-fields. The rest was a red dirt landscape, much like the Pilbara, where I grew up.

The team commander held up two fingers, crossed, and shouted, 'Thirty seconds,' as he unclipped the cable from his earphones that connected him to the helicopter. Everyone shouted, 'Thirty seconds'. People shuffled into position, freeing weapons from their legs. Last adjustments were made by nervous men, checking antennas to avoid snags, flexing fingers, checking safeties. Beige mud buildings dotted the landscape and I could see men in light blue robes and prayer caps running between them. They were in a hurry. I felt a hot ball in my guts when I saw the men running. Goats and sheep retreated to the corners of their pens.

My heart rate was climbing, chest tightening. I maintained a neutral mask, though – you had to keep fear, and the impression of it, at bay. Panic is contagious.

The gravity pinned us to the floor like a slowing elevator, and we landed in a dusty brown-out. We jumped from the helicopter and ran; I felt like I was floating. The feeling in my legs was gone, and I felt only a jolt in my hips and chest cavity when my feet struck land. My weapon was on my shoulder and aiming forward. I looked over the sights and made sure I could see the tip of the barrel so I could shoot without aiming if I had to. I squinted to keep the whipping sand and dust out of my eyes.

We each ran towards the closest mud compound, the walls towering over us, mammoth compared to our top-down view. I propped in the gap at the compound entrance, and dropped to the hard-packed mud of the walkway. I extended the bipod legs of the gun, flipped up the shoulder mount and looked down the long alley. With the safety off, and my finger on the trigger, I stared over the sights, waiting. I knew what I would see would be a flash, 20 per cent of a man, a metal weapon, ready to fire. I would have a microsecond to respond. My world became the alley and the doorways that led into it.

The man kneeling behind me had put his foot in contact with my thigh. I knew my back was covered, another barrel pointing out at the rest of the battlefield. No words were exchanged, just a light physical touch to indicate presence. My heavy pack was pushing my head forward and I could feel my body still tingling from the exertion.

'Waler.' I knew from the footsteps behind me it was a command to stand up. He was a trooper, technically junior, but the rank did not matter. I stood and turned, barrel down, and another man was standing beside me, rifle up, covering the alley. He had uttered the command. He stepped to the side in one motion, keeping his sight picture and barrel up. I walked past him and saw the team was collapsing back towards a compound of interest. He stepped back and knelt in my spot, placing his leg against the man behind me. I stopped and covered an open field nearby, where my weapon could be used to much greater effect. An alleyway can be covered with a rifle, so the team leader had put me in a spot to get full use of a belt-fed machine gun.

We took the prisoners, and then stood up and swept towards the river. The fruit groves were surrounded by terraced mud fields and we pushed forward to cover the deep washout of a river. In the river bed that ran alongside a mud wall, one bloke motioned towards a blanket on the ground. He checked for booby traps then pulled it back to reveal an AK-47 with a canvas chest rig, standard for Taliban soldiers. The retreating men had left it there to fall back to. I covered the river with my machine gun, the sweat dripping from my forehead onto my clear ballistic glasses. I could hear my heart pounding. I kept my mouth open a fraction and listened.

The walkie-talkie came to life reporting that the enemy had

an ambush in place and were very close to us. The men on the walkie-talkie were whispering. I believed them.

Over the next few hours we gathered more prisoners, then it was time to head back to the landing zone.

This was the dangerous part. Getting there and landing, even fighting, was not always the hard part. The extraction: that got dangerous. We would be collected in two lifts of two helicopters. When the first lift went, the enemy would try to decimate the now-halved force.

The Apaches found some work. They hated going home with missiles in the rack, and after spotting communicators on the high ground, they swept in and unleashed a barrage of rocket fire on a hill right beside us. The noise was deafening and I flinched at the explosions, a familiar sound from three years earlier.

The birds landed and we marched the prisoners through a red dust storm and into the Black Hawks. They were blindfolded, hands bound in front with black cable ties, urine and faeces staining their garbs. The attack dogs yelped and butted their snouts against the trembling prisoners, sniffing and snapping at them.

I was already seated when a prisoner – a slight adolescent – was shoved under my feet. His whole body shook on the floor of the helicopter. His black flip-flop had fallen to the ground at the skid of the aircraft. I could see it tumbling away into the dust storm. I imagined how the prisoner must feel as the engine revs boosted and our stomachs dropped during the ascent, warm air blasting through the open doors. This would be his first ride in a helicopter, I assumed.

Some soldiers stomped on the prisoners' bodies and limbs a couple of times, hard, as the helicopter began its ascent. This was not to assert dominance, but simply a quest for more leg room.

After we had landed and processed the prisoners, I was glad we had survived that op with no casualties. I thought about the prisoners. Most would be farmers recruited by the Taliban.

'You look after those people,' I remembered my mum saying when I was young; she was talking about those less fortunate than us. I could still picture Mum in her dressing-gown with morning hair, clapping as I rode my skateboard for the first time as a kid: 'Look, Mum, look at me!'

Look at us now, Mum. Look at us.

The good war was turning bad. Like a team losing in a footy match, if we couldn't win it, we would make life hell for our opponents. I never did anything, nor did I directly see anything worse done to Afghan civilians than rough handling as prisoners, and a kid with some blast injuries. But my disregard for their humanity, even in a small way like this, was one example of diminishing moral standards.

I survived the trip – physically, at least.

It never occurred to me then that you could come home intact and upright, but still be damaged. I truly felt like I was losing part of myself the longer I stayed in Afghanistan.

23

THREE STARS

By the end of the trip, I had met an Aussie girl from an aid organisation. A pretty blonde with a runner's body, I had struck up a conversation with Joanne – known to everyone as Jo – at Windmills, the Dutch cafe at Camp Russell, as we waited to order lattes with burnt milk and stale coffee grinds. By the end of the trip, we had made plans to meet in Paris. We wanted some more privacy to get to know each other, and she was fluent in French, so I knew it would be a magical trip. I finished our final job, heart in my throat the whole time. I knew it would be the last time I would be in the field in Afghanistan, possibly ever. I was never coming back.

Jo left for Paris a few days ahead me. I hopped onto a strategic air flight to Dubai, sitting in business class. Nobody laughed or smiled or chatted with the Portuguese hostesses. We all had our headsets on, lost in our own thoughts. Next to me was a young psychologist who had joined the army as a captain. She wanted to know all about my trip. I spoke in vague terms for the most part, but she knew I was with the SOTG.

She considered me for a moment. 'Do you want a Xanax? I have heaps on me.' She pointed at her backpack on the floor.

'Nah, thanks,' I said. I was puzzled. Had she just offered me prescription medicine? I had chosen not to take medication when I was depressed after my first trip. I wasn't suicidal, I reasoned, and I was terrified they would inhibit my ability to function properly. Protecting my dream job was way more important to me than alleviating some suffering. It was common knowledge by this point that some soldiers were displaying symptoms of burnout, in some cases trauma. Soldiers were excellent at masking the symptoms – I know I was. I would do anything to keep my job. It was my identity. We were fraying, though, and the senior leadership knew it; it was being reported to them by psychologists debriefing our troops. My guess is that army leadership hoped we could hold it together a bit longer, until the war was over. One of the unit medical officers told me the unit regularly ran out of sleeping pills, and they were ordered in bulk.

Jo and I sat at a pavement cafe, the sort that has cane chairs and white tablecloths. The waiter wore a black vest and was very polite. I ordered onion soup and a large glass of sparkling mineral water. I sipped it and stared at the Parisians walking past. My mind was still parked in the mud-walled alleyways of a village in Kandahar. My forearms were tanned and hard and strong from holding a rifle and cleaning weapons. I wore a pair of jeans and an olive t-shirt. Berets, scarves and manicured facial hair was the order of the day in Paris. I held Jo's hand, and it seemed foreign. Her fingers were soft and cool, and as she rubbed the back of my hand it felt very soothing.

'I'm taking you out tonight,' said Jo, 'so you'd better dress up.' She gave me a promising smile.

'I'll need some new clothes – this is all I have.' I hadn't exactly packed for Paris when I left Perth for Afghanistan.

We walked to a store and I bought a blue-and-white-checked

shirt, grey jeans, and a pair of black Converse high-top sneakers. Jo thanked the sales assistant in fluent French.

That night we walked down a pavement lined with ornate streetlamps that had lit the boulevards since the guillotines had clunked on the Place de la Concorde, and entered an intimate, dimly lit restaurant with eight small tables, each illuminated by a single lamp casting a small disc of light over the starched white tablecloth. We followed the maître d' over plush carpet. Before I knew it, I was perched in a velvet-upholstered chair with a napkin draped across my lap.

I could feel my face warming. I could hardly make out my surrounds, but I could sense movement in the shadows. As my eyes adjusted, I was aware of the occasional pair of hands in the darkness, and I heard murmurs, but I could not see anyone.

'Good?' Jo asked. She was happy; when we were back in Afghanistan she had dreamed of the two of us coming to this restaurant together. It had three Michelin stars.

'Amazing,' I said. My back felt very exposed. I could hear movement behind me but I could not turn to see who it was.

Jo ordered the degustation menu in French, and we sipped wine as an array of small but luxurious dishes was brought out. When our plates were cleared, a hand would appear under the light with a metal object that looked like a cut-throat razor. The waiter used it to scrape the crumbs from the stiff, white tablecloth. The hand and its owner would then melt into the darkness without a whisper.

The final dish was an avocado sorbet that was a perfect balance of savoury and sweet. Although the dishes had been miniscule, I was stuffed; I wasn't used to such rich food. At one point I was struck by the realisation that while I was here eating truffles, the rest of the squadron would be waiting for the next job. Browny had been buried by his parents in the Karrakatta Cemetery. I sat, weaponless and without consequence. I was nowhere at all.

I swam out of my funk after a question or two from Jo. She understood how long it took to return from a trip in the mental sense. We sipped a dessert wine, and after a while I stopped caring about the fact that I didn't have my back to the wall. When the bill arrived on a silver platter, Jo paid immediately with a credit card. I protested and stole a look at the receipt. It was 610 euros. Jo signed the bill without hesitating and thanked the waiter in French. I thought her accent was pretty hot.

'Thank you,' I said to her. I meant it. I was very, very grateful. No-one had ever done such a thing for me and I really appreciated it.

We spent a few more days in Paris. We slept late most mornings, and in the afternoons we walked along the Seine wearing scarves and jackets against the crisp autumn air, Jo pointing out all the landmarks. We stopped on the Pont des Arts and I looked at the mass of padlocks attached to the railings, each one symbolising a couple in love.

I had been missing love for years, leaning on my mates instead. I knew I would not love anybody until I had recovered from Afghanistan – the walls I had built around myself were too vast by then.

Jo and I both moved to Canberra in the dry summer of 2011. I had agreed to take a job at Duntroon as an instructor, going full circle to where my career began. After attacking my own troops as a cadet, dropping grenades and ruining ambushes, the army decided it made perfect sense for me to guide junior officers. Driving through the city in my LandCruiser, I couldn't help but notice the sterile buildings and empty roads. It was a soulless city, and I'd hated the four years I'd lived there at ADFA and RMC after the beauty of the Western Australian coast.

I stopped at a zebra crossing in Braddon and watched in disgust as a flock of office workers waddled across the road to the cafes on their lunchtime breaks. I fixed on one man in particular with bulging neck rolls and broad flanks, his tie fluttering in the breeze.

'Look at these fuckin' lemons,' I muttered, using the standard SAS insult.

I was in a foul mood. Before leaving Perth I had watched the annual Stirrers Parade at Campbell Barracks. Normally a fun affair, it was now being used to settle scores by some of the soldiers running the show. Pete, an exacting and disciplined officer, had been nominated for 'Cock of the Year'. Pete had rightly tried to correct a culture where in his view some soldiers were wielding too much negative influence. It would have been a terrible way to end his two years working his arse off for 1 Squadron. I was starting to question whether the Defence Force was serious about its lawful obligation to ensure the wellbeing of its employees outside of war.

I had two years in Canberra to think about what more I was going to offer Defence.

Arriving at my apartment in Kingston, we unloaded the car. Jo had rented an apartment on the other side of the road; I didn't want to move in with her immediately.

The only good thing about being in Canberra was that Stano, my mate from my 2007 trip to Afghanistan, was here too. He was single, so I knew I could rely on him for plenty of support.

My new job in Canberra would mean leading a staff of twenty or so officers as we prepared hundreds of cadets to assume command of their platoons. The curriculum would include drills and lectures, assessment of tactical exercises and mentoring troops. I didn't give one shit about the curriculum; all I wanted was to get them in the field so they could make their mistakes now, and not in combat. When you trained one platoon commander, it directly affected the lives of 30 soldiers down the track, so the stakes were high.

I was burned out, though. I could barely wake up in time for work most days. I felt like this posting might be a crossroads for me.

24

SCORPIONS

My apartment was brand new, with white walls and fresh carpet. If I had to live in Canberra, at least I could stay in a great apartment. As I hung framed pictures of my mates, I thought about the last rotation. Ten Aussies had died in the space of three months in 2010 – in helicopter crashes, blown up by mines, shot by their Afghan partners or, like Browny, shot by the enemy. There seemed to be no end in sight. I was glad to be out of it.

My phone rang.

'Hello? Is that Walesy?' It was a senior officer from the SAS. I never got social calls from him. He asked about Canberra and my last tour, as I waited for what I guessed would be an ask of some sort.

'Do you want to come back to the unit at the end of the year? You'll be able to lead a squadron,' he said.

'Yeah, which squadron?' I asked. Despite my exhaustion, I was interested. It was a real job: I could lead a 90-strong sabre squadron with a decade of combat experience. I had to keep growing in my role as an SAS officer, and this was the only logical step to promotion. But I had already achieved what I said I would: I'd led troops in war.

'It will be a support squadron just for the first year, then you'll compete to go to a sabre squadron.'

I lost interest; I didn't want a support squadron. 'Ah . . . I'm not so keen on that idea,' I said.

There was a pause, then: 'I would recommend taking this, if I were you.' I detected the finest trace of an order. 'Have a think about it.'

I called him back the next day. 'Yeah, I'd rather wait for a sabre squadron,' I said. 'I don't mind doing two years here.'

'Okay, no worries. So, for your second year in Canberra, we'll need you in the J5 position.'

'Yeah . . . I don't know about that,' I responded, even though this amounted to disobeying an order. The J5 slot was a tough position. It was interesting work, planning future operations for the whole of Special Ops, but it would mean long, long hours and a commute out to a paddock in a place called Bungendore, where someone had plopped the high-tech Special Ops headquarters building in an open field within a marginal political seat.

The colonel's response was crisp and direct. 'It's a service need.' In other words, it was an order. 'Service need' was a phrase rolled out when posting someone to a shit spot.

'It's a great opportunity,' he continued. 'I don't know what it will mean for your career if you don't take it.' This was tantamount to a veiled threat. It was clear this was a turd they were trying to jazz up with a garnish of fresh parsley.

If things were not going to progress on my terms, I decided, I would have to take control of my next steps.

The next day, a military police colonel called me. She was responsible for officer staffing positions.

'Hi, Mark, so it looks like in 2011 you'll have the chance to go to the J5 position – that's a good opportunity for you to compete for a sub-unit command position.'

'Yeah, I don't think I want to do it,' I said.

'Well, it's a service need, so it has to be filled,' she replied.

'I understand, but I don't want to go to the J5 slot.'

'Okay, but it's a service need, so you'll have to accept it.'

'Yup, I know. I'm not going to the J5 slot.'

And so it went.

I said no to the position. I would stay at Duntroon for twelve more months while I figured out what to do with my life.

In my new job as the lead officer at the famed training academy, Duntroon, I would be the visible face of the army to some trainee officers. During my time, the role was filled by the dashing SAS captain who was a Buzz Lightyear look-alike – everyone wanted to be like him, and he was responsible for a bunch of officers joining the SAS later. I was taking over from my mate Billy, a model officer: this was a four-year deep recruitment strategy for the SAS.

The problem for me: I was hardly a role model. I was suffering a deep fatigue. A couple of hours of work a day was all I could manage. And this town was not my favourite place. I agreed with travel writer Bill Bryson: 'Canberra: why wait for death?'

Stano and I spent the winter weekday evenings parked on my couch, watching *Mad Men* and drinking Old Fashioneds. One morning I drove to work to lead a tabletop exercise with cadets – I'm certain I was still drunk. I wore Ray-Bans to hide my red eyes. Not my finest hour as an instructor.

During a field exercise, I was in combat gear, storming a room with cadets – I grabbed a captured soldier around the neck with a bit more force than I meant to. I could tell from his dinner plate eyes that he was afraid. There was a simmering violence in me; I could summon it easily. The experience of the last few trips was smouldering away – it was hard to shake it off and move on.

An army colonel seconded to a Prime Minister and Cabinet position gave a presentation to my staff. He wore a boxy grey suit and spoke with great confidence about Australian policy in Afghanistan.

'Australian contributions to Afghanistan have been ongoing and the coalition is driving towards consolidating the "surge" gains.' He went through a list of gains in the government and indigenous forces, and talked us through the withdrawal plan. As he meandered along, I realised he had no idea how badly the war was going.

I put my hand up. 'What's Australia's strategy in Afghanistan?' I asked. I was looking at the colonel, but I felt several sets of eyes on me as those in the front seats turned.

'Well, I'm glad you asked.' A slight edge crept into his voice. 'The aim is to produce a stable government and to prevent a sanctuary for terrorism – that's why we're there.'

I had my comeback ready. 'So we ejected al-Qaeda from the country in 2002, and there have been twenty to forty al-Qaeda fighters in country ever since. So why are we still there?'

Everyone was looking at the colonel now, awaiting his response.

'Well, our presence as an ally is important. Our relationship with the US. They're both important reasons . . .' He trailed off, sounding less assured.

I knew our strategic aims in Afghanistan had been fulfilled since about 2005: eject al-Qaeda and hand over to the government. Now we were nation building, and it was a waste of time. You didn't need a PhD in military strategy to know that

Afghanistan was not a fight you could win unless you wanted to spend a generation there.

Meanwhile, I knew more people would die in an operation that had no strategic clarity.

That night, Stano came to my place and we looked at some snaps from the Deh Rawood battle and reminisced about the war. A photo came up of Stano and me standing on a barren hilltop the day I'd written in my diary that it was good to *PUNISH THOSE CUNTS*. A lifetime had passed since then, yet I still had not processed the intensity of that struggle. I had hardened myself to suffering. When I wrote those words, I wanted to live, and I wanted the rest of my team to live as well.

I told Stano that I wanted to leave the military. He was the only one I had ever told, and the only one I would trust with the information. Of all people, I knew he would understand my hesitation about remaining in the army. Stano was a contrarian. During his selection course in 2003, the instructors had asked him his views on the Iraq War. Instead of being intimidated, he chewed them out for supporting the invasion, insisting the campaign was unjust and illegal. Some of the men in the room had fought in the Western Desert that same year. He was as incendiary as his hair was red, and I loved him. We had been inseparable for years.

'I think I want to leave, mate,' I said.

Stano sipped his favourite Laphroaig whisky and thought for a long time. 'Have you heard the story about the scorpion and the frog?'

I hadn't.

'A scorpion is standing by the edge of a river with a frog. He needs to get across, but he can't swim. "Can you carry me over?" he asks the frog. The frog says, "No way, you're a scorpion – you'll sting me." The scorpion says, "Nah, I won't do that – we'd both drown!" So the frog agrees to carry him. Halfway across the river, the scorpion stings the frog, and they both start sinking beneath the water. The frog was like, "Why did you do that?!" The scorpion replies: "I couldn't help it. It's in my nature."'

I laughed. 'That's good.' I had known him fifteen years and he still pulled out the occasional gem.

'We're soldiers,' Stano reminded me. 'That's us.'

The following evening I received another call from the MP colonel. She offered me an even worse position than the J5 one. I could see what was happening: I was being punished by the careers managers. I declined the offer.

As I hung up, I saw I had four missed calls from Jo. It wasn't only my career that was suffering; I was missing in action in my relationship. It was grey and bleak outside, the trees bare. I decided to go for a run along the edge of Lake Burley Griffin. As I ran in the biting cold wind, I kept seeing a city skyline, a really dazzling one. I felt a bit lost, like I did not belong in the army, but I did not know where else to go or how to break out. I remembered the book I had read in the command post about the Harvard Business School, recalling that it had sounded like the best fun you could have as an adult.

It was the United States – that was the skyline I'd been picturing. And then I knew: I would not try to change the game; I would change the field of play entirely.

25

EXILE

I WAS 32 YEARS OLD. IF I STAYED IN THE ARMY, I HAD A DECENT idea of where that could lead. After Afghanistan, I was not even certain I could survive a second war. I remembered an afternoon sitting with Angus Campbell in Timor, when we were discussing the potential of conflict in the world. 'War brings nothing but misery,' he'd cautioned. I'd thought at the time it might be true. After Afghanistan, I *knew* it was true. War brings many things, but misery first and foremost.

If I was going to jump from Special Ops, it had to be to a top-tier school – the Ivy League. I only knew the Ivy League from the movies; I had no idea what it meant, only that it was highly regarded. And I knew the US was the place to be. I'd heard the saying: If you want to be a gladiator, you have to go to Rome. The US was ground zero for capitalism. Wall Street and Silicon Valley, Nike and Apple, Amazon and SpaceX: the Yanks loved to swing for the bleachers. Industry titans were 'Made in the USA'. The Americans celebrated endeavour and ambition, and I knew that my service would be respected. I would have extra cachet in any job hunt, and being fresh out of military service would be a distinctive advantage when I applied to business school.

When I thought of the US, all I could see was a majestic city skyline. Black with neon trim, and the sparkle of nightlife and aspiration. People excited about the future. Half a million American workers had chipped away for ten years to put a man on the moon, and you couldn't do that with a weak, negative mindset.

The idea took root that day and immediately formed a critical mass. The hours evaporated as I researched the best schools, looking for my ticket out of the Canberra winters that would haunt my future in the army. That city skyline was important, so it had to be a good city. And it had to be Ivy League, because after a career in the special forces, I knew I wanted to be surrounded only by the best. This wasn't just ego – you swam harder around the big sharks.

I narrowed it down to Harvard in Boston, Stanford in the Bay Area and the Wharton School in Philadelphia. The three were known as 'the Holy Trinity', consistently rated as the top three institutions for an MBA. The average applicant had a 10 per cent chance of success – not dissimilar to SAS selection – and it would cost me thousands of dollars and take years of work to secure a spot.

The application process was elaborate. For each school I applied to, I had to pay a US$250 fee, fill out a long sequence of forms, complete a standardised test, write three specialised essays, gather professional references, undergo a police check and fact verification, and attend an interview. And I only had four months in which to get it all done or I'd miss the application window.

The clock was ticking.

The biggest hurdle was the Graduate Management Admission Test – the GMAT. It was used to rank the intellectual horsepower of each candidate or, officially, 'to assess certain analytical, writing, quantitative, verbal, and reading skills in written English for use in admission to a graduate management program, such as an MBA program'. It was a four-hour mental marathon, and the stakes were bloody high. The GMAT was scored out of 800, but I needed to land inside the range of applicants at these top three business schools, which was 650 to 790. It would be fucking hard to do that well. It would take a lot of study, and a lot of trial and error.

In May 2011, I took the bus to Sydney to do the GMAT test online, without study. I got 570, which was enough to start with. I went home and bought a solid carpenter's desk, added a computer monitor, and bought a foot-high stack of books on GMAT exercises. I called my desk the command post, and every night after work until the early morning, I pursued the extra 80 points I would need to get a GMAT score of 650.

The questions were mind-bending, and drew on none of the fast and loose decision-making I had used as a troop commander. Take the question on data sufficiency; that is, could a problem be solved if you were only given a couple of pieces of information. For example:

Of the 75 houses in a certain community, 48 have a patio. How many of the houses in the community have a swimming pool?

1. *38 of the houses in the community have a patio but do not have a swimming pool.*
2. *The number of houses in the community that have a patio and a swimming pool is equal to the number of houses in the community that have neither a swimming pool nor a patio.*
   a) *Statement (1) ALONE is sufficient, but statement (2) alone is not sufficient.*
   b) *Statement (2) ALONE is sufficient, but statement (1) alone is not sufficient.*

c) BOTH statements TOGETHER are sufficient, but NEITHER statement ALONE is sufficient.

d) EACH statement ALONE is sufficient.

e) Statements (1) and (2) TOGETHER are NOT sufficient.

My brain started smoking the minute I read it. As you progress through the question, it becomes obvious that both logic and algebra needed to be applied. The question was how many houses in the community had a swimming pool. That was *x*. We were then supplied with two overlapping pieces of information that might tell us what *x* was, if we could turn it into an algebraic equation. I couldn't do that initially. I could not see it as a maths problem. My instinct said: *Well, I guess it's about 30-ish, based on the two statements.*

The military operated in extreme uncertainty, so mathematical problem-solving was new to me. Gradually, I learned to play the probabilities. I had to learn to 'triage' my answers, allowing myself only one or two minutes to respond. Calculators were not allowed in the test, so I downloaded a year three video tutorial on how to do long division. I was going back to primary school.

It was the first of many lessons in humility I would learn on this path to a new career.

After a month of study, I took a bus to Sydney to do my second GMAT test. This time I got 600. I was short at least 50 points. That was my hurdle. If I got over that, I knew the rest of my application would be ready.

I studied even harder, and a month later I took the test for a third time. At the end, the computer spat my score out: 530. I had gone backwards by over 10 per cent!

On the bus back to Canberra, the negative self-talk started up: *Maybe I'm not cut out for this. Maybe I just can't learn this stuff.* I had already failed to meet my target on three tests, and

I was almost out of time. Business schools have three rounds of intakes each year. You wanted to be in the first or second round. The third round was just filling the last few seats. To add to the mess, I would need to complete three essays and secure three recommendations for business school.

I decided I would take the test at the latest possible moment: 30 November 2011.

Jo came over to my apartment and I made her chicken strips with garlic and red chilli and a salad. As we ate, I complained a bit about feeling ragged from study.

'I know a good psych here. You want me to reach out to him? He's a neuroscientist, too.'

It was a kind offer, and I thanked her.

We talked over my plan to enter business school in the US.

'If you get in, I could think about coming too,' she suggested. 'I could probably get an aid position there.'

I didn't respond.

She pushed her plate away and looked at me. I think she knew what I wanted.

I wanted to exile myself, to leave behind any trace of my old life – and that included her. It was selfish, but I wanted to begin my new life alone. I knew that if I made it, I would be celebrating having escaped with my life intact. For the two of us, that meant it was over.

I visited the neuroscientist that Jo recommended. A laid-back Queenslander, he had helped intelligence officers live double lives and treated trauma as well. He listened as I described my experiences and symptoms, including sleeplessness and constant recollections of the fighting, then he jumped to his feet, went to the whiteboard and drew a sketch of a brain.

'This is your amygdala.' He circled a small patch near the spinal column. 'This is an ancient, reptilian part of your brain that controls fight or flight responses. It keeps you alive when you face danger.' He tapped it with his pen. 'You have been overusing this for years, or at least the time you have been in combat. So, you're more lizard than human at the moment.'

I laughed, interested.

'That's why you can't concentrate and you're apathetic,' he continued. 'Trauma and depression do that to humans. We evolved these responses over time. Don't worry about the recurring memories. When people experience trauma, as you have, that experience is hardwired.' He tapped his temple as he sat. 'It's stored as a DVD-quality image and can be recalled at any time. The quality does not degrade with time.'

Now he really had my attention.

He repeated: 'DVD-quality images that can be recalled any time. That's how you remember what can kill you. This is useful for our species. It's a reminder of what you need to avoid to stay alive.' He pointed at his head again. 'You are not crazy – the intrusive thoughts mean your brain is working as it should. I know it doesn't feel great, but it's designed to save your life.'

I exhaled when he said this, feeling a grip release from my neck and chest. It was the first time in three years that I'd felt I was not on the verge of madness.

'This,' he went on, pointing at his upper temple, 'is your prefrontal cortex. It is responsible for cognitive functioning, problem-solving, decision-making, empathy, rational reasoning and logic. We call it the CEO of your brain. These executive functions have been benched since your life has been under threat. This part of your brain has probably atrophied. But we're gonna rebuild your mind, and I'll show you how.'

The relief was overwhelming: *I'm not mad.*

'You will recover,' he assured me. 'Most people do. It just

takes time. I'm going to get you started with some tips and routines I want you to follow.'

I was sitting on the edge of my chair. This was the best counsellor I'd ever had. He didn't give a shit about my feelings; he just wanted to explain the science and talk about solutions.

'First: you're gonna exercise more. Keep it at 120 minutes vigorous training each week. You do CrossFit? Okay, good. Keep it up. That will improve cognition, and your mood. You'll concentrate better too.

'Second: you're gonna eat better. Leafy greens, lean meats, fruits etc. Keep processed foods to a minimum and cut out the sugar. Also, drink less. How much do you drink?'

'Too much,' I admitted.

He shook his head. 'Reduce it right down. That will improve the symptoms of depression too.

'Third: you're gonna rest more. Seven to nine hours a night, no excuses. I want you to follow a bedtime routine. Thirty minutes before bed, write in a diary, just to process your day. Then I want you to stretch for five minutes, have a shower, and do some breathing exercises sitting on your bed – ten breaths maybe. Then I want you to read a novel for a bit. Something mindless. No devices. Then you go to bed. The bedroom is for sleeping and sex. Nothing more. You can have a drink at night, too, if you want – just one.'

I was taking notes, loving this approach.

'Try a G&T,' he advised. 'A white spirit is the go. Nice and clean.'

I left feeling invigorated. I had a plan.

I looked for any edge in study – it was 'advantage in the aggregate'. Like special ops training, I knew that a hundred small disciplines, well executed, compounded to a game-changing advantage. I read that walnuts improved short-term memory and blueberries increased cognition, so I ate both of them by the kilo. I trained harder at CrossFit. I ran up Mount Ainslie every other day, time trialling my sessions. I slept as much as I could to reinforce short-term memory of my study. I stopped drinking on school nights. The aggregate effect was improved retention of knowledge. I was getting faster and more accurate at problem sets.

I had one last chance at the GMAT before my application window would close. One month. I had one month, and it was my last roll of the dice. I signed up for an online GMAT class that had homework and sat once a week during the day. I left work early, telling my boss at Duntroon I had medical appointments. I took my books to cafes. One night, I sat in a fish-and-chip shop working away at problem sets under time limits. A work colleague walked in, a tall, genial Brit with side-burns and easily the biggest shitbox of a car on the base.

'What the hell are you doing in here, Walesy?' he asked.

I put my pencil down. 'Studying for a test, mate. I'm trying to get into business school overseas.'

'Really?' He went up to the counter to order his fish and chips then came back to sit on a stool near me. 'You want to leave?'

'Yup. I think I can do it.' I could tell he was surprised. People don't expect SAS officers at Duntroon to throw away their careers – it's a pathway for a run at the top ranks. But the more I studied for the GMAT, the less I cared about my officer career potential. I had achieved my original goal, set way back in year nine: I'd joined the SAS and gone to war. That didn't mean I had to keep doing it. I still had time for a second act.

I packed my overnight bag and took the bus to Sydney for my fourth and last test. It was late November, summer beckoned. I sat at a cafe and had breakfast while I waited for the test centre to open. As harried office workers with briefcases and smartphones rushed past, I felt a sense of calm wash over me: the same feeling I used to get when all the pre-battle planning was done. I would sit the GMAT in twenty minutes, but the result was already determined. I knew the battle had either been won or lost in the hours I'd spent at my desk over the past twelve months. The test was just a formality.

I walked in to the test centre and completed a palm-print recognition test to ensure I was not a fake test taker representing 'Mark Wales' for a small fee. The lure of the Ivy League invited all sorts of illegal innovation. The test administrator gave me a locker key. I walked through a metal detector to enter the test room. The administrator handed me a pen and paper, and I took my seat in the computer booth. One of the other candidates was wearing yellow earplugs to block out the tapping of keyboards. Another glared at me from over the top of the cubicle as I crept past. The kids were deadly focused.

I entered my details and stared at the start screen: *Do you wish to commence GMAT Test?* My hand hovered over the keyboard. I felt fresh and well rested. I was ready. I hit enter, and began. I focused only on the questions and nothing else. It was gruelling, but the hours flew by.

Four hours later I sat exhausted, buzzing. The final question gave me the option to either record or delete the test score permanently. I looked at the question for a full minute to make sure I was clicking the right one. I clicked accept, hoping I had finally achieved my goal of 650.

My score popped up on the screen.

670.

I bounded out of the test centre.

On the long bus ride home to Canberra, I thought about how hard it had been to build my career in the army. Was I sure I wanted to leave it all behind?

Still, I kept seeing those city lights. Once distant, they were now within reach.

After the GMAT, I completed the essays; veterans from the Wharton Business School helped check my rough work. Then it was time to complete the application. Watching the cursor blink on the screen with the form, I felt a spark in me that had been missing for a long, long time. I was excited again.

I hit the submit button, and I waited.

Two weeks later, I was in a Canberra bar, ignoring the phone vibrating in my pocket as I tried to chat up an attractive blonde diplomat. Unsuccessful, I walked back to my apartment, checking my phone as I went. The missed call was from a US number; a telemarketer, no doubt. I was getting ready for bed when I checked my email. My heart stopped when I saw an email with the title: *Congratulations from Wharton!*

> *Dear Mark,*
>
> *I hope this note finds you well. I was hoping to speak with you in person, but was unable to reach you by phone. I'm thrilled to let you know that you've been accepted into the Wharton MBA Program – congratulations! We're excited to offer you a place in our 2012 intake!*

I'd got it.

'YES!' I shouted to no-one. I fell onto my bed with my phone in my hand, and flapped my arms and legs a bit in pure relief. Then I stopped and reread the message, just to soak it in, and to make sure it was not a cruel hoax. The email was gone. I had deleted it somehow when I fell on the bed. I scrolled in cold dread for five long minutes before I found it and was able to reread the words. *Congratulations!* That was all I needed to see.

I'd be discarding a career for this acceptance letter. It was a good trade.

I texted all my mates and started planning a party. I did not tell Jo about it – we had already parted ways.

The move to the US was going to be costly. After fifteen years of service, I was allowed to apply for $1100 in training costs to be covered by Defence. A qualification ticket to become a hairdresser cost over $12,000 at the time. I claimed the expenses for one of my four GMAT tests with that money and planned how I would find the rest.

The US had been smart enough to educate their soldiers after World War II. Over 16 million service personnel had to hang up their uniforms, and walk, hobble or wheel back to civilian life. Worst of all, the recovering fighters lacked purpose. They had been in charge of Sherman tanks on D-day and flown strategic bombers over Japan, saving and taking lives, and now they were stacking shelves in supermarkets. The GI Bill was activated to retrain these soldiers, and to avert another Great Depression – it provided low-cost tuition and housing for returned soldiers. By expanding the education system, it thrust these hard workers into corporations around the country. I would be following in their footsteps. It was an ideal off ramp.

I finished all my jobs in a frenetic last month. A colonel who had served with me in East Timor on my first-ever deployment drank with me at the officers mess with a handful of staff, and was kind enough to officially farewell me from Duntroon. He thanked me for my hard work, and said that even as a 21-year-old I had been 'no talk, all action'. I loved it. I felt proud of myself, and very grateful to him; it was a moving gesture, one I'd never had from a unit before. I did feel a pang of regret at leaving my career – I would never be a six-star general – but I knew it was time.

*

Two mates from the SAS volunteered to come with me out to the airport in Canberra to see me off. We walked to a waiting cab through the fog of a Canberra morning. It was 5 am and the cars lining the road had white frost on their windshields. Denis and Billy helped me shove my bags and surfboard into the boot.

'Where to?' the cabbie asked.

I was about to answer, when Denis shouted: 'The United States of America!'

We all laughed, even the cabbie. For the first time in years, I was very bloody happy.

26

BAREKNUCKLE CAPITAL

IT WAS A STEAMING HOT DAY IN PHILADELPHIA WHEN I stumbled out of the airport bus. I was on Spruce Street in the downtown area, and spruce trees lined the road, a naming convention from a time when literacy was rare. I hauled all my gear to my walk-up single-bedroom apartment and stood in the main room. It was basic, but new and neat. This would be home for the next two years. I could hear a baritone singer rehearsing opera at the studio across the road. Corner stores had craft beer cases in the window displays, and brewed coffee. My first beer in Philly was Dogfish Head Ale. It was a two-mile walk over the Schuylkill River to University City with a thousand other kids in my class. I could see the famous Rocky Steps leading up to the Museum of Art as I walked.

I went to Starbucks and bought an apple slice and a coffee and carried them back to my bare apartment. There I sat on the floor and logged in to my school curriculum. I was 32 years old and it was my first day of school.

I took in the classroom. I had my own printed name plate on my desk, and I sat with 40 other students in a horseshoe, triple projector screens to our front. The professor was centre of the cauldron and pacing the full length of the classroom. He was a rock star faculty member. In his spare time, he was an economics commentator on NBC and CNN and a columnist for the *Wall Street Journal*. He had long grey hair and wore a Hawaiian shirt and sandals. He was Californian, so it seemed right.

'Do you get points for your working out, even if the answer is wrong?' one student asked.

'No! In this class you are either right or you're wrong. There are no points for "trying"' – the professor put this last word in air quotes – 'this is *capitalism*. We are either right or wrong, and at Wharton we're never fuckin' wrong. No points for *trying*.'

The class erupted into cheers. Some bankers with slicked-back hair fist bumped one another. I was slumped in my seat, jetlagged, but this jerked me awake. I was used to stone-faced briefings from the war; emotional statements were akin to blasphemy.

The professor shook his head. '*Trying*,' he repeated. 'Get your communist tail outta here.'

The class cheered even louder.

My classmates were bareknuckle capitalists: financiers, bankers, consultants and marketers from S&P 100 companies. Many had risen through family dynasties. One classmate was a whisky heir; his family bourbon, Templeton Rye, was Al Capone's favourite, and bottles were smuggled to him during his incarceration on Alcatraz. The daughter of the Michael Kors CEO was a classmate, too. With model good looks, she walked into class like she was dressed for the runway. There was a Bollywood actress and the dapper son of the Danish prime minister – he wore chic aviator sunglasses and a silk scarf year-round (even during a 100-metre sprint at the school carnival, which he ran barefoot, the scarf trailing in the wind).

There were kids from all over the world. Chinese, Indian, Canadian, English, Saudi Arabian, Lebanese and Aussies – of which I was one of ten in my class. The military contingent was strong. Each Thursday night was Pub Night. The entire 1000-strong class gathered in a Civil War barracks halls downtown for free keg beer and pizza. At one event I witnessed a Lebanese start-up executive almost come to blows with an Israeli F-16 pilot over Middle East foreign policy.

The veterans club was wild. We had marines, Green Berets, submarine engineers and pilots. I had a close buddy who was an instructor from Top Gun – the school, not the movie – and swore at people when the Maverick quotes landed. Another was a Black Hawk pilot; quick-witted, he did great impersonations of our teachers. He was from the 160th Special Ops Aviation Regiment – the Night Stalkers. He planned to head back to Texas to join an oil company. Navy SEALs from the year above filled me in on all the traps and trials of the school. The club argued over whether to admit a former CIA analyst, a Steve McQueen look-alike, the issue being whether the CIA was an 'armed force'. He was gay, and also a member of the LGBTIQ+ club. They had a reputation for throwing the best parties, but there was also a pecking order and it irritated the shit out of him. 'If another one of those queens calls me a female name again, I'll fuckin' destroy them,' he said.

The school was diverse, fun and had an unending sense of excitement to it. I bounded out of bed each day. It was the new world I had hoped for. Unlike the army, nobody shouted, cursed, stared at me or was angry. It was welcoming.

Then that little thing called 'academics' started to get very hard.

Wharton was known as a 'quant school': derivative equations, statistics, bundling science, macro and microeconomics calculations. There was a science to business, and Wharton excelled at it. The alumni there included Elon Musk and Warren Buffett.

Class performance was ranked, and if you were in the bottom 10 per cent of results in a core class, like accounting, you were awarded a Lowest Ten, or LT. If you got six of these in your first year, you were sent packing. As a survivor of a small war, this did not worry me. I had got by in fighting; I would figure out the academics as I went.

I blanched when I saw my results for the first semester. I'd got five LTs. I'd only scored 37 per cent on the microeconomics exam. The lecturer was concerned. I was humiliated; I felt like a dumbarse. If I repeated that performance, I would lose my place. I'd be going back to Canberra, cap in hand, looking for work.

My results warranted a visit to Maryellen Lamb, the school admissions and careers officer. I needed her help. Maryellen's job was to make sure the best and brightest got into Wharton and graduated to become successful alumni. I was now an impediment to her mission. I'd first met her when I arrived at Wharton and was damn impressed. She was a hair shorter than me, and I am 6 foot 3 inches. She had been a varsity rower. I liked her right away – she was in her mid-40s with bright eyes and an intellect to match. She delivered her sentences in tight, high-energy packets, not an ounce of fat in them. *Economy of words*, we called it in the SAS. She had learned to communicate as a currency trader on Wall Street, where seconds wasted talking could mean the difference between a million-dollar loss or gain.

Maryellen's assistant greeted me at reception and showed me into her office.

'Okay, it looks like you had a rough term,' Maryellen began. 'I saw your Magic exam score.' I winced. MGEC, or 'Magic', was microeconomics, the toughest of quantitative subjects, feared even by the investment bankers. It was a great leveller.

'Look' – she leaned forward in her seat, hands flat on the desk – 'the first semester is hard. Especially for vets. You missed

By my fourth tour of Afghanistan, in 2010, the high tempo of deployments was causing burnout and trauma, but my confidence and capabilities had improved with experience. In this image we are returning from a strike mission, now flying rather than driving to targets as the IED threat increased.

Smiles with Stano. By 2010, deployment grooming trends had gone full circle, with shorter hair back in vogue. Over time the role of the SAS had shifted from long-range reconnaissance to aggressive, time-sensitive strike missions.

Into the storm. I snapped this photo of a soldier standing in a dust storm somewhere near Kandahar province, mid-2010. You could see a lot of surreal things in one day – this was one of them.

At the range at Camp Russell. By 2010 my entire life's work was in Afghanistan – my girlfriend lived there, all my mates were there. When I returned to Perth, all I wanted to do was head back. My family barely saw me.

Heading out on a commandeered motorbike for a shoot on the range. We had all the best toys, vehicles, weapons and jobs – despite the hard times, it was often a boy's dream.

Extracted from a hot landing zone by a US Chinook helicopter. My clear ballistic glasses were practical, but not so fashionable.

Heading out again. Each time I went to Afghanistan I saw new threats, more violence and more killing. Our impact on the country was short, fragile and totally reversible. It was becoming clear our mission was unlikely to be successful by any metric.

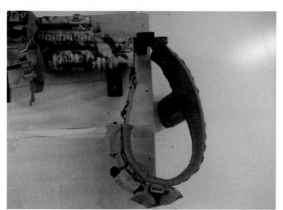

Trooper Jason Brown's pistol belt, my costly $6000 win at the post-wake auction. It was considered tradition to buy parts of a fallen soldier's gear to support the loved ones left behind. That night in August 2010 we raised US$99,000 in cash for his family.

The green belt was the dense vegetated terrain where the farming and irrigation was done, a dramatic contrast to the surrounding mountains and deserts. It was easy for enemy forces to hide, move, attack and conceal weapons in the thick cover. This cornfield was somewhere near Kandahar.

Getting ready for extraction. I was the Squadron XO on this tour, but it was not unusual to fill a position in a team if they were heading out and had a man injured or sick.

Apache attack helicopters were used extensively in the campaign. This one had been firing in support of us during a mission in Kandahar – note one of the Hellfire missiles missing from the pod rack on the stub wing.

This was one of the last jobs I did in Afghanistan. I'm covering a creek line as my mates work in a compound nearby. Creek lines were quick, easy methods of moving through the green belt so they had to be watched closely, despite my posing for a shot.

In 2011 I agreed to take a job at Duntroon as an instructor, going full circle to where my career began. After attacking my own troops as a cadet, dropping grenades and ruining ambushes, the army decided it made perfect sense for me to guide junior officers. I was burned out from my overseas deployments, and the adjustment to life in sterile Canberra proved too challenging. I hatched a plan to make an escape.

In 2012 I began studying an MBA at Wharton, a US Ivy League school in Philadelphia. Wharton was a real dream, and a surprise pivot late in my career. I knew it was a ticket to a new life.

The classroom environment at the Wharton School was full of possibilities, and the staff and people were supportive. Here I am about to talk to my class about my family and my experiences in the military.

In the rush of new friends, faces and a supportive culture, I definitely kept the party going. This may have led to my academic probation after the first semester!

I pulled the gloves on after a long hiatus and started training. It saved me. My grades improved, my focus was better and I was a happier person. I squared off against a US marine, a former MMA pro, in downtown Philly. It was a brawl, the main event and it was livestreamed across the internet.

I retained my 4–0 record. Four losses, no wins.

The debut of Kill Kapture, my 'tough luxury' fashion label. The idea of building the values of special forces into a brand appealed to me. I created a professional leather jacket in the Garment District in New York City and I rolled it out at the Wharton Fashion Charity Show in 2013.

Kill Kapture was targeting a new market segment of men and women who love the culture of high performance teams, especially the military. Here I'm manning a desk at a Philadelphia start-up convention. It was the new purpose I had been looking for.

A sense of purpose won't always pay the bills, so I joined the elite McKinsey & Company. It was a stellar firm, but a crushing workload. Twenty-hour days were not unusual in New York. Here, in 2015, I'm at a client's office, at 10 pm, with mismatched trousers because I had torn my pants getting into a cab.

Consulting for McKinsey involved long absences from home, frequent travel, hotel rooms, long work hours and drinking to make it all feel better. I was grateful to have a job, but the incessant stress reminded me of SAS deployments. This is me on my birthday in the Le Méridien hotel, New York City, 3 November 2015.

Kill Kapture was one idea I could not shake, and as I worked at McKinsey I kept it alive with some content development and photo shoots like this.

Behind the scenes of a Kill Kapture photo shoot in Laredo, Texas. Weapons and helicopters were cheap and easy to get in the Lone Star State.

James 'Mad Dog' Mattis is a celebrated Marine Corps general who has fought in every war since the First Gulf War. We met him at Wharton and he exhorted us to get into the economy and build strong businesses as it would support national security. I convinced him to come to a Kill Kapture photo shoot and we snapped one picture of him wearing a jacket.

Working hard on the beaches of Samoa without much food, in 2017. Quite a pivot from the corporate world of New York. I was not sure what I would find in the game of *Australian Survivor*, but I knew it would be an adventure.

I spotted Samantha Gash on the boat when we first walked onto the set of *Survivor*. She was engaging, smart and good looking. She also could not sit still – ever. Sam and I joined forces in the jungle. The further we went, the more in love we became.

Despite my SAS survival skills, I did not survive the game and I did not win. Or did I?

Sam and I formed a close connection after leaving Samoa. A former lawyer and endurance runner, she had the biggest heart in the world. Before long, we were in love and on a road trip across California. We went back to New York to pack up my apartment and take one last cruise on the Hudson.

My best creation ever – little Harry Locke Wales, born 23 March 2018. Sam and I named him after both our grandfathers, his middle name in memory of Matthew Locke.

Pushed by Sam, I started speaking to corporations about my experiences in the army and the crossover into the business world. I spoke on leadership and teamwork, and this shifted quickly to resilience as people, men especially, related to my story about burnout and mental illness. I got more nervous speaking than I used to in battle.

With Sam and Harry for Anzac Day 2018. Being a father so quickly was a surprise, and it changed me in many ways. Now I had purpose, and the sense of tribe I'd been longing for since leaving the SAS.

Sam and I tied the knot in Victoria in late 2019, bringing together the tribes of the SAS, my original family and my new family.

Dad giving a wedding speech, glad to have me home after all those years away. He has been a present father my whole life.

Jarrad Seng

A rare family gathering as Sam and I wed in regional Victoria. From left: Dan Wales, Steve Wales, me, Sam and Cassandra Gash.

Harry in full flight, taking a walk through the scrub in Mount Dandenong. Some of the old habits of fieldwork never left me: scanning the vegetation for movement or any exposed skin. Eventually I calmed down and learned to enjoy the time with my family.

In the major COVID-19 lockdown of Melbourne in 2020, I wrote about Matt Locke for this book, a promise I had made to his son Keegan in 2007. This is Harry and I sharing a moment in the bunker that Sam and I made to be able to work remotely.

Years of experience have taught me that resilience is investing in yourself and your health, consistently. Keep your eyes and ears peeled for your purpose: it may not shout in your face, it's probably just a whisper in the distance that never seems to leave. Hard times don't last, but you will. It's been a long journey to reach this point, but it's been worth it for the little wisdom I've gained to pass on to my son.

too many classes. You can't get any more LTs. Seriously.' She was pleading with me: *I don't want to kick you out, but if you do that again, I'll do what I have to do.*

I was crestfallen. 'Will I get kicked out?' I asked point blank.

She paused. 'If you don't get your shit together, possibly.'

I felt my stomach turn.

'You're on academic probation now. You need to study – you still have core subjects left over. More than that, show us that you *want* this. We kick people out all the time.' She raised her eyebrows. *Fuck this up and you're next*, was the message. I understood. This was a 'learning moment' at Wharton, which I translated to 'arse-kicking' in military parlance. Maryellen cared a lot about veterans, though, and while her support was conditional, she truly was on my side.

'I know you took a chance on me. I'm sorry.' I was looking at the desk surface. I was upset that I had let her down.

'Submit an academic probation plan to your student life director. And stop chasing girls.' It seemed nothing escaped her, not even our private lives.

I left her office and walked past her assistant without saying goodbye.

I felt two feet smaller than when I had walked in there.

It was my first post-war lesson: respect the field of battle you enter. You might have been good in your old field, but this was a whole new game and I was just a rookie. It was an embarrassing lesson in humility.

27

STILL IN THE FIGHT

MY ACADEMIC PROBATION PLAN WAS TO STUDY MORE AND focus less on extracurricular activities. I thought about what the neuroscientist had advised only a year earlier: eat well, exercise and rest. Instead, I had been eating Taco Bell and peanut M&Ms during exam prep. I was drinking most nights with my mates. I was getting about five hours sleep a night, surrendering my time to the local bars in Philly. I was exhausted and my clothes were getting tighter.

I had heard stories about the famous charity Fight Night held between Wharton business and Penn Law. It was a black-tie fundraiser, and easily the most revered event at Wharton. It was held in the oldest boxing venue in Philadelphia, where *Rocky* was filmed. I knew I had to focus more on my studies, but this felt like an important exception: it was a goal to train for. I needed this. In my academic probation letter I sought permission to train for it.

My request was approved.

I cornered the trainer at a local boxing gym. Matt was a former UFC fighter, who had retired at 27 years old after damaging his back in the ring. His buckled nose and chipped front tooth signalled to me that he was legit. I talked him into training me, opting for one-on-one training over group training, despite the expense. I remembered from East Timor how hurt you can get if you don't commit all the way.

In the winter dawn, I would head away from the pristine sidewalks of Rittenhouse Square, observing how the pavements crumbled the further south I went. Twin sneakers hung from the low-slung powerlines. This was a crack dealer's patch. I knew if I was going to learn how to fight in Rocky's home town, I couldn't train in the clean gyms of the city. I had to head out to where the street kids lived. I walked nine blocks until the razor-wire fencing of Matt's gym came into sight. I loved the rawness of it, and the contrast to the Ivy League college kids only blocks away. This felt real to me.

For months we sparred, danced and skipped in the MMA gym. I paid $600 for the lessons, and Matt was worth every penny. I soon changed shape, easily running the nine blocks and pulling an hour-long session before school started at 9 am. I was faster, fitter and more accurate with my punching. I stopped drinking. I cooked clean meals twice a day in my tiny apartment kitchen. My energy improved and I was studying longer and with greater focus. The prospect of a secret project I would wheel out in a few months time was exciting. The old discipline of soldiering and training came back to me. I welcomed it; I knew I needed it.

Fight Night the year prior had pulled a crowd of 1200 students, most of them cheering for Wharton. I was facing off against a heavyweight opponent for the main event. He was a marine with a Purple Heart, wounded by a roadside bomb in the Al Anbar Governorate in Iraq. He was also a former MMA fighter and had fought professionally. The fight was being promoted as a veteran brawl – Aussie Special Ops vs a US Marine Corps hero. It was unusual to have paired two veterans, but there we were.

The fight was a risk – I could get flogged in front of my mates. But with the renewed focus and health benefits it had brought me, it had already paid off.

'Okay, you're up.' A stern official with a clipboard was pointing at me. The crowd behind him roared as two heavyweights danced on the boxing ring canvas. It was the Wharton Fight Night of 2013, and I was next in the ring.

Fuck, I'm not ready. I was no stranger to the boxing ring – I had three fights in the army, and I had a flawless fighting record of 3–0. Three losses, no wins.

In East Timor an immense corporal had belted me in front of my entire battalion, all of them cheering *against* me. Tonight was different: I had supporters, and almost all of them were drunk.

I surveyed the crew that would walk me to the ring. The veterans club guys were all wearing uniforms. There was a ranger, a marine bearing a Marine Corps standard flag, and a few slouch hats, including a staff member from Duntroon who had come all the way from the West Point Academy to see the fight. I wore my ceremonial jacket and medals for the walk out, to add a bit more theatre. My brother Steve had even flown in to Philly, and he was walking me out with a boxing kangaroo flag.

The crowd started clapping as we emerged from the changing rooms and weaved our way through the crowd to the ring. The room was gritty, a warehouse with a low roof, and a single light hanging over the ring. AC/DC's 'Highway to Hell' reverberated off the ceiling. The referee was waiting by the side of the ropes in a blue shirt with sweat patches, and a skewed bow tie.

We climbed the stairs and as I slipped under the ring ropes I saw the canvas: it was bloody. Like, murder-scene bloody. One of my Italian mates from the rugby team had fought in a late round and near broken his nose. I was the last of eight fights and the crowd was berserk after a night of drinking. Men in black tie with neatly combed hair screamed and whooped. Women in thousand-dollar dresses fist pumped, straps falling from their shoulders.

I took deeper, forced inhalations to slow my mind, a trick I'd learned from combat. Matt, my trainer, yelled the battle plan again as he pulled my gloves on. 'Score in the first, come out hard. Listen for me in the final thirty seconds. Hit and don't get hit. Don't go for the knockout yet. Okay?' He whacked my shoulders. 'Breathe. Relax, man.'

There was a cameraman in my face; he was clinging to the outside ring ropes as he livestreamed the event to thousands of Wharton alumni.

I was ready for this – at least I thought I was, until I saw my opponent. He was dark-skinned with thick triceps and muscled shoulders. A tattoo of a green globe with an eagle perched on it adorned his left shoulder. The crowd hissed. The marine sauntered towards the ring, nodding and smiling at the spectators. He climbed into the ring with ease, throwing a few fast jabs after he stood. He was shorter than me by a full hand, but he was a nugget.

Shit, I thought. It wasn't his size that worried me; it was the relaxed jabs and the smile. He was having a grand old time. He had been a killer once before and this was just a bit of fun.

Matt strapped my headgear down and shoved my mouthguard in. I started hitting my gloves together, palm to fist, forcing my knuckles tight against the leather. A cut man rubbed Vaseline into my nose and cheeks. A few encouraging noises came from the crowd. The referee called us to the centre. The marine stood well inside my personal space. We touched gloves and went back to our corners. Matt tapped my shoulder and told me to relax.

The bell rang.

We danced into the middle of the ring as the crowd screamed. I threw some jabs for ranging. We tacked and stepped and slipped and ranged each other, looking for weaknesses. At one point the marine threw an overhand right that cleared my guard and landed squarely on my forehead. I was rendered dumb for an instant. I could taste a metallic tang in my mouth. The first-round bell rang.

The cut man was kneeling in front of me, working Vaseline Q-tips into my bleeding nostril. He patched a few cuts and rubbed my legs down. I looked over to my opponent. His breathing was shallow and normal. His skin was matt, no sheen of sweat visible. He laughed at something his trainer said.

'Up the work rate – he won that round,' yelled Matt.

'Really?' I asked, incredulous. I'd felt like I was throwing ten punches a second.

'No, up your rate. Ones and twos. Use your range. Watch out for the overhand right.'

I climbed to my feet as the stool and the cut man were swept away. I hadn't been knocked out; winning was possible.

The bell rang. I threw more jabs, face and body shots. The marine threw full right crosses then another wild roundhouse right. I dampened the impact with my forearm, but it rocked me. We started brawling, my hard-earned technique gone. I connected with a right to his forehead as he slipped a punch. I had hurt him. The crowd roared.

The bell rang again. The cut man went to work on my face. Now I could see sweat running in streams off the marine's chest and arms.

'Better!' said Matt. 'It's even. Last round!'

Round 3.

I stepped forward. We touched gloves and commenced swinging. All respectful facades were now gone. I went for a body shot but missed by an arm's length. The ring bounced and heaved as we dodged. The crowd was chanting my name to help me, but I was slowing – my legs were gone and my mobility with them. He was in close, mitigating my reach and stifling me. It was smart – Taliban tactics. We propped in the corner, and he landed a few strong punches in the last seconds of the fight. The bell rang, and we paused for moment, and then embraced. I was relieved. I staggered to the corner. Matt leaned over the ropes to hug me. 'Excellent, man. I think you got it.'

We met in the centre as the referee held both our hands. The marine was announced the winner in a split decision. We shook hands and our respective entourages joined us on the stage.

The marine and I stood in the middle of the ring with our wrists wrapped, talking. I thanked him for agreeing to come out. He complimented me on a blow I'd landed that stung him. 'That rang my bell, homie.' He had a cool Hispanic accent. He told me that he'd started fighting after leaving the Marines. He didn't know what else to do with his life. He missed the excitement of the war. He had a wife and a baby daughter but, after Iraq, fighting was all he knew.

I knew exactly how he felt. I too was done with the war, but I had missed the culture of relentless excellence in the SAS. The striving was an end in itself. It was the constant pursuit of excellence, the discomfort of it, that really drove us.

A month later I finished the semester with a credit average. No more LTs.

I walked back into Maryellen's office and she sprang from behind her desk, beaming, with open arms. 'Great,' she said, hugging me. 'Really great. I was worried for a bit there, but I knew you could do it.'

I was relieved.

I would need to maintain the good habits I had established for myself, because survival would not be enough.

I had two more battles ahead. There was the battle that would begin in fall semester; the battle most important to my wallet and my future: the job hunt. If I got this wrong, I would be going to the unemployment queue.

But the immediate battle was far more personal. I wanted to run my own start-up. This would enable me to apply some of these amorphous concepts I'd learned to a real business. Wharton was a safe place to get started. If I continued with it, it would give me a sort of combat experience of the business kind. There was risk – that was ever present. Yet this next battle wasn't just about adding some credentials to my résumé. I'd had a vision since the war that I wanted to test in the marketplace.

28

MAD DOGS

When I arrived in the US, I had put aside money to buy new clothes for school. After deploying for years, my wardrobe was bare. I wanted a school uniform, edgy and different. A leather jacket was a must: timeless and rugged, they were a single man's essential. I shopped around the heritage brands: Burberry, famous for the World War I trench coat; Belstaff, who made leather jackets for motorbike cops in the UK; Barbour, with its hunting jackets for rich people, with stuff pouches for quail in the back. Problem was, they all sucked. Impractical, not rugged, too shiny, poorly made and not even close to being masculine. I began to realise I disliked most fashion brands. Their marketing values were bizarre, the quality was weak. I finally settled on a Rag & Bone leather jacket. Lambskin, and made in China, it cost $1000. I wanted to see how a thousand-dollar jacket looked and felt.

I knew there was a market for rugged outerwear that wasn't being filled. I toyed with a few brand names as I walked to school. Kill/Capture sprung to mind. That had been our mission profile in Afghanistan. It was a nasty, edgy name, but I loved it, and there was a truth to it. It also had two hard C sounds in the name, which I'd learned was both appealing and easy to remember: brands like Calvin Klein, Michael Kors and Marc Jacobs all capitalised on this.

I emailed Jim, my old mate from the underage brothel escapade, who now happened to be an IT gun. I asked him how to buy domain names. KillKapture.com was available, so he bought it for me and then transferred it over to my name: two errant kids still causing mischief.

To keep costs really low, I would be going direct to the consumer via the internet, cutting out the middle man. There would be no shops, no expensive ads, no inventory. This would allow me to compete on both price and quality in a way that other brands could not, resulting in better value for the consumer.

I paid attention in my new classes, looking for gems of knowledge I could apply to the business. I learned in accounting about 'inventory shrink'. Inventory is valuable, but disappears over time due to spoilage and theft. For Kill Kapture, I would not hold inventory; our products would be made to order.

I completed a case study on Lego. They had been nearly bankrupted when they went overboard expanding their range of block sizes and types. The insight: complexity = cost. I decided to reduce complexity by avoiding seasonal clothes, instead making long-lasting garments. I would use the same fabric, zips and lining for all products, the economy of scale meaning I could buy the raw materials cheaper.

I had learned in marketing that you had to build a strong following with products that were high cost but high priced, aiming for 'top line growth'. That was revenue. Later you could increase your profit by selling higher-margin products to your followers. Eventually, if you did it well enough, you could sell the brand. I decided the pathway to market would be to make the 'hero product' a killer leather jacket, take low margins, and build a trusted base of followers.

The branding should be all storytelling: the nature of war, and soldiers who put their mission, and their team, before themselves. I remembered a moment I'd had in Chora, over-whelmed after battle, wondering how the hell I was ever going to explain this back home. I believed I had found the answer to that: I could celebrate the good things about my old life and make it a business. This was the 'why' behind the brand, and I was excited by it.

The only problem: I had no idea how to actually go about it.

I wrote up a multi-page business plan for Kill Kapture to enter in the school business plan competition. I was keen to see how people would respond.

One of the judges in the contest wrote: *This is horrible. How can you justify a name like this when mass shootings are happening every other day? It's offensive.* Of the eight judges who reviewed Kill Kapture, five of them commented that the name was either mildly or wholly offensive. But I think my financial projections slide was considered the most offensive part of the entry. I showed two lines on a chart that trended upwards and labelled them best case and worst case for revenue, by year. Best case had the business making $43 million within three years. Worst case had us earning a meagre $2 million. At least I was thinking big.

At a time when software and apps were the big money makers in start-ups, apparel was not a category that was attrac-tive to investors. But the market gap when it came to addressing the 'manly men' segment was so big you could send an army division through it. I had second thoughts about the name. It was so acerbic, it could cut out too much of the market. I consulted Pete Winnall, who was now in Sydney doing his MBA and was also considering leaving the army. When I canvassed Kill Kapture with him, he replied in an email:

I think this works against you. It won't get you celebrity endorsements or long-term success. It may initially get you some bad press but it doesn't work. You may also get some extreme groups adopting it because it is so right wing and then your brand is dead.

I was pretty sure he was right. It was aggressive. It went against the rules of branding.

Next I emailed a classmate who was a hotshot in retail branding in NYC. I gave him my pitch, explained why I believed in the name:

I know it defies marketing conventions and is not remotely politically correct, but I keep going back to it. Part of the reason is I hate going with the crowd, and I want something that stands out. This does stand out, but maybe for the wrong reasons.

I asked for his opinion. He didn't respond.

Dismayed, I shelved the idea for then, but I kept the website domain name. The future was still a blank slate, but I could see something exciting in Kill Kapture.

One morning before class, nine members of the veterans club gathered at an upmarket hotel in Philadelphia to meet General James Mattis. The general had attained mythological status in the Marine Corps. Decorated in both Gulf Wars, he was a warrior-scholar with an encyclopaedic knowledge of military history, and the nicknames 'Mad Dog' and 'Call Sign Chaos'. In the Iraq War TV series *Generation Kill*, his character was played by Harrison Ford. As the Central Command general, he was now responsible for two long wars America was fighting in Iraq and Afghanistan. The opportunity to sit at a table with him was a rare treat, organised by a marine whose father had fought under the general in Iraq.

There was a disturbance in the Force, as a compact gentleman with grey hair and an intense but warm expression rounded the corner.

'Good morning, troops!' he said, with the slightest lisp.

These hard veterans were all smiles and tripping over themselves to stand up. I saw one marine officer look down dumbstruck at his open palm after shaking the general's hand.

Mattis poured a black coffee and gave us an update on the wars, including an assessment of which allies were failing to pull their weight and what the future of US security looked like. He was relaxed, but could carve his way through an issue in tight sentences. I'm sure that scriptwriter Aaron Sorkin wrote at least some of his legendary one-liners. It was said that during the Battle of Fallujah he had warned local sheiks, 'I come in peace. I didn't bring artillery. But I'm pleading with you, with tears in my eyes: If you fuck with me, I'll kill you all.'

We were all rapt.

After a while, he shifted the focus to us, now re-entering society as former soldiers. He talked to us about our importance in civilian life.

'You all need to make sure you build good businesses and boost our economy. One of the best forms of national security that we have is the vitality of this economy. Make no mistake. Our security as a great nation is built on our economy. And this little experiment we call America: well, we need you all now even more than ever.'

We were all hanging on the general's words, nodding. We still mattered. We were the new Mad Dogs, and he was telling us: *You are still in the fight.*

For a bunch of veterans missing their old tribes and mourning a loss of purpose, it was the morale boost we needed.

*

That night, I sat in a smoky booth in a midtown bar with three other business school mates. One was Sonia, a stunning Iranian girl with long dark hair and another was an Indian girl, Desai. They were talking about the upcoming school fashion show. It was an exclusive gala, and the attendees would include the CEO of Michael Kors. Sonia, who knew all about Kill Kapture, was urging me to participate. 'Mark, you have to put Kill Kapture in the fashion show!' she insisted.

That struck a nerve. It was unfinished business.

'We can add that,' said Desai, who was one of the organisers. 'A Wharton start-up? Definitely.'

I still had no idea how to make a prototype. I asked the women for their advice.

'I'll send you the details for a designer,' Desai promised. 'Jessy will help you.'

I would also need capital, I realised – about $5000, which was the last of my savings.

'Okay, let me come back to you tomorrow,' I said.

I stormed home, headed to my desk and got to work. I did not stand up until first light, some six hours later. By dawn, I had set up a logo design contest and established a limited liability company in Delaware. I had a trademark on Kill Kapture and had emailed Jessy to help with a jacket design.

By midday, I had missed all my classes. I was too busy reviewing the logos that had been submitted to the contest. There were swords and shields and axes. But one stood out: three silver chevrons pointing to the right, silver on black. It was a heritage tribute to the sergeant's rank. To me, it said: *Keep moving, you're still in the fight.* I accepted it, and paid $300 to the designer.

When I collapsed into bed at 2 pm, I was still wide awake. I had three weeks to make a prototype before the fashion show.

We were going to war again. Kill Kapture was alive, and I was too.

*

I wanted to learn more about the fashion world, so a friend sent me a note about an event I should attend:

> The YJP Fashion Network is hosting our Fall Fashion & Luxury Summit with fashion icon Tommy Hilfiger (Founder and Principal Designer of Tommy Hilfiger) and Harry Slatkin (CEO of Belstaff) on 30 October.

She wrote to me: 'YJP is a Jewish networking event program but I don't think you need to be Jewish to attend. Their events are industry specific and a great opportunity to meet and mingle.'

I pulled on my suit, took the $5 Bolt Bus from Philly to New York, and walked into a room with a platoon's worth of fashionistas, all big hair and flapping hands and glasses and lithe bodies. Tommy Hilfiger took to the stage to talk about his life in fashion and building a $6 billion company. At the end of the show, I had a cocktail with a dapper man in a suit. He was polite and interested in me: 'Where are you from, man? That's a hell of an accent.'

'I'm from Australia, but I'm doing an MBA at Wharton.'

'No way! What the hell are you doin' here?' he asked.

I talked about my idea for a military fashion brand. He loved it. A few more guests drifted over to join us as we chatted. Normally shy, I was now warming up to the conversation. I had convinced myself I had them hooked on my accent and my outstanding idea for a new fashion label. When I finished chatting I noticed the guy frowning at me. I could see he wanted to ask something. He leaned forward: 'Hey – you're not . . . Jewish . . . are you?'

'Oh, no, not at all,' I admitted.

'Ha!' The man nodded to himself. 'Man, how did you get in here? You know this is a Jewish professionals event, right?'

'Yeah, I did know that!' I admitted – though I hadn't realised that I had entered tribal territory without a formal invite.

The dapper guy thought it was unreal; no other New Yorker would dare crash a YJP event as an outsider, yet here was a stray Aussie with good intentions. 'Let's get a Scotch, man.'

So the Jewish fashion tribe in NYC took me out on the town and talked me through the fashion industry. They loved the branding play I was going for.

I took the bus back to Philly with one thought in my head: *This might just be crazy enough to work.*

Every day for the next two weeks I got up at 5 am, poured a coffee and looked at my gear laid out in rows on my coffee table. I had a fully charged iPad, noise-cancelling earphones and a small thermos. As I packed my gear, I realised I had been doing this my whole life and it was a process that worked. Then I got on the bus and headed to the Garment District in New York.

The District was storied. In the 1860s it had supplied uniforms to the Yankee soldiers in the Civil War. Now, it was home to the top fashion labels, designers who had emerged from the Parsons School of Design and the Fashion Institute of Technology. Donna Karan, Ralph Lauren, Oscar de la Renta and Calvin Klein had all earned their battle scars in the industry here.

The manufacturing factory was on the twelfth floor of a pre-war building, and the manufacturer's name was Barry. His rooms were packed with leather jackets and leather pants and scraps of leather. I showed him the prototype designs.

He shook his head. 'This is gonna be hard to make and I have back orders to meet all week.'

'I really, really need this by Friday,' I told him. 'The show is on Saturday night.'

He thought. 'I can do it, but it'll cost extra. Like I said, I gotta lotta work on.'

'I'll pay a thousand dollars,' I said. It was ludicrous. Most places would dodgy it up for $150. But I wanted Barry because I'd heard he was the best leather maker in NYC. He made leather dresses for Beyoncé.

Barry looked at me. 'I'll do it for five hundred. See ya Friday.'

The day before the fashion show I picked up the jacket from Barry and pulled it on. It smelled of cut leather and dye. It fit like body armour. I had made it matt black, minimal, no fruit, streamlined and mean. The silver chevrons gleamed off the collar. It was everything I wanted in a jacket. This was my new uniform. I was 24 hours early, under budget and overexcited.

I held it in my hands the whole bus ride home, precious cargo. I was proud of this pile of leather. I'd swum against the current the whole way, but it was done. That tiny devil on my shoulder that wouldn't let the idea go – I thanked him. I'd almost surrendered the concept.

Years later I read a passage in which Bear Grylls talked about the first time he'd tried and failed to pass the SAS selection course. It had been his dream, and people encouraged him to drop it. Instead, he went back and finished the job. He said, 'Every dream has a birth, a death, and a resurrection.'

The next night, I stood backstage at the fashion show. The crowd was loose, like on Fight Night, but even more agitated because of all the swimwear on show from the models at school. I was nervous, and had overindulged in Jack Daniels beforehand. I was unsteady, but excited. A handler with a clipboard and headset was directing human traffic.

I held on to the banner frames to stay upright. I checked the zip of my jacket and pulled it halfway; it felt amazing still. The handler held his hand up to his ear.

'Okay, stand by, this is your one,' the handler said.

My intro song boomed over the speakers: The Killers, 'All These Things I've Done'. I let the intro riff play for a while then I climbed up to the stage and began to walk, staring hard at the apron at the end of the runway so I did not veer off the stage into the nosebleed seats. My mates howled. Sonia had her fist in the air, shouting. I started to walk offstage, then turned on my heel and strode back to the end of the catwalk, my heart thumping in my chest.

That feeling – pride, I think – had eluded me for a long time.

29

THE HUNT

'So, looking at this table' – the consultant pointed with a manicured finger – 'which product mix will have the best incremental profit margin on the semi-conductor chips once production is scaled?'

A bespectacled man waited for my answer. I felt a creeping heat under my suit. The table he referred to had five columns, twelve rows and a seven-digit number in each. Numbers. Big numbers.

'Well, I can see the product mix along the top, and the scale improvements along each category when I look vertically.' I was playing for time. I scanned the table, looking for patterns. 'In column A, I can see the margins optimise the most out of the five different categories. I would choose the quantities in A. It's about a 10 per cent improvement in margin.'

'Okay, so let's assume we activate this plan.' The bespectacled man was driving the case along. 'What will the incremental profits be over a three-year period? It will cost $25 million to change the factory moulds.'

I scrawled the numbers on my blank sheet of paper as he continued talking.

'In year one, I expect to sell 30 million chips. The net costs will drop 5 per cent a year, and the sales volume will increase by 8 per cent year-on-year for the next three years. Should I take this course of action, or preserve the CAPEX and run the factory as is?'

I had to interpret the next layer of the question. He wanted to know if it was financially viable, with an estimate of the expected return. I rounded the figures up and down, and ran the numbers, multiplying them out. I felt like I was spinning a whole lot of plates at once, and one false move would see me drop the whole lot.

'Okay, the CEO has just walked in – what's your recommendation?'

My time was up.

'I recommend you implement the factory mould change to scale production.' I turned my page to face him so he could see my calculations. I started with the most compelling number. 'So, this will generate eight million dollars in incremental profit over the three-year period.' He was nodding. 'Your risks for the implementation program might be a slow uptake in training for the new moulds, but you can mitigate that by educating the influencers in the company to lead training.' He was nodding still.

Phew. I think I got it.

'Okay – that's wrong,' he said. 'The incremental margin gain in category A was not 10 per cent. That was the cost increase. You read the table wrong. So, if the CEO followed your advice' – he pointed at my calculations – 'it would have been a fifteen-million-dollar loss in year one alone.'

Boom. A mental IED detonated somewhere in my addled brain.

Fuck. Fuckin' SHIT. I had committed the business equivalent of attacking my own fire support troops.

'So that advice alone is not optimal.' He jotted down a few notes as I waited.

I'm done. No McKinsey & Company for me.

'Thanks so much for coming in, it's really great to meet you. I want to thank you for your service, too.' He was a decent man.

I thanked him, left the office and walked into the 34th floor lobby. I stood at the immense glass windows, gazing out. My brain was mush. Two hours of thinking, listening, calculating and trying to look 'high energy'. An introvert, the effort had ruined me. There were four other candidates in the lobby, wearing suits and fidgeting with leather folios. Two hours earlier, the room had been full of buzzing candidates, all class-mates of mine.

McKinsey & Company was a top strategy and management consulting firm. It had a reputation as a tough data-driven company with highly personable consultants. They had the ears of the CEOs of the top companies in the world, and the job spots were coveted. The year prior they'd had 200,000 appli-cants and took fewer than 2000. I had been in the running for a position with 'the Firm', but I doubted I would be coming back now. I'd screwed my chances with a couple of basic errors.

A woman walked me to the elevator and thanked me. She told me to expect a call before 5 pm to let me know if I would head to the second and final round of interviews.

At home, I peeled off the suit and dressed for school in jeans and a Kill Kapture jacket. I pulled my grab bag together: a 16-inch MacBook Pro with an iPad as a back-up – *one is none, two is one* – plus a notebook and a small thermos filled with hot coffee. I slipped my Bose earphones on and cranked some Public Enemy before heading out the door. It was all the kit I needed in this new life: caffeine, music and processing power.

I finished the day with a class in microeconomics – my old nemesis – and walked past the Georgian-style frat houses that lined Locust Walk on the college grounds. Students manned plastic tables with banners, selling tickets to events and protest marches.

My phone rang. 'Hello, Mark?' It was the recruiting head from McKinsey. 'We want to extend an invitation for you to attend the second round of interviews for the Australian office. The interview will be held in New York in October, with the Australian team.'

I was stunned. I thanked her and said I would love to attend.

'Our feedback was that you delivered well in the fit presentations, but we noted a calculation fault in the business case study. Aside from getting the margins incorrect, your calculations were right overall.' She sounded like she was reading aloud from written comments. 'Your logic was sound and you defined the problem clearly, broke your analytics down to support your answer. You also added a clear recommendation to the CEO, which is rare. Often candidates don't want to commit to a course of action. Overall, well done. We'll reach out again soon to arrange second round interviews.'

It seemed the Californian professor was wrong – apparently McKinsey did give points for trying!

This was a surprise. If I landed a spot with the Firm, it would open a lot of doors in the future and give me the skills to run my own business.

I had researched my round two interviewers. One was Geraldine Buckingham; I looked her up on LinkedIn, and almost fell out of my chair: Rhodes Scholar. Emergency room surgeon. Senior partner at McKinsey & Company NYC. McKinsey appeared to be rolling out an Abrams tank to a knife fight. I knew I would be intellectually outmatched, even physically outmatched.

I had expected a battered corporate veteran, but when Geraldine Buckingham strode into the lobby she was genial, bright-eyed and compelling. She welcomed me and led me to the interview room.

'You've had some good experiences from the look of it,' she said, referring to my army service.

We started the business case interview: cheese manufacturing. I had to run the numbers on changing ingredients, improve the quality and find creative uses for excess cheese. I bolstered my energy by nodding, speaking in clipped sentences and using hand gestures. The military valued deadpan communication; this kept teams calm in times of chaos. This habit translated badly to the modern workplace, which valued expression and vigour.

My next interview concerned mining volumes. The Australian office was helping to drive the mining boom back in Western Australia and Queensland.

In my final interview, a junior partner talked me through brewing company operations.

After three hours of interviews I had a dull headache from all the calculation required and the high-energy interactions.

When I was done, the executive assistant thanked me and said I would receive a call by the end of the day. I was amazed. These guys were fast.

I headed downtown to the cobblestoned streets of the Meatpacking District and browsed the fashion stores in the back alleys, researching my future competition.

At 5 pm, my phone rang.

'Hello, is that Mark?' It was the junior partner.

They must be getting their junior people to do the dirty work.

'Mark, it's my great pleasure to extend to you an offer to join McKinsey & Company as an associate in the Australian office.'

I stopped in my tracks.

I thanked him. I over-thanked him. Shock was my overriding emotion.

'Great! Well why don't you go back to your hotel and dress yourself up, and we'll head out for dinner.'

I got in. I actually got in! From being on academic probation after my first semester, eighteen months later I had a job with the Firm. All I had to do now was be charming and professional at the company function that night.

Three hours later I was a slurring mess in front of my new employers. The start of the evening was innocuous enough: we piled into a bar humming with young, good-looking professionals. The women were all in black dresses and blazers, with one or two subtle pieces of jewellery. The men all had combed hair and pressed suits. It felt very exclusive. Was this my new tribe? Could I belong here? I ordered the first of many Old Fashioned cocktails, hoping to find out.

Before the night was through I was stupid drunk, and I had Jonno, the most junior of my interviewers, in a headlock. He escorted me from the function to a cab, propping up his 107-kilogram recruiting error. He asked me where I was staying.

'Holiday Inn,' I said.

He winced. 'That's a disgusting hotel chain. There's tons of them in the city. Which one?'

I had no idea. We stopped at four Holiday Inns, not one of them mine.

Jonno sighed. 'Come back to mine – I'll put you on the floor,' he said.

I woke up on a couch in the same hotel I had interviewed at twelve hours earlier, shirtless. Jonno was nowhere to be seen. I scanned the floor for vomit. None. Good. *I think I got away with it; no-one will remember what happened.* I staggered back to Penn Station and boarded the Amtrak back to Philly.

Hours later the train pulled in to Philadelphia's 30th Street Station, and I wandered into the cavernous terminal, commuters striding in all directions. An immense bronze statue rose a storey high from the centre of the room: an angel, lifting a wounded soldier from the ground. It was a memorial to the fallen. I was feeling fragile, it tore at my heart. What was I doing? I had left one tribe for another, and I just wasn't sure about the move anymore.

Later, I wrote to Jonno, apologising.

He replied: *If you'd spewed, we would have sacked you.*

I believed him.

Years later I met Geraldine Buckingham again, this time in the Chinese Tuxedo in Manhattan's Chinatown. It was another exclusive Firm dinner. I scored a seat opposite Dominic, the director of McKinsey. Geraldine Buckingham was nearby. The last time I had seen her was the evening after she'd recruited me. 'You interviewed me in New York!' I said.

'Oh, I remember you,' she said. 'You passed out in Jonno's hotel room.'

I felt my face turn hot. 'Yeah, that was a big one.'

The McKinsey associate sitting next to me leaned over. 'Do you know her?'

'Yeah, she was my round two interviewer.'

'Really?' he said. 'The Buckinghammer?'

'The Buckinghammer?'

He explained that she had a reputation for being bloody tough in interviews, hence the nickname.

I stood in a sea of black gowns and mortarboards. For some absurd reason, I had worn scuffed Converse sneakers to my graduation. I think I was clinging to a start-up uniform, informal and gritty.

I felt pride, but a sense of loss too. After two years, the dream run was over. I knew I couldn't stay a student forever; it would ruin the memory of this place. I had survived some near misses, only to emerge with a great job. Best of all, my family had flown over to watch me graduate.

This place had given me the time and the space to start over. To heal some of the moral fatigue that came with organising for war. More than anything, it had restored my faith in humans. We were off, and the road was calling us.

30

IMPACT

'MAKE SURE TO LOOK AT THE VOLUME FROM THE SITE FOR 2014 and map it against these costs right here. Here's the tonnage, here are the operational costs. Transfer that chart to PowerPoint. Map it in one chart, by month, and put the costs in a bar chart. Just add a circle under each one showing the mega tonnage. Add the units to the top left of the chart. Not there – under that bar. In italics, please, would you? Goodness. Afterwards, get it scrubbed by visual graphics. Sound good? Let's have that slide before lunch.'

It was 11.10 am. I had understood about 10 per cent of what my team leader had said to me.

It was day one on the job with McKinsey and I was in an iron ore mine in the town where I was born: Newman, in the red dirt of the Pilbara. It was the same place my dad had driven ore trucks. I was back in the desert, I realised, surrounded by chunky men with beards and oversized machinery. The only difference was that I had exchanged low-visibility clothes for high-vis, and instead of carrying a weapon I was hauling a laptop around. By lunchtime, I was starving; my brain had consumed all my energy. No-one had told me to pack my own lunch. That day my lunch consisted of sachets of Milo and glasses of milk I took from the staff fridge.

The sheer volume of computations was mind-bending. As a company, McKinsey generated more outputs in a few hours than most companies could produce in a full working week. By eight each morning I had developed a headache which lasted until my head hit the pillow at midnight.

Months passed. The harder I worked, the more those essential habits I'd learned in order to maintain my mental health were falling by the wayside. Diet, exercise and rest were all thrown by the long hours. I knew I could sustain this lifestyle for a while, but not indefinitely. The numbness of depression was creeping back to me.

From iron ore in the Pilbara I moved on to outback coalmines. My mission was to boost the running hours of the giant haul trucks so they could move coal 24/7, probably headed to the iron furnaces in China. I rode shotgun with a truck driver as he drove the interminable loop. I wore my high-vis outfit. I wondered if I had been hired as a 'knuckle dragger': I could speak the language of bearded men and machines, and that was useful to the Firm.

Between shifts, I lived in a single-storey motel in Central Queensland. My neighbour was an immense bearded man squashed into a plastic chair on his porch. He was still in his high-vis clothes, shoeless, smoking a cigarette – and waiting to go home to his family. Had I really gone through all that shit in my life just to end up in another desert, this time with a profit motive?

I was deflated, and lonely. If this was the best there was on offer, the future looked grim.

I applied to take leave so I could head to the US and do another Kill Kapture ad campaign. I had devised how to launch the business and wanted to go out all publicity guns blazing. It would be a rallying cry for the brand and help me to leave the coalmines. Planning for the photo shoot was in full swing, and I had reached out to General Mattis to invite him to it in NYC. He had left his position in Central Command and was a free agent.

I had arranged a call with him from the coalmine in Queensland, and I snuck away from my laptop to have the conversation.

'Where are you now, soldier?' he asked in his familiar lisp.

'I'm in Moranbah, in Queensland. I'm in a coalmine.'

'Okay, I can have a drone strike there pretty quickly.' He chuckled.

He was utterly devoid of ego. Talking to troops gave him energy. We talked about my start-up idea. He referred to the business name, Kill Kapture, and the call to action under the logo: 'Hold the Line'. He had done his homework.

'I don't know about the name. It might limit your market. I love the phrase "Hold the Line", though!'

He agreed to come out to the shoot in New York City, pending his availability. I believed him when he said he wanted to be there.

I wrapped up my calls and started the two-hour drive to the tiny airstrip in the outback. It took two flights to get back to Sydney for the office dinner on Thursday night. There were rumours about a big announcement from the Office Boss.

Every McKinsey consultant in Australia flew in to Sydney for the dinner. The usual characters were there: crisp-looking folks with wavy hair and bright smiles. In one corner there was a group of peppy frat boys, probably the business analysts. The beers were tall and cold in crystal glasses. The crowd was swelling as I joined my mate. He was a marine officer from the Royal Navy and had been quick to spot a former soldier. He considered the crowd. 'What a shit show,' he said. 'Look at those blokes.' He nodded towards the frat boys and girls. 'What's this announcement, anyway?'

I admitted I had no idea. I gravitated towards sceptics for their grim humour.

The head of the Australian division stepped up to the stage.

'Welcome! We don't gather often in McKinsey, but when we do, we do it *well*!' said the British gentleman to the 200-strong crowd. Whoops and cheers. 'So, we're "lavish, but *lean*". We believe in impact, but we also like to have a good time, and that's why we're here. Lavish but *lean*,' he repeated.

The room buzzed.

'We've had a *massive* year.' The director thrust his arms forward for emphasis. 'Australia has been a leading driver of client *impact* globally.' Everything in McKinsey was *impact*. 'And that's why I am pleased to announce that, effective today, every consultant will be getting a *10 per cent pay increase*.'

The crowd erupted before he had finished the sentence. 'You've all earned it! Well done!' he said. The business analysts were fist pumping and men and women were hugging each other. I stood and clapped, worried that a lack of gratitude might lead to the firing squad. I saw a partner wiping his eyes. I expected a brass band to burst through the doors at any moment. Even veteran consultants were cheering like teenagers.

Most people believed in their jobs, but it was a tough playing field – you delivered impact, or you were 'managed out'. Financial incentives drove behaviour more than people realised, and I was not exempt. The army had a purity to it in that sense: there were no profit motives, just capability and outcomes. But those days were gone, and there would be no heading back. I had to keep driving ahead and build something I believed in.

I went to strange places with the Firm. I spent my 35th birthday walking on top of a nickel smelter in Kalgoorlie, sweating under helmet and overalls. That night the Canadians in my team took me to a 'nice fried chicken restaurant', which I soon realised was Chicken Treat – far inferior to my native Red Rooster. One team member was a genial Frenchman who ate quarter-slices of carrot cake for breakfast. He had rarely left the chic arrondissements of Paris, yet here he was in Kalgoorlie. I took him to a saloon dive bar to complete his cultural immersion.

'This is a uniquely Western Australian experience,' I shouted above the jukebox as I handed out a round of beers. I saw a horrified expression sweep across the Frenchy's face. I looked over my shoulder in time to see a fistfight erupt between two bearded miners by the entrance to the men's toilet. It was like watching two bears grappling in high-vis outfits. The fight careened across the bar for a full minute as a topless waitress skirted around them holding a drinks tray. The fight ground to a stalemate and ended in handshakes. Nobody was watching them but us.

'Is this a safe place to be?' Frenchy asked, still frowning.

I laughed pretty hard.

A year had passed, and I was starting to hurt. It was hard, grinding work. On flights home to Perth, I would make sure I had a window seat. I would be teary from exhaustion as I stared out the window and wondered what the hell I had done with my life. I could not reconcile myself to visiting remote client sites for the next decade, destroyed every Thursday night as I flew home to an empty apartment. Qantas had already sent a bottle of Krug champagne to my house to reward me for being a platinum flyer. I was not proud of that achievement. I was catching six flights per week. All the while, I thought about my old career.

Had I made a mistake? It was an unthinkable notion.

I planned a second photo shoot in the US. I'd always wanted to do a post-apocalyptic shoot, *Mad Max*-style imagery with leather jackets, weapons and helicopter. I canvassed a couple of NY-based photographers and received a cracking proposal from a young kid, Evan Robinson. He had studied media at the University of Pennsylvania, where Wharton was based. He understood what I was going for. We planned to do it at a ranch in Laredo, Texas. A Navy SEAL classmate owned it, and it was wild country. I booked a small helicopter for the shoot. Even if it was just for the short term, it would keep the Kill Kapture dream alive.

From the all-consuming nature of my new job, it felt like my personal life had taken a back seat for a while. I had not been looking for a relationship, but I soon walked into a workplace romance. I met Vicki at one of McKinsey's Thursday dinners. She had the finely honed intellect that young business people have when they are seasoned by their late twenties. We stayed in the Sheraton on the Park during our weekends off. I didn't even bother flying back to WA; it was too far to travel and I liked being in Sydney with Vicki.

She was headed to Harvard Business School at year's end, so I was expecting it to be a short-lived romance. But as we spent more and more time together, and her trip drew nearer, I started to think about the US for myself. I missed the hum of the business scene there. Australia felt staid by comparison. I started cooking up options to head to a McKinsey office in the States, scanning the internal noticeboards for a slot. I found a post-merger project at a large chemical company. It was NYC-based – a three-month project, starting the following week. I emailed the job placement people, and spoke with the British manager of the project. 'Ex-SAS, hey? Brilliant,' he said. He considered it. 'Okay, let's move ahead.'

I went straight from the coalmine and, on the drive to the airport, called McKinsey's travel cell and booked a flight to

New York City. It was that simple. I was heading straight to the US without even stopping off in Perth to pack up my apartment.

I landed at JFK 24 hours later. It was dark and sleeting. I took a cab to Manhattan. As we approached, I could see the Chrysler Building lit up. The Empire State dominated the middle of the skyline, its crown flashing in red, white and blue. I checked in at the W Hotel in Union Square, pulled off my suit and stepped into jeans and a t-shirt. I had build-up research to do for the project, but the true mission was undisclosed: planning the photo shoots for Kill Kapture.

I was in full insurgent mode, back in the battlespace.

I was home.

31

HOLD THE LINE

I WALKED THROUGH THE AIRPORT IN DALLAS, LOOKING FOR the photographer, Evan. He was easy to spot – a true creative often has a black uniform: torn jeans, sneakers and black t-shirts. He looked like a baby – fresh faced and oblivious to life's challenges – but I was wrong: in his mid-twenties, he was a world-class photographer and drank like a soldier.

We rented a car and headed south to the Mexican border, where the ranch was located.

The ranch manager greeted us at the gate; he was a polite Texan on a break from Harvard, with combed hair and an outsized belt buckle.

'I heard y'all wanted some weapons,' he said.

'Sure,' I said, thinking he might have an old shotgun that would be handy for a shoot. I also had a few veteran mates driving in from around Texas, bringing their uniforms and some weapons.

The guy went to his truck bed and pulled out an SR-25 sniper rifle and an M4 assault rifle with a 10.5-inch barrel. In his bag was a Remington tactical pump-action shotgun and another M4, this one with a 7-inch barrel. He had a large duffel full of ammo, and a tub of powder with explosives symbols on it.

Don't mess with Texas.

He gave us a short safety brief. 'If you see a pallet with a parachute attached, don't touch it. It's likely "merchandise", and the cartels have airdropped it here by mistake. They got GPS trackers on them, so leave 'em alone and they'll find it. If you see any bodies on the ranch, it's likely immigrants crossing to the US who've died from exposure. Y'all just lemme know – don't touch anyone.'

Hell of a briefing, I thought.

The helicopter was due the next day, so we settled in for dinner and some of Evan's margaritas, which could have stripped paint. We went to bed in the early dawn, in total disarray.

We stumbled through the first day of the shoot. We ran one serial where four of us would walk towards the camera with weapons and jackets, while a Navy SEAL buddy was detonating explosive canisters behind us for the smoke effects and the helicopter buzzed us at head height. It was an Oliver Stone film redux.

My Navy SEAL mate, looking for an apocalyptic background, set fire the to the earth with a bottle of fuel. In one photograph you can see his silhouette, out of focus, but dancing away from flames with both sneakers ablaze.

It was the most fun we'd had in a decade. *This is something, this is really something good*, we were all saying.

I wanted more. 'Let's get the New York shoot going!' I shouted to Evan over the rotor wash.

For the city shoot, we secured a Chelsea bar owned by a famous war correspondent, Sebastian Junger. I had put the call out to veterans from Wharton to come and model in a photo shoot with some jackets, the first iteration I called the Pathfinder series. Having seen the mean and dark images from the Texas shoot, people were keen to join.

Halfway through the shoot, I was standing near the front of the bar when a short, grandfatherly man with a cheeky smile walked up and offered his hand. It was General Mattis.

'How goes it, young man?'

I was shocked. 'Thanks for coming, sir. Can I get you a drink?'

General Mattis walked into the studio area with me, holding his beer. Half a dozen veterans waiting to be photographed all turned and fell silent. I noticed some were standing at attention. This was déjà vu from the last time I had seen the general interact with soldiers. Our lighting guy was an outgoing former US Army Ranger, and he was rendered speechless. General Mattis shook everyone's hand, and gave an extra polite greeting to a pretty intelligence captain who was attending the shoot with her Navy SEAL boyfriend. The boyfriend whispered to me: 'I think Mad Dog just hit on my girlfriend.' He seemed proud.

The general held court and spoke about his time in Central Command, the rise of ISIS, and the state of defence affairs. He even mentioned his 94-year-old mother, reminding us that she was the only person who outranked a five-star general. He also commented on life after service and what his own experience had been like. He was now an envoy to the Middle East and, after years of war, he wanted peace in the region.

'Ask him to try a jacket on!' whispered Evan, but I wasn't game. Evan took control and asked the general if he liked my jacket. Mad Dog said yes, and he even tried it on. Evan took a single photograph.

As he prepared to leave, the general turned to us and said, 'You have to make a difference. Keep growing. Keep charging, marines.'

His hour was up. He put down his drink, which was still full, shook hands with everyone, and left the bar.

*

In between working at my day job with McKinsey, building Kill Kapture and enjoying New York, I was on the Amtrak train up to Boston to visit Vicki. She was in full Harvard Business School mode, and as her partner I got to attend some of the events. On weekends we stayed in a local hotel, close to the river. We had grown close. I was finally slowing down for another person. I had often shirked commitment, knowing that the demands of my career were too great. Now I wanted to stop, to commit. The emotional drift that had afflicted me as a soldier was coming to an end.

I was in love with Vicki and was going to build a life with her.

In New York the days were growing short and cold. I was wrapping up the McKinsey project, and I decided I would take three months unpaid leave. It was time for me to work full time on Kill Kapture. I crammed myself onto subway cars to head to meetings with smooth-talking venture capitalists. The McKinsey and Wharton stamps would get me in the door, but getting funded was hard. *So this is a niche market? The name is aggressive. We're interested – work on revenue more and let's speak soon.* My skin got thicker and pitch deck sharper by the day.

I called a hedge fund manager in Australia with a strong affinity for the military. He wanted to help. 'When I saw this,' he said, 'I thought: *finally*. Someone has done it. "Tough Luxury" – this is a good idea.'

It was what I needed to hear, after months of little feedback. He talked probabilities and bet sizes.

'You have built a "biased coin". That means your probability of success is not guaranteed, but you've improved the odds. Bet your capital accordingly; don't go all in.'

I told him I was afraid: I was running out of dollars and was going to leave my job. If I didn't succeed, it would mean heading home. That would be the end of the start-up, and my time with Vicki too.

'Good – you should be afraid. There's a lot at stake. Keep the business alive, no matter what, and focus on the leverage points. It's not always a case of "the harder you work, the further you go". Sometimes it's the opposite. One day some rapper'll be caught in a sex video wearing your jacket, then you take off. That's a leverage point. Stay alive until then.'

It was sound advice. I calmed down, and stopped burning money by trying to launch the business in a year. I settled in for a long haul. Evan and I worked on the website and sold a bunch of jackets. In those early days, Evan quickly outgrew his role as the brand photographer. We spent our days in the factory, running design iterations, cutting threads, boxing jackets and writing notes to our customers. It grew into a real business, and we built on the vision of developing a full men's capsule wardrobe of Tough Luxury goods.

After a day of pitching, Evan and I sat on a rooftop bar among the neon skyline and stared downtown as the after-work crowd fill the balcony. We drank the cheapest beer on draught. A few blocks away, Freedom Tower reached to the heavens from the gritty Wall Street district. The long war had started on US soil, in this city, and having returned from it, we were now hungry, lean and ready for the next contest.

At the end of my three months of leave, I had nine days left on my tourist visa. I had to find another project with McKinsey or head home. Then I saw a job for an internal start-up called McKinsey Academy. It was a small team, in a fancy WeWork office facility down on Wall Street. This bought me another twelve months in Manhattan, time with Vicki, and more runway with Kill Kapture. Best of all, it gave me a paycheque. I had racked up $6000 on my credit card by the time I joined McKinsey

Academy. After a career on government income, I was learning money management the hard way. I moved into an apartment in Hell's Kitchen, and every morning I rode a bike south along the Hudson River to box in an underground Cuban gym.

New Yorkers know how much of a grind life in the city can be: traffic jams, queues, arguments, beggars, taxis and subways. Sirens filled the streets and stabbed your eardrums. The streets were endless rivers of stressed humans. This bled into me over time, and soon my bi-weekly trips to Vicki in Boston were no longer a source of joy; we were finding the distance hard.

We walked along the Charles River after lunch one weekend. As the silence between us stretched on, Vicki stopped walking. 'Are you sure you want to keep doing this?' she asked.

She had confirmed to me what I already knew: we were falling apart.

Vicki arrived from Boston the following weekend with an overnight suitcase. We sat down and, over wine and cheese, she broke up with me.

'I need a partner who is a source of joy,' she said. I hadn't been. I was in a race to nowhere. I was not caught out – I'd known it was coming – but it still burned. I loved her. Unrequited love is one of life's painful tragedies. I did this to girls, not vice versa. Being on the receiving end was a lesson in what I had only ever inflicted on others. I was reaping what I had sown in the years prior.

At work, I was a ghost. The loss of Vicki was sinking in, and I had not shared the news with anyone. The city was hard, just like Afghanistan, with one difference: this story was meant to have a happy ending.

My workmates knew me well enough to get me out of the office. They walked me to a famed hole-in-the-wall eatery near Chinatown.

Three of us sat in the tiny shop under flickering neon lights amid the aroma of basil, chilli and garlic. The concrete floor was pitted, grit piled in the corners. The waitress brought us Chinese beers, all of them warm.

My phone beeped with a message and I checked it, hoping it was Vicki. Instead it was Horse, the dog handler who had crouched beside me in that ditch in Chora. His sidekick, Rischa, had yelped every time I shot a grenade at the enemy.

Last night I had family and friends with me as we put Rischa to rest, he wrote. *If a dog could tell stories, this dog would share them all. I love you, mate.* He had sent a photo of him hugging Rischa in a dusty Afghan field. The dog was grinning.

Rischa.

She understood us and cared about us more than anyone from home ever had. We were all she cared about, and now she was gone. I put my phone down, and I wept for Rischa: in that shitty restaurant, with my concerned mates watching me, I wept for my lost girlfriend. I cried for Matthew Locke, for his robbed son Keegan and his bereaved wife Leigh. I wept for the humiliation of this whole selfish dream. I had lost my way, and I was even further behind than when I'd started. Six years of clawing away, to land on a plastic chair on dirty concrete, a million miles from home.

It dawned on me: none of this had worked. For six years I'd tried, but no amount of MBAs, sleep routines, positive thinking, exercise, good eating, top management consulting jobs and psychologist's tissue boxes would work. I was never going to outrun those losses in Afghanistan. They would dominate me for good.

If there was a lower moment in my life, I don't remember it.

On the train home, wondering what the hell I was doing with my life, I recalled a recent visit to a friend's house in Brooklyn.

An enthusiastic Texan, Zac was a film buff who was obsessed with bear attacks. He made me watch bear attacks on YouTube, as he shouted in fear bedside me. Reality wilderness shows came up at one point.

'One of my buddies in San Francisco got on to *Survivor*. Dude, he said he got up every morning on a tropical island and swum for a kilometre before breakfast. He freakin' loved it.'

Survivor. I was aware of the show from when it debuted a lifetime ago, but I had never watched it. *I could do that*, I thought. *Actually, I could do that really well*.

On the train ride home, I googled 'Survivor Australia'. I found out a season had just finished and casting for the following season closed in five days. I knew I was going to apply for it. I considered the risks. I might be humiliated on TV, for a start. It would mean a career switch – *again* – and for what? I wasn't sure. So far, for all the career switching, all I had was an unprofitable business, $200,000 of school debt and a rented single-bedroom thousands of miles from my family.

Maybe it was time to go home.

ACT III

THE PATH LESS TRAVELLED

I couldn't hear, but it was clear what the shades were saying: We, the dead, are telling you – your lifespan is short. Make of it everything you can. Before you're one of us.

Oliver Stone, *Chasing the Light*

32

UNREALITY

BACK IN MY HELL'S KITCHEN APARTMENT, I SAT AT MY DESK with the application form for *Australian Survivor* open on my laptop, explaining why I would be a good 'castaway'. I pitched myself as 'special ops and fashion designer'. I knew I wasn't really a fashion designer, but that didn't matter – it was make-believe. It *had* to work. As I hit send on the email, I felt a little thrill, similar to the one I'd had years earlier when this foreign land was just a skyline in the dark.

The next morning was bleak. Snow was bunched on my windowsill and fire trucks blared down Tenth Avenue towards downtown. I started going through my morning emails and noted one from the casting company for *Survivor*. They wanted me to do a Skype call. The email continued:

> In the event that you do make it past the Skype stage, which is
> a casting tour, are you planning on returning to WA anytime
> soon? Or would you be prepared to fly yourself there?

They had actually read my application. I had shouted into the void, and it had talked right back to me. I typed back: *Yes of course! I had planned to head home soon anyway.*

I was lying. At McKinsey people feared taking a few days out of their ten-day annual leave allocation. We arranged a video call for that evening.

I had ten hours to learn about reality TV. I started by watching YouTube highlights. The show had legions of fans with clubs and costumes and families dressed up as castaways. I bought an e-book on 'Reality TV Show Casting'. The advice was simple enough:

Be a character: know what that character is, and own it.

Make it two words: lawyer nerd, smart jock, hot cheerleader.

I'd already nailed that with 'special ops / fashion designer'. *That's four words you idiot.* But it had a dichotomy that I knew would catch their attention.

Understand that you can be depicted however they want.

You can be transformed into a villain, a hero or a fool in the editing process, through shot selection, sound effects and music. There was risk: no matter what I did I could still be made to look a villain or, worse, a fool.

At the appointed time, I logged on to the call and spoke with the casting agent, Jade. She seemed relieved to be speaking to a sane person, and was interested in my background. She asked about my character idea and my strategy. I had no freakin' idea, as I hadn't thought that one through, so I said I would be a 'useful idiot', hiding my skills and attributes, to remain unknown, and then whack them all at the end and walk away with the $500,000 cash prize. I was making it up as I went along.

Jade looked intrigued when I said I would not mention my background in special forces to my tribe. I took a mental note of that – I was looking for leverage points. It sounded like a 'storyline'.

After an hour of talking she asked if I would come home for an audition.

'To Australia?' I said.

'Yes, I would recommend it,' said Jade, a hint of promise in her eyes.

I said I would.

'You can't say why you're headed home either. You'll have to make something up. Say your brother is sick. And no social media. *Don't tell anybody.*'

'I'm a vault,' I promised. 'I was cleared to Top Secret.'

'*Survivor!* That's amazing!' my boss said when I explained why I was asking for a week off. My operational security had lasted 24 hours. He was thrilled about the audition. 'Let me know how it goes.'

In Perth a week later, Dad let me borrow his car so I could drive to the audition being held at a hotel in town. I wore my full New York uniform: jeans, a Kill Kapture jacket and snake-skin boots I'd bought before the Texas photo shoot.

In the hotel lobby, I approached a desk with a placard reading *Endemol Shine.*

The woman behind the desk said, 'Go upstairs and wait – don't talk to anybody.'

I climbed the stairs to the second-floor lobby, where I saw a barefoot man with a shaved head and a Hare Krishna outfit leading eight other barefoot people in what appeared to be a silent interpretive dance or a yoga session. They performed synchronised lunges and twirls and it just looked fuckin' weird. *Oh no.* I edged along the walls and avoided making eye contact with the group. I was terrified I would be pulled into the dance cult.

I took a seat in the lobby with a group of applicants who had avoided the dancing. The bald man ended the class. He glided over to me and offered his hand. In a thick Aussie accent, he said his name was 'Chicka'.

'No talking, please,' an assistant called.

Chicka sat next to me and started typing on an iPad, humming. He bumped my elbow with his then he made a show of looking away, like a primary school kid passing a note. I glanced at his iPad. On the screen was a note: *You and me to the end.*

We've got a live one here, I thought. I glanced towards the stairs and considered making a run for it. *What am I doing? Even if I get in, I'll be trapped on an island with these nutbags.* If I went ahead with it one thing was for sure: it would be reputational suicide.

A producer approached the waiting area and pulled ten of us into the hotel conference room. We split into two teams of five, and I pulled my cowboy boots off and put them against the wall.

'We're gonna do a mini *Survivor* challenge,' the producer told us. 'So you need to choose a person for the twenty burpees, the next person untangles this rope, the next person completes a puzzle and then two people need to build a three-layer structure of cards.'

I argued with a young surfie bloke over the burpees. He got the burpees; I got the card house, and was partnered with a short woman called Jessica, whose trembling lips told me she had been unable to quell the terror that I also felt. 'I'm a dental technician, so I have really steady hands,' she assured me.

The challenge unfolded, both teams cheering on their members. Three producers watched from behind a desk, taking notes. It was my turn. The dental assistant and I lay on our stomachs as we assembled the house of cards. I handed cards to Jessica, whose hands were shaking. I looked over at the other team. The red-headed kid in charge of their card house was even worse than us; he was so nervous he could hardly hold the cards. I took over after Jessica collapsed the card structure three times. She appeared to have stopped breathing and her hands were still rattling away like she was hypothermic. I made a mental note not to get a root canal from her. I bent some of the cards into a curve, and they sat on their edge well enough for us to build three levels. We won the challenge and I mock-celebrated with the team.

We were gathered into our teams of five again, and the producer told the losing team to vote a tribe member off the island. They voted unanimously to send the red-headed kid packing. He crumpled lower into his seat, ashen as the verdict was delivered.

The producers kept us waiting as they conferred, then they told us that four people would be asked to come back the next day. One of the producers read the names from a list; mine was one of them.

I pulled my snakeskin boots on as everyone started to leave. 'Nice boots,' the senior producer commented. I had been fishing for the compliment: special ops/fashion designer was still the hook I wanted them to remember.

The next day I returned and sat at a table in the same conference room with three large video cameras pointing at me. A couple of producers chatted to me, relaxed, as a cameraman gave a final thumbs-up. 'Buttoned on,' he said. I felt a tiny rush: this group held my fate in their hands; I remembered the feeling from the SAS selection course all those years before.

'So, Mark, we're going to ask you more about your application,' one of the producers said. She was holding an A4 page with three large images across the top, each a picture of me from social media, along with a handful of bullet points. 'You say you're from the army, but we already had someone from the army last year. Why do you think you'll be any different?'

I had anticipated this question. 'I don't think you've ever seen a creature like me before,' I said. I dialled up my facial intensity a bit; I was playing crazy. 'Comparing an ordinary army person to me is like comparing a house cat to a leopard.

Same animal, but different breed.' I died a little bit inside. I was exploiting my career for a slot in a reality TV game show.

'What are your strengths?'

'I was made for this environment. I've survived the greatest game of all: war. I'll do it again in this field.'

Oh please. It was absurd, a repeat of the high-energy facade I'd presented the McKinsey interviews, with one difference: the excitement was intrinsic now. This was totally unconventional, but the further I went, the more I wanted to be on the show. It would be a dangerous gamble with dignity, though. This footage – braggart garbage, uttered with the aim of self-promotion – could show up anywhere. I had not burned my boats; I had torpedoed them with a tactical nuke. There was no heading back. Not to special ops, not to Vicki, not to my old life. I had no idea where this was headed; I was in uncharted waters.

That evening, Dad and I went to the Ocean Beach Hotel, my old hangout in Cottesloe. I had left home twenty years ago and sitting with Dad, content, I realised my mind had finally come home, too. We talked about life as we watched the sun dip into the Indian Ocean. Dad asked if I thought I would get selected for *Survivor*. I said I wasn't sure, but if I did, I would be coming home.

Home. That was a concept I'd forgotten. I'd spent the last two decades running away. There had been hard times, starting with losing Mum. At one point I'd doubted I'd see my thirties. I'd survived the war, but in moving on I'd left my tribe and I had felt adrift for years.

Trying out for *Survivor* was a cry for help – a potentially entertaining one . . .

*

I landed at JFK and rode a bus into the city. The road was lined with banks of snow as high as my chest. I was back in New York, but in my mind I was already gone. I wanted that show. A new direction.

More forms arrived by email. Swim tests, police checks, cardiograms.

At 10 pm I had a call from an Aussie number. It was the executive producer, Amelia, who had interviewed me a month before in Perth. She told me that a record-breaking 20,000 people had applied to be in the series. Only 24 of these had been selected, and I was one of them. The show would be filmed in Samoa. Was I in?

I was thrilled. 'Thank you so much for choosing me. I won't let you down.'

She warned me: 'Once you're on that island, we can't speak with you. You promised me a character – I need you to deliver on that.'

I promised I would.

I pulled the first Kill Kapture jacket I'd made from the wardrobe and tried it on again. It fit perfectly.

Is it right for the jungle? I wondered. *Probably not – but who gives a fuck?*

I had a new character to live up to, comfort be damned.

33

WELCOME TO THE JUNGLE

I CLIMBED OVER THE GUNWALE OF THE BARGE AND STEADIED myself on the rolling deck. It was pitch-black, a dense tropical rain was teeming down, and the visibility was 3 metres. I scanned the deck as a bolt of lightning bathed the scene in crackling light, and there it was: the opening set of *Survivor*. Barrels of green coconut and bamboo were stacked in bundles on the deck. Two cargo net rafts were tied down in the centre, and a rusting 1950s pick-up truck was bound to one flank.

A dozen other contestants were scattered around the deck. A young woman shivered in a thin sundress, her blonde hair plastered to her neck and shoulders. An old man with a bushy grey beard and tattoos stood next to a vast anchor, looking stoic. A producer led me across the deck; I stepped carefully around the puddles in my snakeskin boots. She seated me on the bonnet of the pick-up truck and left without a word.

Whoa, here we go. It seemed only five minutes since I'd been in my apartment in Midtown, New York, planning a night out in the city. Now, the tropical air and smell of the ocean brought my city-battered senses back to life.

The wind billowed hard across the Pacific. I pulled my sleeves down and zipped my leather Kill Kapture jacket right up to my neck. It was an unconventional wardrobe for the tropics, but it aligned with the fashion designer persona I would roll out in order to conceal my true identity.

I scanned the multiple characters, labelled them offensively to remember them: Giant male with steamed-up spectacles: Old Accountant. Slight male with tortoiseshell glasses, dancing to no music in the dark: Camp Dancer. The large-jawed male with a tattoo snaking up his arm: Rugby Lad. Female in a red-sequinned cowboy top: Cowgirl Mum. Old guy with the beard: Anchorman. Muscled male with hair tied in a bun, flowing robes and wrist beads: Yoga Man-Bun. There was Gritty Athlete and Champagne Grandma. The woman right near me – attractive, with a white Panama hat like you might see on a South American drug lord – was Short Hottie. She turned to look across the ocean, and I stole a look at her sleek body and bulging calves.

A man crept up on me with a shoulder-mounted camera. The light array on it blinded me as he recorded my face in the rain. I felt awkward. *Look staunch*, I reminded myself. He filmed, and I stared into the distance, frowning. It was absurd. Eventually, without having acknowledged me in any way, he slunk across the deck and lit up Anchorman, who made a show of scanning the Pacific Ocean.

The sun rose over the magma cliffs of Samoa, and the light green jungle and clear water came into relief. The barge tracked along the coast and we watched the waves pummel the reef and waited for the opening challenge.

I looked over at Short Hottie, sitting on the edge of a crate of eggplants. She was unable to remain still: she stood up, squinted at me from under her oversized hat, then walked in a circle and picked up an eggplant to inspect it. She tied her jumper around her waist and asked a producer for a drink. She stared at my boots and then held her hands up to the sun, looking for the drone that was filming us. She checked her fingernails and

312

looked out at the beaches. After climbing the edge of the boat railing, she laughed at nothing in particular. I wondered at her beautiful bronze skin, and her developed calves. *Olympian?* I guessed.

She later she told me she had looked at me and wondered what the hell I was doing wearing a leather jacket in the tropics. I discovered I was tagged by one contestant as 'Flog' and by another as 'Fonz'.

We all watched a speedboat power alongside the barge. Jonathan LaPaglia, the show's host, climbed up the rope ladder and stepped onto the deck, all perspiration and biceps. We cheered and clapped. Cameras were pointed at us by the dozen. The sun was high in the sky by now and I was sweating through my t-shirt. The host arranged us in our groups and I smiled as he recited his lines for the opening of the show. It was a surreal moment.

'Welcome to the world's greatest game!' he shouted, arms wide.

More clapping; we were all ecstatic. Some contestants had waited their whole lives for this moment. I was terrified of the cameras. My mouth flapped away as I mentally rehearsed my lines. At the same time, I was trying to smile. In the replay, I look like I'm in the midst of a mental episode. I was in sensory overload only two minutes into the show.

The host explained the first challenge. We had to collect stores, jump off the boat and push a raft to shore. The winners would get a shitload of rice and food.

'Survivors ready!' The host raised his arm.

This is really it! I thought.

'Go!' he shouted, and off we went.

It was mayhem, with people tripping over bamboo and fighting over bunches of green bananas. I stripped my boots off and jumped into the ocean. I almost landed on a scuba diver pointing a fish-eye camera at my face. We pushed our battered raft to the shore, leaving a wake of coconuts and squashed bananas behind us.

We were gassed, shipwrecked. I had barely hung onto my jacket and boots. My shirt and socks were lost. One of the rafts flipped in the breakers and squashed fruit was washing up on the shoreline as bodies of unfit contestants were pulled from the water. Producers shouted at contestants who ran along the beach stuffing squashed fruit into their mouths. It was a tropical D-day landing. Reality TV carnage. My tribe lost the challenge.

We were sent along the white sand to our tribal beach, where we all met and spoke for the first time as a group. Short Hottie was in my tribe, and I learned her real name: Samantha. She was vivacious and smart. She was so tiny I had to lean right down to hug her.

The tribe wandered about aimlessly for two hours picking a shelter site, dehydrated and carping about the heat. I was thirsty and out of patience. I could feel the soldier in me waiting to break out, to lay waste to this crowd of dithering millennials, damn it. But I stuck to my cover story: consulting and fashion. I hated pretending; concealing my past meant I couldn't really relate to anyone. It would keep me safe, though – for now.

At dusk, I stared at the reef break in the dying light. A lone palm tree protruded out to the beach, hunting for sunlight. The clouds on the horizon were ablaze with every shade of red. The ocean was a special place for me: it felt calming. I joined the tribe for a meal of steamed rice on a banana leaf, scooped up with a clam shell. I had been sent on a 'fire challenge' that day with Champagne Grandma and we'd won a striking flint for the tribe. Our rice was cooked, while the other tribe starved.

What a day. I was surprised at how much fun I was having. This was a bizarre detour: to go from the business of national secrecy, weapons handling, counter-surveillance, sending intelligence briefs that would go as far as the prime minister to this – reality TV. It was a professional death sentence in national security circles.

I began to see that the career I'd had was not the most important part of my life. It was just another chapter. I could stand apart from it now. In fact, I would have to.

Nobody on the island gave a shit about what I had done – my uniform was gone, and with it my identity of twenty years. They didn't care about what I had done before; they only cared about the person I was right now. This was a reframing of an identity that I had chosen when I was fourteen. I was here, and I had nothing to lose.

The tribal challenges were elaborate, the competition intense. One challenge started with an immense plastic slide coated in a slippery gel. Two squares lay on the sand beyond it. We had to chase a ball down the slide and then wrestle it into our team's square. I was up first. The other team put up Rugby Lad, who was my size. We walked to the top of the slide, and I noticed Rugby Lad was wearing near-transparent red undies. The tribes waited at the sides of the sand pit; cameras and microphones and scaffolding lined the edge of the challenge. It was scary.

'Survivors ready . . . Go!'

We threw ourselves headlong down the slide, which I realised was laced with detergent. Rugby Lad slid ahead of me, so I reached out to slow him. I reached for his undies and stripped them off in one fluid motion. We landed at the end of the slide and I grappled with the slippery nude man in the sand. The crowd bayed. He was unfazed, and fought with great strength. *Stop the challenge!* I pleaded.

Rugby Lad recovered the ball and dived for the square. As he launched forward, I slid down his body, and face planted in his arse cheeks. He slammed the ball down. He had won, and I had been forced to handle the naked contestant the whole time. Even the production crew was laughing, and they had seen it all before. I felt somewhat violated – it was the TV nightmare I had been dreading.

By the end of the first week, I realised there were only two other tribe members I could rely on. One was a rascal of a bloke who'd grown up not far from me in Perth. The other was Sam. Together we plotted and analysed the tribe.

Sam and I grew close. We talked for a long time about our lives around the tribal fire. I found out she had worked for World Vision and was a professional runner. *That explains the calves,* I thought. She was funny and articulate, and a veteran expedition runner. A former corporate lawyer. Her drive and intelligence were apparent; I was drawn to her vision of what an exciting life looked like. In a game where you could never be sure of people, I trusted Sam. Still, I sold the consulting and fashion cover story. She knew there was a missing decade in there, but she never pushed me about it. 'Do you want to sleep together?' she asked. The dozen of us slept packed together in our tiny lean-to shelter. The nights were long, freezing. I pulled her in tight so we could share body heat. I gave Sam a kiss on the forehead that night. I noticed that cameras seemed to be following us an awful lot, and the producers would often bring Sam up in the interviews.

By day seventeen, I was starving, down at least 7 kilos. We'd had no food apart from white rice and coconut. I was now used to interviews, and settling into the life of a filmed scenario. Sammy had shown her resilience and tenacity in the challenges, and we had won four times in a row.

We were in an alliance of six people. I did not trust any of them but Sam; I could tell the others were lying about their intentions. Some conversations were obviously bullshit, full of fake assurances. It was all askew. My life had once depended on reading a person's intentions, and I knew they were throwing smoke to hide something.

We lost a challenge and had to vote out a tribe member. I was pretty confident; I was an asset in camp life, and muscle for the challenges. But I was uneasy.

'Boys are voting Ben, girls are voting Michelle,' one of the guys whispered to me when we were stoking the campfire. *Too simple*. This was too easy. Normally an early vote is called, then the manoeuvring and deception goes on to figure out the real victim. I just didn't know who the target was.

I interrogated Model on the beach. The cameramen and sound boom swept in on me as I approached her. I hated dishonesty, but here it was our best weapon.

'Who is it?' I asked. 'Who's being voted out?' She couldn't look me in the eye.

Fuck it, I thought. I knew we were in trouble.

I went back to Sam. She too had sensed something was up. 'Do you think it could be me?' she asked.

'Possibly,' I said, feigning calm as I ate coconut flesh. I really hoped it wouldn't be her. She was my little lover and the only person I trusted on the island. We were very close now; we watched out for each other.

We walked into the tribal council in the dark, our fire torches lighting the path ahead. The tribal area was all fire and smoke and vines and stone huts. It was immersive, persuasive; I now believed it to be a real contest of survival.

The host probed us for our feelings about the vote. We didn't know it, but Yoga Man had assembled a coalition to vote Sam out after she'd exposed him for a lie he'd told about his yoga certification. He too had a false identity and was trying to protect it.

We each cast our votes and waited for the host to tally them up. It was Sam. Yoga Man had got her.

She didn't look at me as she picked up her bag and walked away. I was devastated. My little lady was gone. Ratty and tired after three weeks of not eating, I was in the mood for blood. I was also alone, my partner banished.

The following day, we lost the challenge again, meaning we would be headed back to the tribal council to vote another person off the island. I knew I was in trouble because of my affiliation with Sammy. Yoga Man was putting together another coalition to get me, I could feel it in the air. I was vicious now, hungry and wild from three weeks in the jungle. That night would decide my future: an early departure from *Survivor* meant a return to New York, pleading for my job back, another career pivot in tatters.

I prepared some talking points. My plan was to convince the tribe to vote out Champagne Grandma, since she was Yoga Man's sidekick. She'd hurt her shoulder in the challenges, so I planned to kick her while she was down. At camp, I rehearsed my talking points, mouth flapping away as I prepared my argument in silence.

We arrived at the council again, and I made my pitch to the tribe.

'Vote out the grandma and keep me,' I urged. 'I'm useful.'

The votes were cast and the tally read out: I was done, five votes to three.

I stood and carried my torch to the host, who uttered the famous line: 'The tribe has spoken.' He snuffed out my torch.

I met the rest of the crew out the back of the set. There must have been 50 of them, all applauding. I was stunned, grateful to know they cared about us. This had been real, and I was part of the show. I felt like my effort had been appreciated. A lot of crew came and shook my hand; I had been with them for three weeks, and we had never spoken until now. But I was at the end of this journey, and for all my fear about it, I realised that had been my ego talking. In truth, it was all just a bit of fun – we were here to entertain.

It's an exaggeration to say I was reborn in those tiny island battles in Samoa, but to say that I destroyed my old identity in order to find a new one: that is absolutely true.

At the airport waiting for my flight back to Australia, I looked up Sam online. I shot her a note on social media: *Hi, Gorgeous*.

34

TRIBE

'YOU DIDN'T BLOODY TELL ME YOU WERE IN THE SAS!'

Sam had stalked me a bit online, and had seen an article on Kill Kapture from when I was based in New York. I filled in the blanks from our conversations in Samoa, telling her everything I'd got up to. She was surprised, but she'd guessed I wasn't telling her everything.

In return, she told me more about herself. Sam had run across the width of India, assisting child education in remote areas. She had appeared in fashion magazines, was an ambassador for numerous organisations and was an experienced public speaker. She wanted to live a big life and take a path with a lot of uncertain outcomes.

I invited her over to Western Australia. 'I'll take you down the south coast,' I promised.

Sam flew in from Melbourne a few days later and I met her at the airport. She looked as good in real life as she had on the island. I drove her all the way south to my favourite corner of the planet: Margaret River, famous for big waves and bigger Shiraz blends. We stayed in a caravan park overlooking the Indian Ocean and spent our nights romancing each other, despite our tropical ailments; we both had chronic diarrhoea from jungle bacteria, a farewell gift from Samoa. Sam never skipped a beat, though – she had the constitution of a soldier.

Sam and I escalated our travels with a road trip through California. Sam had planned it long before and invited me to join her. Before that, though, Sam came back to New York with me. I'd had a lot of time for reflection in Samoa, and I'd decided, for all my love of the city, it was time to go home. It was time to start the next phase of my life.

With some time to burn between packing up my life and heading to Cali, Sam and I enjoyed the city as tourists. It was early spring, and we rented bikes. I had clocked 1500 kilometres of travel in Manhattan on City Bikes, accident free. It was the perfect way to transit the city and tour at the same time. The 30-kilogram hire bikes were tough to handle, even for me, but I showed Sammy how to use them and we cranked the pedals to get downtown. As we were cruising through the West Village, Sam crashed her bike into a kerb in front of traffic, body slamming the pavement in her summer dress. She picked the bike up, laughed at herself, and pedalled hard to catch up to me. *She can take a hit*. I approved.

On our last night in New York, we took a champagne boat cruise along the Hudson River. Freedom Tower now soared 110 storeys high, a sentinel over the World Trade Center precinct. We watched black sheets of rain roll up the river, past the Statue of Liberty. The city was magnetic: it drew people from around the globe, as it had me. But I was happy to leave, glad to surrender my spot here to another dreamer. I had loved the city, but it was time for something, someone else: I felt like Sammy was it.

We flew into San Francisco and took off south along the Pacific Coast towards the mountains and redwoods of Big Sur. We had hired a blue campervan with a mattress and kitchenette: we called it the Bang Bus. Sam went on long runs every day; I lumbered up the hills, chasing her. It was a losing game. Sam could run steadily on any grade or terrain, her powerful calves firing her along. Nights were spent parked on a ridge overlooking the coast, cooking up tuna and naan bread. Sam was not much of a drinker; I was happy with that after the excesses of my army career. We stopped in Santa Cruz, where the iconic *Lost Boys* was filmed, and I made her watch the Gen-X nostalgia film on my laptop.

Sam lived an unreal life. Running, social impact programs and paid speaking gigs. It seemed too good to be true, but with drive and passion and a tough negotiating bent, she made it happen. I was inspired. I'd never thought the same could be possible for me. Her optimism and love was a true balm.

When we got home, I headed back to Western Australia. We planned to meet up again soon. It had been a great trip and, although we were a new couple, I knew Sam was special. While I was in Perth, though, she took a turn, calling me when she was teary and unstable. We had only been back two weeks and she was punishing me with these draining calls. I didn't know what was up with her.

She called me again when I was driving back from meeting an army mate for a burger. It was raining hard, a regular Perth winter.

'Mark, I need to speak with you.' She was whispering; I could barely hear her.

'Speak up. What is it?' I was preparing for another round of tears.

'I did a pregnancy test today and it's positive. I'm pregnant.'

'Oh,' I said blankly. It didn't compute. *Oh SHIT*, I thought, as it registered fully.

Rain pattered the car roof. I sat with the phone to my ear. 'Okay. That's amazing. Are you okay?' I asked.

She responded, but I was not really listening. I was going through the internal monologue I imagine is common to many a surprise daddy: *It's okay, you always wanted to be a dad, this will work. Actually, no, this won't work. You're a working man, you do what you want! No commitments, no surrender. I have a career, I've gotta head back to the US – sorry, it's a work thing.* The bargaining phase, I think it's called.

I knew this was a life-changing moment, and a lot hinged on making the right decisions.

I think I handled it well. After the call, I drove home, sticking to the speed limit for once. I thought about my life, and how I might soon be sharing it with a girl I had met eight weeks ago on an island. This would be a big leap.

I considered the alternatives. I could opt out of fatherhood and head back to New York. Keep working. Make money. Let a child grow up without a father, let Sam struggle on her own without a partner. It was a horrible thought. Sam understood the immensity of the decision, and to her enduring credit she gave me the option to leave her. She let me know I was far from perfect: 'I know I'm the best thing for you, but I'm not yet convinced that you're the best thing for me,' she said. It was a challenge wrapped in a truth. I gave it a lot of thought, but really the choice was clear. I was in. I would move to Melbourne, unemployed, and start a family with Sammy and our unborn child.

Dad never skipped a beat when I told him Sam was pregnant; nor did my stepmum Jen. In fact, they were thrilled.

Jeez, Mum would be so stoked too, I thought.

On 23 March 2018, I sat at the end of the operating table wearing a hair cap and blue scrubs. Sam's mother had given me a camera with an absurd foot-long lens, I was about a metre away from the doc delivering our baby. I held Sam's hand and we chatted to dispel the nerves. It was a caesarean delivery, and the room was full of doctors and nurses. I had never loved hospitals: I always thought of my ailing mum. But life's wheel turns, and here we were for the start of a new life.

The head nurse had a tiny fob watch pinned to her uniform, the kind Mum wore when she worked as an aged care nurse. Based on the watch, I declared Mum present and accounted for in the birthing room. A blue screen shielded the view from Sam's chest down as the doctors went to work.

The head nurse was peering over, encouraging Sam. She said, 'Oh, I can see a face! It's all scrunched up!' I got my telescopic camera ready. The squeal of a tiny human called to us, and the pull of that cry set our every cell alight. The doctor held aloft a squealing, kicking newborn, with the biggest balls I have ever seen.

My boy! I thought, as I choked back some tears.

I walked with the nurse to the gurney and clamped his tiny umbilical cord. The nurse was wiping some of the grey matter away from his face, cooing to him, and I watched him as he squawked away. His eyes were closed, but I watched him force one eye open and take in this strange world for the first time. *Welcome, little man*, I thought. It was magic.

A nurse wrapped him in a candy-striped blanket and handed him to me, his face still scrunched up, most displeased by his new surrounds. I was the only male in the room, had done none of the work, but I was rewarded with the baby in his first moments. I held the little bundle up to Sam's face and he gurgled away at his mother. Sam was limp with relief as we both watched our baby, having waited so long to meet him.

The midwife snapped a tiny label to his wrist.

It read: *Harry Locke Wales.*

Settling into life with a newborn was stressful, but Sam and I were ecstatic to be parents. Sam handled the sleepless nights with an endurance athlete's tolerance for pain. It was a special time to hold and grow a life, and to think about where we were headed next. We had the unusual luck of being born in a wealthy western country, and we were determined to make the most of it.

Sam encouraged me to start public speaking. *You have a story, and it's a bloody good one. Talk about recovering from war.* I was reticent at first. Introverted and shy, public speaking would run against my natural inclinations. To stand in front of strangers and admit to all my failings: I was not enthused. I trained for it anyway, however: I needed the money and, more than that, I needed a purpose and a profession. I winced when I saw my first video replays; my voice was flat, and I mumbled, speaking in a monotone as I tried to remember my messages, stories and slides. I needed a new style, one that married education with entertainment.

My talk spanned my first tour of Afghanistan, the battles in Chora, and the long road back from the burnout that followed. I shared the tips I'd learned during recovery: exercise often, sleep seven to nine hours a night, and eat a clean diet. Stay connected to family and friends, and keep looking for your life's purpose. They sounded basic, but I was at my worst when I stopped investing in my health; I knew that from my time in the corporate sector. Having felt the steel grip of mental illness, I knew what was at stake.

I would rehearse my talk in front of Sam as she fed Harry. I only stopped at a couple of parts: my mother dying, and being told over the radio that Matthew was dead. I would snag on them and begin to cry. Those moments were raw, and I didn't share them, especially not with strangers. Sam told me not to worry – she had cried before on stage when explaining a near-sexual assault that had happened to her in a North African race. Her emotion had helped to convey the gravity of the story.

Sam was an experienced speaker and a dynamite performer. In stature, she was about the size of Tony Robbins's left leg, but onstage she was a giant. She had a performing arts major on top of her law degree, so she was a pro. Her message was about hope and transformation, even when you're the last kid picked for the school team. She was a role model for me.

I fumbled through my first talk with a large bank. It was clunky, but the message hit home: *You're not alone; even elite soldiers can experience burnout or mental illness. It's fixable, it can be prevented, and with the right habits, you can come back even stronger.*

Sam and I began to do talks at a prison transition facility, speaking to prisoners about to be released into society. They were all terrified of losing their community. I told my story to twenty ex-convicts, and they were rapt. Afterwards, several approached me and shared stories about their trials in life, their convictions. One young prisoner told me he was in for drunk driving and had killed his best mate. Jailed for seven years, he now wanted to move on to something better.

Once I stopped worrying, I was a better speaker: I was working for my audience, not vice versa. Like Sam, I started speaking to companies all over Australia. The message to them was always the same. Be clear about your mission. Address your team's needs before your own. Invest in yourself by taking care of your basic health. Persevere: the night is always darkest before the dawn.

When I knelt to propose to Sammy, I was only half a head shorter than her. She said yes, though not before checking that I was sure about what I was asking. I assured her I was sober and stable. We were standing on the white sands of Frenchman Bay in Albany; Harry was a year old. We danced on the deserted beach and drank some champagne. It was a stellar moment.

We booked a barn-style property for the ceremony and reception, making sure we got the invites out early to my mates who needed the lead time. It was going to be a rare gathering of my friends from the army and both our families.

On 14 December 2019, Sam walked down the aisle on her father's arm, wearing a stunning, sleek wedding dress. I have never seen a better sight in all my life. She was a picture of beauty and life – absolutely sublime. My groomsmen, including Pete, Stano and Jimmy, had to hold me upright. Harry was right behind her, in the arms of a bridesmaid, howling and thrashing in his cream tuxedo. Sam and I exchanged vows then kissed under wattle and eucalypt and banksia flowers.

My mum's three sisters were sitting in the front pews, each with the granite jaw of a Jackson, and with them present I felt Mum was right there with us.

My dad warmed up for the opening speeches over dinner, flapping his notes and mixing them up. He made a few jokes – including the old one about how Mum had wanted a daughter after me and Steve, but had ended up with Dan: 'a reasonable compromise' he said, deadpan. He described how the first time he met my in-laws was at the maternity ward; while Dad was casual in a Fremantle Yacht Club windstopper, Sam's dad had dressed for the occasion in slacks and a dinner jacket. Dad's first impression was of a 'Melbourne establishment' gentleman, but after hearing he'd crashed a muscle car into a roundabout at full speed, Dad's admiration grew; he referred to Sam's dad as a 'local hoon'. About my mother he said: 'She left us too early, and we wish she was here.' The room fell silent. We all felt her. I knew she was with us, always partial to a gin and tonic, so we toasted her.

Hours later, Sam and I lay awake in a luxury tent near the barnyard, listening as the group of SAS men near our tent howled over war stories, recalling tactics of battles fought and anticipating the battles to come. Years earlier, I would have been scrambling to join them. Now, though, I was content not to join the fray. Harry was tucked in bed, I was with my new wife, and I knew that brotherhood would remain for many years.

For all the trials and turns, I was finally home.

A tribe of my own. It was all I'd ever needed.

EPILOGUE

I REMEMBER WHEN I FIRST SAW THE NEWSPAPER HEADLINES about war crimes allegedly committed by special forces in Afghanistan. The accusations were ugly: prisoners kicked off cliffs, murders, torture, dismemberments. Both the media and public were shocked.

The press rightly jumped on the stories, but the context to the war was rarely examined. I doubt these incidents occurred in a vacuum. Men were not waking up, heading to the team rooms and laying out their deliberate plans to destroy civilians in the field. More likely, it was the result of a creep in psychological damage, moral standards and culture over a decade – in line with the mission creep we experienced over the years.

We had fought Australia's longest war by double. I deployed there every year from 2006 to 2010. If the smattering of combat I had engaged in had unhinged me morally and mentally, what did people think would happen if we sent the same unit back into combat time and again over not just a couple of years, but a decade?

We became brittle. In some cases, we snapped. Even elite soldiers have limits. I know I found mine.

We wanted to survive the war. To improve our chances, we had to be vicious. I shudder to think how many other Aussie troops would have died had we not fought as hard as we did. Did we create more enemies? For the most part, yes. We buried a lot of enemies too.

That's war.

If soldiers commit war crimes and are convicted, then punish them. But in my view the leadership at all levels, military and political, must be held accountable. I hope that the same people who opted to send special forces on deployment continuously for over a decade have the courage to admit that they knew we were losing for many years, but reinforced that failure anyway.

As a kid, I was a keen young soldier in the making. If I had the chance to speak to that kid about life as a soldier, knowing what I know now, I would tell him: The army will offer you a full, rewarding life, but there is also the prospect of death, trauma and exile from your own society. If you're going to do it, do it properly, be the best you can be and fight like hell – but be aware that it's a long road back.

The impact of fighting on soldiers is well known. In my case, no amount of running from the problems that plagued me helped; the traumas simply calcified. At some point, you have to do the work required to heal. There are no 'hacks' for recovery. It takes time, effort, discipline and patience. The hardest step for me was recognising and admitting I was in trouble in the first place.

I would go on scenic bush runs in the hills with Sam and Harry, but I could never stop scanning the vegetation. Looking through branches for movement, some exposed skin, a crouching soldier. The habits from my time in combat endured. Sam would get the shits with me for not wanting to head out into the scrub. 'Just relax,' she would say. 'It's meant to be fun.' But for me it meant revisiting moments that were seared into my brain. For so long my life had depended on being constantly alert, on edge, and that hyperawareness never left me. It was an unwelcome war souvenir.

Even in the decade after coming home, I still carried the residue of fighting, and it made it hard to handle the ordinary stresses of life. I had bad weeks. Overwhelmed by parenthood, I shouted at Sam and Harry. I went looking for therapy programs. I wanted to get on with life.

One of my mates had almost died in a helicopter and for years after, he was terrified of flying. He tried prolonged exposure therapy and told me it had saved his life. I was reluctant – I wasn't all that keen to revisit some of the causes of my trauma – but I booked a ten-session treatment in Melbourne.

The psych, a polite man with bifocals, had reviewed my files and he was upbeat. 'You're doing a really great thing. This treatment works, and it works because when we avoid things, we leave them unfinished. The only way through is to confront them.' He paused. 'Freud might have been something of a pervert, but he was certainly right on that: humans go back to what is not finished. By avoiding things, we achieve the opposite to what we intend. We *must* confront our trauma.'

I believed him. Already, I felt lighter.

I have always found writing to be a useful way to process my emotions and experiences. When you join special forces, operational security is one of the first concepts that is hammered into your mind; concealing identities, tactics and equipment is critical. We are told not to keep diaries of our operational work, but I didn't always follow the rules. I kept a diary during most of my deployments, and I wrote notes directly into a field message notebook after combat. Perhaps, alongside the therapy, I could confront my traumatic experiences by writing about them, I reasoned.

I attended a writing workshop at a small publishing house in the streets of Melbourne in late 2019. Most of the other participants were older women and their stories were inspiring; there were abuse survivors and wartime wives. Respected author Arnold Zable lectured us on the craft, from building characters to searching for the threads that can bind a story. He asked us each to write a short piece on a person who'd mattered to us.

I wrote about meeting two army men after a presentation I gave at a defence base. One was a medical warrant officer who was in Tarin Kowt during the battle when Matt died. He told me he had washed Matt's body and dressed him in uniform for his final flight home. I thought it was the gentlest thing you could do for a fallen soldier. I was so moved.

The second was a handsome commando who had been in an adjacent valley to us when we had fought in Chora and Matthew was killed. His unit had wanted to join us in battle but were unable to get there. I could tell from his eyes and the way he wrung his hands that he felt guilty about it. His guilt was needless, and I told him so.

I told the group about my 33rd birthday in Philadelphia, when it struck me that I had outlived Matthew. He had died in that cornfield, so far from home, stolen from his family.

Everyone was silent when I was done. Finally, Arnold asked me why I had written about those particular experiences. I explained through tears that after Matt died, I had written a note to his son Keegan. I said I was sorry for his loss and promised that one day I would write about his dad. It was an important story, I told the class, and I felt it was time to share it.

The author considered me for a moment. Then he said, 'Perhaps this is a story about fathers and sons.'

*

One morning in early 2020, I called Keegan Locke, Matt's son. He was a young man now, and he had the same clipped, direct, no-bullshit tone his old man had possessed. Keegan worked in marketing for a veteran health start-up. I remembered how technically proficient his dad was, even as a dirty team leader. Keegan now lived on the Gold Coast, and he told me he had just chased and tackled a bloke who had stolen a scooter parked on his street. *A chip off the old block, another bloody action man*, I thought. I had seen a picture of Keegan online, cresting a sand dune in his dive gear, all bearded and barrel-chested. I was looking at Matt in his twenties.

'Well, stay in touch, mate. I wrote a few words about your old man – I would love it if you could check them.'

'For sure,' he said.

Some nights, Sam and I would take Harry onto the balcony of our home to look at the full moon. One night, I held him close in the cool air and pointed to the silver disc just visible through the branches of the eucalypts in our yard. 'Moon!' Harry called, pointing, his eyes alive with wonder. He saw the beauty of life all around him, in plain sight. It reminded me that it was good to be alive, and that there was a lot to live for.

I dreamed about Matthew on some of those nights. I was now older than he was by seven years. I always pictured him in the green, camouflaged weapon at the ready, eyes full of life. A happy warrior. In one of these dreams, I spoke with him. 'How have you been?' he asked me from across a cafe table, mischief in his eyes. He was glad to see me, and I him. He'd been watching me, he said.

'I'm better,' I said, looking at the scar over his eyebrow.

He just smiled.

Like my mother, he gave me a gift that lasted well beyond his passing. They had both taught me to treasure every waking moment. The dead never really leave us; they just light the way ahead. I woke up feeling better. We must throw off the chains of that old war: regret and bitterness are poor travelling companions, and will only tarnish the days we have left.

It's still a good, good world, and worth fighting for.

ACKNOWLEDGEMENTS

I LEARNED EARLY ON THE VALUE OF A GREAT TEAM ON A HARD road. With some luck, I have found the best of teams in my life, and this book is filled with their contributions. I felt this was an important story, and together we have breathed life into it. Thanks.

Alex Lloyd. A veteran of many book campaigns, I thank you for a podcast that later became an idea and, four years later, a published memoir. You gave me the courage to build a story worth reading. Few people have the desire to tackle a project with the vigour that you have. Thank you for patiently guiding me through the publishing process as a rookie author, and my thanks to the rest of the team at Pan Macmillan.

Ali Lavau. Thanks for your outstanding copyediting, and for unravelling some tangled chapters. Your encouragement, speed, accuracy and assimilation of style is uncanny and was the polishing this rough little manuscript needed. Thank you.

Kelly Irving. Thanks to you for taking me on and sending me out the door with a strong proposal, an outline, and some overwhelm. Your encouragement in what can be a lonely endeavour was all the inspiration I needed. Your outstanding book proposal work generated new excitement in an old genre.

Stano. You're the best roommate I have ever had. Your enthusiasm for any activity – literally any activity – and your love of surfing kept me sane and honest for many years. I admired your verbal sledging of enemy forces in the Battle of Cheksai; it was vicious, personal and unrelenting. Thanks for giving me a home when I was an MBA student, and for hours of debating contrarian positions just to annoy me. Your promotion of Random Acts of Goodness to the East Timorese people has been my model of how to be a good person. Your friendship saved me, especially when we were finding our way home after a long war.

Pete Winnall. I have to thank Pete for being a true friend and mentor since I was a seventeen-year-old at ADFA, especially for the mock interrogation you gave me over dinner one night to prepare me for selection. To be asked back to 1 Squadron as an XO was a career highlight, despite your grounding me from operations for many weeks for walking around the base drunk one night. I believe it was my detour to the mess to eat many pies from the pie warmer that got me caught. Your leadership was underappreciated at the unit, and your work since has been an inspiration. You're a true mate, and you always will be.

Ben Pronk. A special thanks for your great leadership in 1 Squadron. As a fresh face, I needed the guidance. Your high-speed review of the manuscript was super helpful. Thanks for taking me on as a junior troop commander, and dealing with both Stano and me on a lengthy deployment to East Timor. Your recommendation that I be pushed into the recon squadrons resulted in a career highlight. Our raw amateur push into the CrossFit Games of 2010 was a game changer. Your enthusiastic avoidance of any form of warming up both inspired and injured me in many ways. Thanks for your guidance and friendship.

Nick. Thanks for coaching me through what was my toughest deployment ever, and for trusting E Troop and me with jobs that were exceedingly hard. Thanks for not firing me in Deh Rawood; you easily could have, but you let me run a bit further and I always appreciated the extra rope. We did our best, mostly due to the example you set and the trust you invested in us. Your ability to mark a person with a villainous nickname remains unchallenged, and I will pursue that level of sledging perfection for many decades. 'Arch Fuckwit' remains my favourite and one I reserve for only the worst villains in this life.

Buzz. I thank you for your guidance and support over the years, especially in those dark hours in Chora. Your encouraging words after Matt died helped me when I needed it most. As my long-suffering surf coach, you helped me recover from the hardest times. I'm grateful to have been mentored by one of the self-proclaimed 'Top Five Toughest' SAS soldiers ever to have lived, despite the metrics for measuring that still being unclear. I note that no-one has ever contested the veracity of this claim. Thanks, you're a true mate.

Thorpey. You were delegated to look after me by our footy coach, Eddie, when I was a mere seventeen-year-old officer cadet. I believe I never fully outgrew the role of the first-year mentee, but I thank you for taking me on despite your initial distaste. Your ability to cut through any issue with several comments is without peer, and you kept many a squadron conference entertaining. In your general berating of Canberra and its occupants I have found an ally for life. Thanks mate, for all the laughs.

Robbo. You have been there through the long road out and I appreciated your good will and mateship. I do not appreciate your placing me with Afghan drivers intent on killing me. You and Ginia have been an anchor for me for many years. Thanks for being a great mate.

Irish. Your steady guidance during my early days in the unit made you a calming influence and a fantastic leader. You were also the first-ever civilian to employ me, and I believe you awarded me the honour of being the first-ever intern at Omni. Your skill, wisdom, generosity, faith and patience was a gift then and it still is today. Thank you.

Vando. I thank you for your tips in the surfing line-up, and your super-wide board stance that earned you the nickname Crab Cakes. Our surf trips were a much-needed escape from the endless deployments, and your enthusiasm for them was first class. I look forward to seeing you on the other side of all this.

The Special Air Service Regiment. Thanks for having me. I'm not mad; I still love you. Best job I ever had.

SOCOMD. I never loved you, but thanks for authorising all our jobs and for all the outstanding equipment and training.

The 2nd Commando Regiment. To our annoying little brothers: you're not little anymore. You fought as hard as anyone, and you lost many along the way. For that, you will always have my respect. Vale. Please send me a formal notice admitting I was BOB (Biggest on Base) at Camp Russell from 2007–2010.

Jimmy Keam. Thanks for being my exam supervisor for Calculus. I believe you got me into business school, and you will always be known as The Proctor. You, Jo and The Prince were also kind enough to house me for almost a year when I was a distraught consultant, and we found solace and watched *The Bachelor* as a little family.

Clay Watts. Thanks for encouraging me to do this, and for your leadership in Chora. Your grenade throws are questionable, but your grit, tenacity and leadership are not.

E Troop, Rotation V. You fought hard, well and fiercely. There are many to thank here, and you all know who you are, including all support members, who were right alongside us. I'll never forget you – thanks.

Horse and Rischa. Thanks for your encouragement, and for the steady, sustained heavy weapons shooting that attracted much fire at our car for most of a deployment. Your guidance was a huge help and remains so to this day.

Dominic Skerritt. There is no doubt you got me into both Wharton and McKinsey & Company. Thanks for the stunning chance. I have always appreciated the boost and the friendship that you gave me over the years, including the berating over the many substandard practice cases you trained me in. Priceless.

Alex Sonnenberg. Thank you for taking me on a long tour of the Wharton house parties, including the fall you took down two flights of stairs. Your guidance at school was a rare gift, and you left us way too soon. I miss you every day.

Maryellen Lamb. Thank you for shepherding lost veterans through your school system, and supporting us despite our excessive drinking, arrogance and generally weak academics. Your exhortations to do better and to be grateful for the position I was in helped me snap out of it and get the work done. I count you as a surrogate mother, and one of my closest friends.

Zac Peckham. Thanks for the night in Brooklyn when you showed me bear attack videos, and talked about *Survivor*. You changed the course of my life in the best way possible.

General Mattis. I am yet to meet another military officer who appreciates the place that soldiers hold in civilisations like you do. Your example in generosity, courage, wit, kindness and savage one-liners will be remembered for a thousand years. I also thank you for not hitting us with a drone strike after your Kill Kapture photo went viral in the US.

Captain Morgan. The battlefield currency. Thank you.

Bear Grylls. Thank you for your enthusiastic words about the memoir. I took a lot of inspiration from your own stories, and the risks you have taken yourself to inspire others. Well done and thanks – NGU!

Steve. Thanks for being the most supportive brother ever. Both you and Dan have helped me pull this together and have stood beside me since we were tiny. Although I feel I was taken advantage of as a young pilot in some of your go-kart crash programs. You held us together in many ways. Your loyalty and good grace saved us – thanks.

Dan. I am still astounded as my little brother that you survived being used for both target practice and as a crash test dummy for Steve and me. You can thank us later for the toughening up we gave you from a young age. You have been there the whole time when it matters most, and I love you for it. You have suffered through my *Call of Duty* war stories many times. Thanks for your big heart and for being a good man.

Dad. Only a father knows what it is like to be hugged by a son. In having my own, I realise both the joy I must have given you, but also the fear in watching a young man who thinks himself invulnerable. We both know otherwise. Thanks forever for your love, guidance and your advice at the half-time huddles of sport and life. Sorry about the brothel, that's the worst secret I have, I promise.

Jen. Thanks for supporting me the whole time and for putting up with the shit that only stepchildren can deliver! You have taken it like a champion and earned your spot in the tribe. Thank you.

Mum. I swam across Cottesloe Beach, trying to stay beside you as I watched our shadows glide across the white sand beneath us. You kept us afloat, us four men in the family. You would have loved Sam, she's as mad as you were and just as much fun. I love you, and thanks forever. I know you were there in Afghanistan, and I know I'll see you again. We love you always.

Leigh. Rarely do you see an army wife with the no-bullshit take on what soldiers do and who they are. We had your most important person with us, and we did not bring him home alive. I thank you for your understanding despite your enormous grief. Your good will, courage, humour and tenacity is obvious to me, and you're an example of resilience, if ever I have seen one. Thank you.

Keegan. A stoic man just like your father, you have his tech savvy, his strong build, and his gruff good humour. We all count you as a son; never feel that you're not being watched out for. You are your own man, but know that your Dad inspired and guided many people, and you can be so proud of him.

Matt. Thanks for being hard, smart, aggressive and patient. You invested in me from the start, helping me with planning missions and setting the example for all to follow. I regret that you did not survive, but in many ways you will live forever. Thanks always, and I won't ever forget you.

My son, Harry. You are the greatest gift of all. You have given me a new lease on life, and your innocence and love have healed us beyond belief. Whatever you choose in life, do your best, look after your mates, look after yourself, and be good to people. Tip from Dad: try to keep the lever of the hand grenade in the the web of your hand between thumb and fore-finger – this will prevent embarrassment and injury. We love you, and we are both so proud of our little man.

My love, Sam. The biggest thanks of all goes to my gorgeous wife. Thanks for taking a chance and trusting me in Samoa; I'm sorry for not telling you the full truth of my past life. With your grace, patience, energy and love, you are the best partner I could ever ask for. You have put up with my relentless planning, writing, editing and fretting through this whole process. You picked up the pieces when it all got too much, and in the winter of the longest lockdown in history, you held us together as a family. You were that light at the end of the tunnel I was living for, and my heart will remain forever in your service. I love you, always. Thank you.

INDEX

INDEX